Public Sector Accounting, Accountability and Gover

Funded by taxation, public spending cannot be separated from politics and ensuring efficiency and effectiveness is always high on the political and policy agenda. Accounting, accountability, governance and auditing are essential ingredients in evaluating public sector performance.

Australia and New Zealand are world leaders when it comes to public sector accounting—such as being the first to introduce transaction-neutral accounting standards. This edited collection considers current issues impacting the public sector by primarily drawing upon experiences of Australia and New Zealand. Then, by combining history (from the time of the Domesday book, early sovereignty and Shakespeare) with current practice (differential reporting, international financial reporting standards, government performance, voter turnout, joined-up government and auditing practices), we use these experiences to illuminate the global issues of public sector accounting, accountability and governance.

Based on rigorous research by top public sector researchers, this edited collection offers a multitude of future research ideas to enable those interested in following this pathway—whether they are in Australia, New Zealand, the United Kingdom, Europe, the United States of America, Africa or anywhere else in the world—an avenue to traverse.

Robyn Pilcher PhD (USyd), FCPA, FIPA, CMA is an Adjunct Associate Professor at Curtin University, Western Australia. Having worked in both academia and as a CPA, Robyn was an academic for over thirty years. She has published both locally and internationally with her research interests centred around public sector accounting, accountability and governance. Robyn also served for several years as a public sector expert with the Institute of Public Accountant's Public Sector Faculty advising on policy to government and the Australian Accounting Standards Board.

David Gilchrist is a Professor at the University of Western Australia, a chartered accountant and an economic historian. He has held senior roles in the public sector, not-for-profit sector and in commerce. Prior to becoming an academic, David held the role of Assistant Auditor-General in Western Australia and is currently a member of the Australian Charities and Not-for-profits Commission Advisory Board. David has published academically and as a journalist across a number of areas including public sector governance and the public sector/not-for-profit nexus.

Routledge Studies in Accounting

Auditing Teams
Dynamics and Efficiency
Mara Cameran, Angela Kate Pettinicchio, Angelo Detillo

The History and Tradition of Accounting in Italy
*Edited by David Alexander, Roberto Di Pietra, Stefano Adamo
and Roberta Fasiello*

The Social Function of Accounts
Reforming Accountancy to Serve Mankind
John Flower

The Role of the Management Accountant
Local Variations and Global Influences
Lukas Goretzki & Erik Strauss

Interventionist Management Accounting Research
Theory Contributions with Societal Impact
Jouni Lyly-Yrjänäinen, Petri Suomala, Teemu Laine, and Falconer Mitchell

Accounting, Innovation and Inter-Organisational Relationships
*Martin Carlsson-Wall, Håkan Håkansson, Kalle Kraus, Johnny Lind, and Torkel
Strömsten*

A History of Corporate Financial Reporting
John Richard Edwards

Public Sector Accounting, Accountability and Governance
Globalising the Experiences of Australia and New Zealand
Edited by Robyn Pilcher and David Gilchrist

Public Sector Accounting, Accountability and Governance

Globalising the Experiences of Australia and New Zealand

**Edited by Robyn Pilcher
and David Gilchrist**

Routledge
Taylor & Francis Group

LONDON AND NEW YORK

First published 2019
by Routledge
2 Park Square, Milton Park, Abingdon, Oxon OX14 4RN

and by Routledge
52 Vanderbilt Avenue, New York, NY 10017, USA

First issued in paperback 2020

Routledge is an imprint of the Taylor & Francis Group, an informa business

British Library Cataloguing-in-Publication Data
A catalogue record for this book is available from the British Library

Library of Congress Cataloging-in-Publication Data
A catalog record for this book has been requested

ISBN 13: 978-0-367-58844-1 (pbk)
ISBN 13: 978-1-138-56338-4 (hbk)

Typeset in Times New Roman
by Apex CoVantage, LLC

Robyn
For Verna and Edward. Although both gone, you will always be with me in my heart. Without your support and encouragement throughout my life none of this would have been possible.

David
For Ben, Georgia and Maddie.

Contents

Tables

Figure

Contributors

Robyn Pilcher (principal editor, contact and sub-editor)

Robyn Pilcher (r.pilcher@curtin.edu.au) PhD (USyd), FCPA, FIPA, CMA is an Adjunct Associate Professor at Curtin University, Western Australia. Having worked in both academia and as a CPA, Robyn was an academic for over thirty years. She has published both locally and internationally with her research interests centred around public sector accounting, accountability and governance. Robyn also served for several years as a public sector expert with the Institute of Public Accountant's Public Sector Faculty advising on policy to government and the Australian Accounting Standards Board.

David Gilchrist (co-editor)

David Gilchrist (david.gilchrist@uwa.edu.au) is a Professor at the University of Western Australia, a chartered accountant and an economic historian. He has held senior roles in the public sector, not-for-profit sector and in commerce. Prior to becoming an academic, David held the role of Assistant Auditor-General in Western Australia and is currently a member of the Australian Charities and Not-for-profits Commission Advisory Board. David has published academically and as a journalist across a number of areas including public sector governance and the public sector/not-for-profit nexus.

Michelle Bunn (assistant sub-editor)

Michelle Bunn PhD is a Research Assistant at the University of Western Australia who kindly acted as assistant sub-editor working with Robyn Pilcher to ensure all the sub-editing was as close to perfect as possible. She has more than 20 years' experience in the Western Australian public sector, specialising in policy and legislative development, research and analytical roles in the fields of public sector audit, management, equity and cultural diversity.

Bikram Chatterjee

Bikram Chatterjee (bikramc@waikato.ac.nz) PhD, CPA is a Senior Lecturer at the School of Accounting, Finance and Economics at the University of Waikato,

New Zealand. He has held academic positions at Charles Sturt University, Curtin University, Deakin University and Massey University. His research interests include international accounting standards, public sector reporting, private sector reporting and accounting education.

Joseph Drew

Joseph Drew (Joseph.Drew@uts.edu.au) is a Research Fellow at the University of Technology, Sydney and is also Adjunct Professor at Tokyo Metropolitan University. He has consulted with a number of Australian councils on accounting, finance and economic matters. Joseph has also been called as an expert witness at a number of Australian state and federal government Upper House inquiries into local public finance, as well as working on projects and delivering keynote addresses to governments abroad.

Sasindu Gamage

Sasindu Gamage is a Researcher at the Institute for Public Policy and Governance at the University of Technology, Sydney. Her interests centre on in-depth qualitative analyses and applied statistics for social research and she has conducted a number of complex externally funded research projects for public and non-public entities.

Karen Knight

Karen Knight PhD is an economist, historian of economic thought and part-time academic. She has interests in welfare economics and social choice theory, the Cambridge School of Economics, and the sociology of scientific knowledge. Karen has published in academic journals and book chapters and is currently Research Director for the Independent Centre for Applied Not-for-Profit Research. She also lectures and researches at various universities in Perth, Western Australia.

Mary Low

Mary Low PhD, CA, FCPA Australia, is a Senior Lecturer at the School of Accounting, Finance and Economics at the University of Waikato, New Zealand. Mary is the Accounting Convenor. Her research interests include accounting education, accounting and business ethics, corporate social responsibility, financial reporting disclosures, public sector reporting and integrated reporting.

Janet Mack

Janet Mack (j.mack@qut.edu.au) is an active researcher who regularly presents papers at both Australian and international conferences. Her research interests are public sector accountability, infrastructure asset management in the public sector, measuring and reporting on the contribution of volunteers in nonprofit organisations and the applicability of private sector based accounting standards for government and nonprofit entities.

Nicholas Pawsey

Nicholas Pawsey PhD is a Senior Lecturer in Accounting at the School of Accounting and Finance, Charles Sturt University, Australia. Nicholas has previously held academic positions at La Trobe University. His research interests include international accounting standards, water policy and management, public sector accounting and accounting education. Nicholas has published a number of journal articles, industry reports and book chapters in relation to these topics.

Glennda Scully

Glennda Scully (G.Scully@curtin.edu.au) PhD FCPA CAANZ is a Professor in the School of Accounting, Curtin University. Her research interests (and subsequent publications) are varied and include behavioural decision-making in auditing; corporate social responsibility reporting, not-for-profit accounting; ethics; accounting education; and financial disclosure in developing economies. She participates in multiple committees both within and outside the University, including volunteering on not-for-profit boards.

Harjinder Singh

Harjinder Singh (h.singh@curtin.edu.au) PhD is an active researcher at Curtin University and has research interests in audit fees, audit quality, corporate governance, internal audit and initial public offering underpricing. He has many academic publications including a number in highly ranked journals such as *The International Journal of Auditing*.

Ross Taplin

Ross Taplin PhD is a Research Professor in the School of Accounting, Curtin University and an Accredited Statistician (AStat) with the Statistical Society of Australia. His research interests are diverse, including developing new quantitative methods and the application of statistics to a diverse range of subjects including accounting, tourism and economics. He has over 100 publications in highly ranked journals.

Grantley Taylor

Grantley Taylor PhD is a Professor and Deputy Head of the School of Accounting, Curtin University. Prior to his academic career, Grantley worked in the mining industry and the Australian Tax Office. His research interests include corporate taxation, financial reporting and disclosure and he has published in several high ranking journals.

Peter Wilkins

Peter Wilkins (p.wilkins@curtin.edu.au) is an Adjunct Professor at The John Curtin Institute of Public Policy at Curtin University. He has served as Western

Australia's Deputy Ombudsman and prior to this had been the Assistant Auditor-General, Performance Review, Western Australia. He is a National Fellow and Western Australian Fellow of the Institute of Public Administration Australia, and Deputy Chair of the Board of Australian Volunteers International. He has published several books and multiple academic papers and industry reports.

Elnaz Vafaei

Elnaz Vafaei PhD is a risk consultant with one of the large accounting firms in Western Australia and a part-time instructor in the School of Accounting, Curtin University. Her research interests include auditing, governance and financial accounting in both the public and private sectors.

Acknowledgements

The development of this volume arose out of extended work and discussions with a number of people worldwide over several years. These dialogues were essential to our recognition of the gaps in the literature. Respecting the source of this challenge, we sought to fill these gaps via an edited volume rather than an authored book. We are grateful to these scholars who are too many to name but who were generous in giving their time and their opinions which helped shape this edition.

Some of those we spoke to became the authors included in this volume and to these we owe a special debt. Each chapter was reviewed, then submitted to a blind review. The authors made applicable revisions after which the chapter was submitted to a second review if deemed necessary. Their patience and dedication, despite their multiple other obligations, ensured they produced chapters of the highest quality and met all deadlines. Their contributions have brought great learning and erudition to an array of topics applicable to researchers throughout the world.

We also acknowledge Dr Michelle Bunn who has been very important in the finalisation of this volume. She has provided her support and scholarly input generously and unreservedly, for which we are very grateful. On a more personal note, I (Robyn Pilcher) thank Professor Graeme Dean for his supervision and mentoring many years ago. His attention to detail and experience as editor of *Abacus* was invaluable and paved the way to my becoming a better writer and editor. Also, to Christopher Barrett who kindly acted as a sounding board on many an occasion and enabled me to see the end picture more clearly.

Finally, we thank our publisher Routledge of the Taylor and Francis Group, and, in particular, Jacqueline Curthoys (Commissioning Editor), Laura Hussey (Editorial Assistant) and Jessica Harrison (Editorial Assistant).

1   Introduction

Robyn Pilcher[1]

Introduction

This book brings together works by authors specialising in various aspects of the public sector. It integrates experiences of Australia and New Zealand (NZ) in such a way as to conceptualise topics relevant to the western world. There are three main themes presented here—accounting, accountability and governance—and accounting is where it begins. The history of *accounting* is long and vast with the scientific, traditional side being traceable back to mediaeval times (for example, Martinelli (1983) and his review of 1340 and 1341 Genoese ledgers). Yamey (1994) considered accounting at a slightly later date with his review of double entry accounting and the manuscripts transcribed by Cotrugli in1458 and Pacioli in1494.

On the other hand, it has been argued (see, for example, Hoskin & Macve 1986) that *accountability* didn't appear until much later in the 1800s. However, there is enough evidence to prove this was not the case. For example, Seidman (2005) traced accountability back as far as the 13th century: 'most significantly, the 13th century presented England with the constitutional crisis that forced serious consideration of questions of royal power and accountability' (Seidman 2005, p. 11). The securing of the Magna Carta in 1215 ensured the King (allegedly) became accountable to the English barons (Seidman 2005).

Finally, we have *governance*, a buzz word introduced into the public sector with the reforms of the 1980s and 1990s. According to Blackie (1989), the term governance was first used in an effort to improve public sector efficiency—such as in Sub-Saharan Africa. This report from the World Bank defined governance as 'the exercise of political power to manage a nation's affairs' (Blackie 1989, p. 60). Although this links in with Aucoin's (2012) definition of new political governance (notwithstanding, he takes it further than just political, referring to it as 'sleazy governance' (Aucoin 2012, p. 178)), it is too narrow a definition to be the only one considered here. Governance, although not adopted by the public sector until recently, was said to be used as far back as Shakespeare (Edwards 2002). In fact, journals such as *Public Integrity* have published special issues on whether Shakespeare's plays teach students and practitioners of public administration important lessons on ethics today.[2] According to Osborne (1999, p. 38), in the 17th century it was simply 'a method of management', whereas now it includes 'performance, accountability, transparency, participation, relationship management and . . . efficiency' (Edwards 2002, p. 52). Hence, we can see how the three themes integrate closely with each other and are all essential components when referring to the public sector.

This chapter begins with a review of the public sector in Australia and NZ. We then consider each of the themes and how the various chapters contribute to the overall objective. Although we recognise the differences between Australia and NZ, there are also many similarities regarding the way the public sector report.

The public sector

To fully understand the public sector in Australia and NZ one must firstly have a brief knowledge of the countries themselves. Australia became an independent nation on 1 January 1901 when the British Parliament passed legislation allowing the six Australian colonies to govern in their own right as part of the Commonwealth of Australia. The Commonwealth of Australia was established as a constitutional monarchy (Parliament of Australia 2012). These colonies became the six states of Australia (New South Wales, Queensland, Victoria, Tasmania, South Australia and Western Australia) with the addition of two, limited governing, territories (Australian Capital Territory; Northern Territory). In NZ, this independence occurred several decades earlier in 1852 with the passing of the *New Zealand Constitution Act 1852*. However, it was not until 1907 that NZ became a dominion within the British Empire (NZ Ministry for Culture and Heritage 2014). In 1986, the 1952 Act and the *Statute of Westminster 1931* were repealed and replaced with the *Constitution Act 1986* (NZ). This meant the British Parliament was no longer able to pass laws for NZ. Interestingly, it has been said that NZ turned down several offers from Australia to become part of the Commonwealth (NZ Ministry for Culture and Heritage 2016).

The actual definition of the public sector is one that changes not only from within countries with several states, such as Australia, but between countries as well. According to Funnell, Cooper and Lee (2012, p. 2), 'public sector organisations can be identified according to financing arrangements, ownership, management and accountability arrangements'. Government departments that provide a service to the public are traditionally known as being part of the public sector. In Australia these include education, policing and defence (Funnell, Cooper & Lee 2012). Other areas are not so obvious. For example, in Australia the railways are part of the public sector, whereas in other countries (such as Britain), they are not. In regards to differences between states, the electricity suppliers are a good example of where there is a blurring of the lines between the public and private sectors. Behind much of the reform process was the thought that the private sector's practices, managerial styles and objectives were superior to those of the public sector (Funnell, Cooper & Lee 2012; Pilcher 2011).

The Australian Bureau of Statistics (2016, p. 3) offered a more definitive definition of the public sector: public sector agencies are all those 'owned and/or controlled by one of the three levels of government'. In NZ the definition is very similar with the public sector consisting of local government and state sector organisations. Within the wider state sector lie the Offices of Parliament (e.g. the Auditor-General); state-owned enterprises (such as NZ Post); tertiary education institutions (TEIs); and legislative branch departments. These four areas are governed at arms-length from ministers. Also, within the state sector there are the state services such as Crown entities (other than TEIs); other departments (such as NZ Police); *Public Finance Act 1989 Schedule 4* Organisations and others (such as Reserve Bank). Finally, there is the public service which consists of all other departments working closely with the ministers (Dovey 2003).

One major difference between Australia and NZ is the lack of a federal/commonwealth government in NZ. In NZ there are the state and local governments whereas in Australia there is the addition of the overarching federal government. Still, in essence, the public sector is similar in general; it is only how it is structured that occasionally differs.

Once Australia and NZ became constitutions in their own right at the beginning of the 20th century, there was a period of incremental change within government administration until the mid-1970s. It was then the public began to expect more accountability and transparency from its governing administrators. In Australia in 1974 the Prime Minister implemented a Royal Commission into government administration which resulted in major changes in the public sector from 1975. It recognised the need for more accountability, better communication, a more economical use of resources, a change in managerial styles and a devolution of responsibility. According to Funnell, Cooper and Lee (2012, p. 129), the report resulted in 'an increase in responsibility for departmental performance . . . and improvements in accountability'. Public servants were expected to be more efficient and would be judged on their performance.

The NZ public sector also underwent major reform in the 1980s when the country was apparently about to default on several international loans. The *State Sector Act 1988* and the *Public Finance Act 1989* were instrumental in change. Based on the need to provide better public accounting practices and managerial accountability (central tenets of these pieces of legislation), NZ moved to accrual accounting and output budgeting in 1988. According to Mulgan (2004), these two Acts, combined with the *State-Owned Enterprises Act 1986*, formed the basis for adoption of a 'radical' version of what is now known as New Public Management (NPM) (Mulgan 2004, p. 1).

In both countries, one of the aims of the reform process was to delineate roles and hence reduce the confusion between politicians, public services and public servants. This, in turn, was supposed to lead to greater accountability for performance.

As mentioned above, NPM was the unofficial basis for the reform process moving many of the public sector processes closer to those of the private sector. According to Bovaird and Downe (2006), the United Kingdom (UK) was the first to launch NPM-type reforms. Since the appearance of the NPM in Australia in the 1980s, all political parties have supported its underlying principles (MacDermott

2007; Pilcher 2014). The acceptance of NPM ideas by government, in particular, allegedly 'added impetus for greater participation by communities' (Aulich 2010, p. 37). Accounting was a key element in NPM since it, purportedly, 'reflected high trust in the market and private business methods and low trust in public servants and professionals' (Hood 1995, p. 94). The development of NPM was seen as a means by which to enhance accountability and transparency of governments and this, in turn, required financial information that was more comparable, relevant and useful for decision-making within the public sector (Pilcher 2014). This leads us onto the first theme of the book—accounting.

Accounting

Whether relating to the public or private sectors, certain financial information is essential for informed decision-making (Pilcher & Dean 2009). One of the key elements of the public sector reforms in both Australia and NZ was the adoption of accrual accounting in the preparation of financial reports. It has been recognised globally that these two countries were not only the first to implement accrual accounting into the public sector but did so more comprehensively than most other western countries (Champoux 2006; Guthrie 1998). According to Cavanagh, Flynn and Moretti (2016), in 2015, 41 governments (21 percent) had completed the transition from cash-based to accrual-based accounting, 16 governments accounted on a modified accrual basis (8 percent), 28 governments (17 percent) used a modified cash basis, and 114 governments (57 percent) remained on pure cash accounting.

One reason for the implementation of accrual accounting in Australia was the perceived lack of usefulness of the cash-based system for making decisions by users (Funnell, Cooper & Lee 2012). Initially in Australia local government was targeted (1991), followed by state government departments (1993) and finally government as a whole (1996) (Walker, Clarke & Dean 1999). This move has been aligned to the 'domino theory' of change (Leeson & Dean 2009; Pilcher 2006a). Another outcome of the reform process was the requirement that the public sector, including governments, establish an asset register and report on all non-current assets and their related depreciation expense in annual reports.

Until 1989, NZ was using a cash-accounting system for its budgeting process. With the introduction of the *Public Finance Act 1989*, the NZ public sector adopted an output-based budgeting process. This allowed departments to use accrual-based projections of cost and revenue for its 'outputs' (e.g. services) so that parliament could then compare these with those from the private sector. Between 1992 and 1994, all accounting in the public sector became based on the accrual system.

The introduction of accrual accounting into the public sector brought with it several benefits. Apart from those referred to above, it allowed a more comprehensive and accurate view of an organisation's performance and the cost of providing services. With this (allegedly) came greater integrity and transparency and made the government departments more accountable to the public (Cavanagh, Flynn &

Moretti 2016). However, along with the potential efficiencies and improved accountability, there were also critics of accrual accounting for the public sector. For example, questions were asked as to its suitability to accounting for long-life infrastructure, something the private sector did not need to worry about (Barton 1999; Pilcher 2006b).

Initially both Australia and NZ had their own standards for public sector accrual-based accounting. Then, in Australia, under the transaction-neutral philosophy (where transactions were considered to be the same whatever the sector), the International Financial Reporting Standards (IFRS) were implemented (with an Australian flavour, A-IFRS) on 1 January 2005. In NZ, early adoption of NZ-IFRS could occur from 1 January 2005 with compulsory adoption from 1 January 2007.

As indicated above, one of the major issues with accrual accounting was the need to establish an asset register for all infrastructure—including those items with very long lives such as roads or heritage buildings. Added to this was the requirement to depreciate such assets. Chapter 3 considers depreciation of infrastructure in detail. The chapter details asset management and depreciation concerns as applied to transport infrastructure (concentrating on roads) in local government in Australia and NZ. Based on Sterling's (1975, p. 28) 'recycled ideas without resolving issues' observation, it traces asset management and depreciation from as far back as the Domesday Book through to current accounting practices. By analysing relevant discussion forums, it concludes that problems experienced by local government today are no different from those confronted by accountants and engineers back in the 11th century. An interesting and informative read, it provides many avenues for researchers to follow in regards to their own research interests – wherever they may reside.

On the other hand, Chapter 2 considers an alternative to IFRS in the public sector. After its introduction, it did not take long for people to recognise that A-IFRS and NZ-IFRS were too complex for many entities (see, for example, Pilcher & Dean 2009; Ryan, Guthrie & Day 2007), including small and medium-sized enterprises (SMEs), not-for-profits (NFPs) and public sector organisations. Hence, differential reporting was proposed, initially for SMEs by the International Accounting Standards Board (IASB), then Australia and NZ each introduced a differential reporting framework. In NZ the framework was established in 2005 whilst, in Australia, the Reduced Disclosure Requirements (RDR) regime was introduced by the Australian Accounting Standards Board (AASB) on 2 July 2010 (AASB 2010) (effective 1 July 2013 but with the option to early adopt). Chapter 2 considers the potential impact of a differential reporting system on the public sector. The main reason the authors undertook this research was to consider the process of reviewing the potential effects of a new/revised set of standards, prior to implementation, on public sector reporting. Their inspiration was the UK Accounting Standards Board and European Financial Reporting Advisory Group (UKASB/ EFRAG) Position Paper (2012) which considered 'effect analysis'. Another reason for the research was to determine possible efficiencies under RDR as well as identify further areas where the idea of an alternative differential reporting system may have merit. At all times the balance between cost and utility is considered, as is the ultimate purpose of the reports themselves (for example, Carnegie 2005; Carnegie & Wolnizer 1995).

Unfortunately, because both in NZ and Australia the differential reporting system remains framed within the transaction-neutral philosophy, the framework retains the decision-usefulness emphasis. Trewavas, Nives and Laswad (2012) claimed that one of the major concerns regarding the introduction of accrual accounting into the public sector was the lack of a conceptual framework. With transaction-neutrality adopted (and hence, by default, the private sector conceptual framework), decision-usefulness is the underlying objective. According to many, such as Pallot (1992) and Rutherford (1990), accountability is a more appropriate objective for the public sector. This is not the case with the current differential reporting systems.

Accountability

Like accounting, the topic of accountability itself is vast and has formed the basis of many a research paper. When it comes to the public sector, accountability goes hand-in-hand with what we perceive to be the role of government. However, the definition of accountability is not so easy to specify. Historically a central question of the sovereign power was whether the sovereign was accountable to law and public judgement. What was known as sovereign immunity forbade suits against the government without its consent (Seidman 2005).

Referring to financial reporting, Bryer (2000) and Meiksins Wood (1981) considered the relationship of accountability to two different meanings of accounts. The first is that of a steward being held to account in relation to the financial side of the business and the production of financial reports (in other words, the organisation is responsible for providing financial and performance accountability to users of those reports (Tooley & Hooks 2010)). The second definition considers accountability in terms of a person's behaviour and how that behaviour is judged (Bryer 2000). It can refer to whether an organisation has complied with a legal or statutory requirement (hence 'legitimising' that organisation (Tooley & Hooks 2010, p. 40)). In the public sector, accountability is integral—as shall be demonstrated later in the book.

If we digress for a moment and consider Dobel's (2015) analysis of several of Shakespeare's plays and concepts associated with accountability, we can see how accountability is entrenched in Western society's system of government. According to the Australian Public Sector Commission (APSC) (2015, n.p.), accountability is 'one of the cornerstone values of an open democratic society'. To ensure transparency and integrity, Dobel (2015, p. 304) claimed 'public institutions should be enmeshed in a web of accountability'. He (2015, p. 305) then concluded:

> Shakespeare reminds us that . . . a realistic public service needs transparency, multiple accountability mechanisms, and active reassertion of the importance of public service as a calling to counteract the limits of the public service and human nature.

Given this, in Australia, NZ and all democratic countries, government account-ability to the public is key (Funnell, Cooper & Lee 2012). When Australia became a colony of Britain, the British way of accounting transferred over with little change. Up until the reforms discussed above, cash accounting 'contributed to the sovereignty of the Parliament' but efficient and effective government was less obvious (Funnell, Cooper & Lee 2012, p. 21). In the public sector, account-ability from parliament to its multiple stakeholders is complex. It is 'not a simple one-to-one relationship between a principal and agent' (Mayston 1993, p. 77) but a relationship between a number of different groups with overlapping economic and political interests (Pilcher et al. 2013).

Chapter 4 explores the concept of accountability, concentrating on the Austral-ian federal government. The Australian political system is based on the Westmin-ster system of 'responsible government'. With this doctrine comes the assumption that parliament is the central body in a chain of accountability that allows the elec-torate to hold those who govern accountable for their actions. Thus, as the central player in the chain of accountability, parliament is accountable to the public (Davis et al. 1993). One of the functions of each Australian parliament is that of control-ling government expenditure by evaluating financial proposals and subsequently ensuring that government funds have been expended appropriately. In practice, the task of scrutinising the appropriate dispersion of funds usually falls to the auditor-general, who then reports to parliament. The audit function can be seen as fundamental to accountability as it offers independent verification of the account presented to discharge accountability. The chapter goes on to compare budget documents and annual reports (both accountability mechanisms) pre and post the introduction of accrual accounting, and the findings may surprise some of you.

Chapter 5, on the other hand, provides an in-depth, historical look at account-ability in countries influenced by the Westminster system of government. We spoke about sovereignty above and this chapter considers fundamental principles relating to parliamentary sovereignty and responsible government (introduced in Chapter 4). Both of these concepts are still used today to emphasise the key attrib-utes of a democratic system that ensures executive accountability.

Parliamentary sovereignty is described in Chapter 5 as referring to the par-liament being the ultimate source, and exerciser, of power within a nation state (Goldsworthy 2010). The Westminster system has also developed the idea of responsible government in which ministers are individually and collectively responsible to the popular house (being the House of Commons in the UK, the House of Representatives in Australia's federal government and the Parliament in NZ's unicameral system). This arrangement establishes what Reilly et al. (2013, p. 18) referred to as a 'chain of accountability', whereby the executive is respon-sible to the legislature which is, in turn, responsible to the public. By exploring the British, Australian and NZ cases in terms of parliamentary sovereignty and responsible government, the author demonstrates that the accountability mecha-nisms used to hold the executive to account are not as embedded in common historical roots or as central to controlling executive government as they may be perceived to be.

In regards to a more focused look at accountability in NZ, Chapter 6 follows on as a natural progression from Chapter 5. It concentrates on NZ local government and investigates the relationship between pre-election reports and voter turnout. Research in the area of voter turnout has grown in recent years (Cancela & Geys 2016) in an attempt to analyse whether more transparent reporting processes (and hence, greater accountability) have an impact on the outcome. The public sector reforms provided a catalyst for users to put pressure on local government to provide user-friendly reports—thereby increasing the accountability and transparency of their reporting. Chapter 6 provides findings that enable further accountability mechanisms to be formed in local government and segues perfectly to the final chapter in this section.

Chapter 7 analyses four recent Australian statutory reviews and presents insights into these reviews and the audit offices involved. Statutory reviews were identified by Whitfield (2006, p. 89) as necessary and 'fundamental for parliament to gain assurance that the auditor-general is carrying out his role in an appropriate way'. Performance audits from the mid-1970s were seen as a direct response to the public sector management reforms (Funnell 2003; Guthrie & Parker 1999). Chapter 7 builds on the argument that parliamentary accountability is important for democratic control and parliamentary inquiries or reviews are an essential aspect of this (Meijer 2003). From a practical and political perspective, it is essential that audit offices select the right topics for their performance audit. There are several reasons for this. First, obviously it is the public's money that is being used and so value-for-money is a requirement. Second, the audit office needs to consider the opportunity cost of auditing some aspects of an organisation's performance compared to others. Put and Turksema (2011) suggested that if the auditor (or auditor-general) wants to have influence, then it should choose topics relevant to the current political climate. Chapter 7 focuses on performance audit and provides some much-needed evidence-based analysis of what performance audit is achieving. Findings reveal audit offices in Australia are contributing to improving parliamentary scrutiny and accountability.

This chapter links effortlessly with the next section as, like the rest of the public sector, it is important that the audit offices are accountable and that there is oversight of their performance. In other words, that an effective governance system is in place.

Governance

The introduction of accrual accounting in the public sector brought with it increased risk and hence the need for more effective governance. Hepworth (2003, 2004) identified various risks in regards to the UK public sector including inadequate audit processes. With a lack of independent scrutiny of policies and procedures, an increased risk of manipulation also became apparent. The complexity of accrual reporting, especially after the simplistic cash accounting systems, meant there were many (including politicians) at a loss to interpret the reports. Earlier, Ryan and Ng (2000) claimed that with a more private sector ethos being forced onto the public sector there was a need for greater governance procedures to be implemented. Clatworthy, Jones and Mellet (1997), Pilcher in Chapter 3 and others (such as Kerr et al. 2009; Pilcher 2014; Revsine 1991) provided examples of manipulation in depreciation calculations with the introduction of accrual accounting, resulting in users receiving erroneous and misleading information. Therefore, in the current context it would seem reasonable to suggest there needs to be improved governance, including improved internal and external audit functions (as discussed shortly).

With high profile United States (US) private sector cases such as Enron and WorldCom and Australian collapses like HIH and One.Tel, corporate governance and related legislation were developed. In the US legislation was by way of the *Sarbanes-Oxley Act of 2002* and, in Australia, the *Corporate Law Economic Reform Program (Audit Reform and Corporate Disclosure) Act 2004* (commonly known as CLERP 9). For some, the public service is considered more susceptible than the private sector to fraud and corruption (PwC 2016). Governance principles developed in the public sector must 'recognise the political and operating environments that differ from those of the private sector' (Governance Institute of Australia 2016, p. 2). Robust internal and external audit functions are seen as key requirements to ensure effective accountability and governance. In Australia it has been the audit offices that have driven governance in the public sector. We saw this earlier with Chapter 7 and the close link between accountability and overall governance.

Chapter 7 introduced the concept of performance audit, however, it concentrated on reviewing the offices actually conducting the audit. In other words, it considered the prospect of reviewing the 'watchdog'. Chapter 8 focuses on the actual performance audit process, not just in Australia and NZ but internationally.

Throughout the world, oversight bodies (supreme audit institutions such as the Office of the Auditor-General in both Australia and NZ) are responsible for improving the performance of the public sector. The US Comptroller General (1994, p. 14, para 2.6) defined a performance audit as:

> an objective and systematic examination of evidence for the purpose of providing an independent assessment of the performance of a government organisation, program, activity, or function in order to provide information to improve public accountability and facilitate decision-making by parties with responsibility to oversee or initiate corrective action.

Others are not convinced the definition is so straight-forward (for example, Guthrie & Parker 1999; Lindeberg 2007). Nevertheless, the 'three Es'—efficiency, effectiveness and economy—form the basis for most performance audits. Vafaei et al. in Chapter 8 consider performance audits in-depth, including an interesting journey back in time when performance audits were said to have originated (1000 BC). They go on to compare performance audits with operational audits and link both to governance within an NPM framework. With performance audits providing external accountability, a controlling mechanism of corporate governance is the internal audit. One of the findings in Chapter 8 was that the mandate for performance audits in the public sector context is essential to the maintenance of constitutional arrangements, while operational audits are very much an internally focused and practised form of assurance. Hence, according to Vafaei et al. there are essential differences and they have offered up ideas for further research which needs to occur.

Performance is a prevalent topic in this section on governance. Following on from performance audits, we now consider in Chapter 9 the actual performance of a different section of the public sector—this time local government. This topic is one that will be of interest to most countries, but in particular the UK where local government is also subject to close oversight and performance management. In the 1990s, the UK government became a target of more performance monitoring with performance indicators designed to identify just how well the public service was performing and whether their policies were indeed improving service provision and effectiveness (Bird et al. 2005).

Performance measurement, benchmarking, corporate governance and improved audit ambits are often researched in an attempt to provide more understanding (Pilcher 2011). Local government is an under-researched sector and so it is timely that Drew has included this chapter within the governance ambit. In Australia, local government is required to report against state specific key performance indicators (KPIs) and data are published annually (Pilcher 2009). With accrual accounting came the need to keep asset registers and so local government was also required to report each year on these assets. Infrastructure, property, plant and equipment is one of the headings used in government reporting. It consists of all infrastructure assets other than sewerage and water. There has been some research conducted on the manipulation of KPIs in regards to infrastructure—in particular depreciation and asset valuation (see, for example, Barton 2005; Pilcher 2009; Pilcher & Dean 2009).

Drew assesses the risks associated with performance management and measurement, including unintended and intended performance distortions, in Chapter 9. He considers the consequences of not meeting targets, in this case, forced amalgamations of councils. The performance paradox has been defined by, for example, Bevan and Hood (2006) as a discord between performance on paper and actual performance and is well attested in the corpus of scholarly literature on performance management. Chapter 9 looks at three causes of the performance paradox, being (1) unintended distortions (measurement error and the like), (2) synecdochical gap (the disparity between the whole entity—comprised of measurable and unmeasurable elements of performance—and the parts which are measured) and (3) intended distortions (which might be either cheating (outright fabrication) or gaming (exploiting the grey areas)). Drew finds (among other things) that, in view of both the unreliability of the performance indicators employed to guide the billion-dollar reform to local government and the fact that flaws revealed might have been avoided, it is clear that the accounting profession needs to engage more fully in the development and scholarly evaluation of performance management regimes.

We have spoken a lot about the public sector and various sections of government; however, another important section of the overall public sector group is the NFP sector. It was this sector, not government, which provided the majority of social services in Australia up until the time of the Second World War. Today the sector is more diverse and covers activities and services including health, social services, education, sport and recreation, arts and culture, environment, animal welfare, human rights and religious practices (Australian Government Productivity Commission (AGPC) 2010).

Although it is difficult to know exactly how many NFPs exist in the world, a rough estimate in 2015 was more than 10 million (Nonprofit Action 2015). In Australia, there are around 600,000 NFP organisations (AGPC 2010) and these represent a fundamental part of the Australian social infrastructure.

The basic precepts of good governance are fundamental to all organisations, including NFPs. The governance of NFPs is undertaken by the board or committee and is different from the everyday work of the organisation. Boards and committees make strategic decisions and management and staff/volunteers then action the governance decisions (Not-for-Profit Law n.d.).

According to the Australian Institute of Company Directors (AICD), NFP organisations are quite different in many aspects to their commercial counterparts. To achieve optimal performance, these differences must be recognised when considering applicable governance attributes. One of the primary differences the AICD (2016, p. 1) recognises is that in NFP organisations:

> [t]heir primary focus is mission driven, rather than primarily driven by financial return to shareholders (although this should not denigrate the importance of prudential financial management).

A NFP organisation's mission forms an essential component of Gilchrist and Pilcher's Chapter 10. One of the main aims of this chapter is to review the impact of regulatory reform in the context of the chapter's purpose: that mission, rather than commercial concern, is the principal consideration for a NFP organisation.

The NFP sector is also a component of Chapter 11 which considers joined-up government in Australia and NZ. The term came into prominence in the UK under the Labour government in 1997. The National Audit Office (UK) (2001, p. 1) provided this definition:

> Joint working or "joined up" government is the bringing together of a number of public, private and voluntary sector bodies to work across organisational boundaries towards a common goal.

Some of the initiatives implemented under joined-up government in the UK after 1997 included initiatives to address homelessness, truancy, the environment, poverty/social exclusion, school exclusion, family breakdown, active ageing, the rural economy and electronic delivery of government services (Kavanagh & Richards 2001; Wilkins 2002). Chapter 11 explores the Australian and NZ experience of joined-up government, the lessons learned from these experiences and considers the future of joined-up government approaches. Specifically, it explores the untapped potential of the NFP sector in joined-up government approaches in Australia and NZ.

Accounting, accountability and governance—global issues

Each of these concepts is not confined only to Australia and NZ. Chapter 12 considers all the issues discussed in the earlier chapters within the relevant themes and uses these to illuminate the global issues of public sector accounting, accountability and governance. The chapter integrates a conclusion for each previous chapter within the globalisation discussion, allowing the relevant findings to be used to inform future research globally.

Notes

1 Curtin University, Perth WA, Australia (r.pilcher@curtin.edu.au)
2 For example: *Public Integrity* 2015, vol. 17, no. 3, published by Taylor & Francis.

References

Aucoin 2012, 'New political governance in Westminster systems: impartial public administration and management performance at risk', *Governance: An International Journal of Policy, Administration, and Institutions*, vol. 25, no. 2, pp. 177–199.

Aulich, C 2010, 'Citizen participation and local governance: the Australian experience', in E Brunet-Jailly and JF Martin (eds), *Local government in a global world*, University of Toronto Press, Toronto.

Australian Accounting Standards Board (AASB) 2010, 'AASB 1053 Application of tiers of Australian Accounting Standards', AASB, Melbourne, viewed 8 September 2016, [updated January 2015], www.aasb.gov.au/admin/file/content105/c9/AASB1053_06-10.pdf

Australian Bureau of Statistics 2016, 'Government finance statistics, Australia, 2015–16', Explanatory Notes 5512.0, Released 27 April 2017, viewed 30 November 2017, www.abs.gov.au/AUSSTATS/abs@.nsf/Lookup/5512.0ExplanatoryNotes12015-16?OpenDocument

Australian Government Productivity Commission (AGPC) 2010, 'Contribution of the not-for-profit sector', Research Report, Commonwealth of Australia, Canberra.

Australian Public Sector Commission (APSC) 2007, *Building better governance*, Commonwealth of Australia, Canberra.

Australian Public Sector Commission (APSC) 2015, 'Delivering performance and accountability', viewed 1 February 2018, www.apsc.gov.au/publications-and-media/archive/publications-archive/delivering-performance

Australian Institute of Company Directors (AICD) 2016, 'Governance issues in not-for-profit organisations', Director Tools, AICD, Sydney.

Barton, A 1999, 'Land under roads – a financial bonanza or fool's gold?' *Australian Accounting Review*, vol. 9, no. 1, pp. 9–15.

Barton, A 2005, 'Issues in accrual accounting and budgeting by government', *Agenda*, vol. 12, no. 3, pp. 211–226.

Bevan, G & Hood, C 2006, 'What's measured is what matters: targets and gaming in the English public health care system', *Public Administration*, vol. 84, no. 3, pp. 517–538.

Bird, S, Cox, D, Farewell, V, Goldstein, H, Holt, T & Smith, P 2005, 'Performance indicators: good, bad, and ugly', *Journal of the Royal Statistical Academy*, vol. 168, no. 1, pp. 1–27.

Blackie, MJ 1989, *Sub-Saharan Africa: from crisis to sustainable growth*, Report, The World Bank, Washington, DC.

Bovaird, T & Downe, J 2006, 'N generations of reform in UK local government: compliance and resistance to institutional pressures', *International Public Management Journal*, vol. 9, no. 4, pp. 429–454.

Bryer, RA 2000, 'The history of accounting and the transition to capitalism in England. Part one: theory', *Accounting, Organizations and Society*, vol. 25, no. 2, pp. 131–162.

Cancela, J & Geys, B 2016, 'Explaining voter turnout: a meta-analysis of national and subnational elections', *Electoral Studies*, vol. 42, June, pp. 264–275.

Carnegie, GD 2005, 'Promoting accountability in municipalities', *Australian Journal of Public Administration*, vol. 64, no. 3, pp. 78–87.

Carnegie, GD & Wolnizer, PW 1995, 'The financial value of cultural, heritage and scientific collections: an accounting fiction', *Australian Accounting Review*, vol. 5, no. 1, pp. 31–47.

Cavanagh, J, Flynn, S & Moretti, D 2016, 'Implementing accrual accounting in the public sector', Technical Notes and Manuals, International Monetary Fund, Fiscal Affairs Department, Washington, DC.

Champoux, M 2006, 'Briefing Paper No. 27: accrual accounting in New Zealand and Australia: issues and solutions', draft, Harvard Law School, Federal Budget Policy Seminar, Massachusetts.

Chartered Institute of Public Finance and Accountancy, The (CIPFA) & The Office of Public Management (OPM) 2004, *The good governance standard for public services*, OPM & CIPFA, London.

Clatworthy, M, Jones, M & Mellet, H 1997, 'The accounting policies of British Gas and the water companies – a conundrum', *Management Accounting*, vol. 75, no. 5, pp. 36–38.

Comptroller General of the United States 1994, *Government auditing standards, 1994 revision*, General Accounting Office, Washington, DC.

Cotrugli 1458, *Libro de l'Arte de la Mercatura*, Venice.

Davis, G, Wanna, J, Warhurst, J & Weller, P 1993, *Public policy in Australia*, 2nd edn, Allen & Unwin, St Leonards, NSW.

Dobel, JP 2015, 'The fragility of public service: a study of *Richard II* and *Measure for Measure*', *Public Integrity*, vol. 17, no. 3, pp. 291–307.

Dovey, L 2003, 'Achieving better social outcomes in New Zealand through collaboration: perspectives from the United States,' *Working Paper No. 16*, State Services Commission (NZ), viewed 26 January 2018, www.ssc.govt.nz/what-is-the-public-sector

Edwards, M 2002, 'Public sector governance – future issues for Australia', *Australian Journal of Public Administration*, vol. 61, no. 2, pp. 51–61.

Funnell, W 2003, 'Enduring fundamentals: constitutional accountability and auditors-general in the reluctant state', *Critical Perspectives on Accounting*, vol. 14, nos. 1/2, pp. 107–132.

Funnell, W, Cooper, K & Lee, J 2012, *Public sector accounting and accountability in Australia*, UNSW Press, Sydney.

Goldsworthy, J 2010, *Parliamentary sovereignty: contemporary debates*, Cambridge University Press, Cambridge.

Governance Institute of Australia 2016, 'Governance principles for boards of public sector entities in Australia', viewed 23 January 2018, www.governanceinstitute.com.au/knowledge-resources/public-sector-governance/

Guthrie, J 1998, 'Application of accrual accounting in the Australian public sector – rhetoric or reality', *Financial Accountability and Management*, vol. 14, no. 1, pp. 1–19.

Guthrie, J & Parker, L 1999, 'A quarter of a century of performance auditing in the Australian federal public sector: a mutable masque', *Abacus*, vol. 35, no. 3, pp. 302–332.

Hepworth, N 2003, 'Preconditions for successful implementation of accrual accounting in central government', *Public Money and Management*, vol. 23, no. 1, pp. 37–44.

Hepworth, N 2004, 'Accrual accounting in the public sector', *CIPFA Presentation*, 22–25 November, CIPFA, Ankara.

Hood, C 1995, 'The new public management in the 1980s: variations on a theme', *Accounting, Organizations and Society*, vol. 20, nos. 2/3, pp. 93–110.

Hoskin, K & Macve, R 1986, 'Accounting and the examination: a genealogy of disciplinary power', *Accounting, Organizations and Society*, vol. 11, no. 2, pp. 105–136.

Kavanagh, D & Richards, D 2001, 'Departmentalism and joined-up government: back to the future?' *Parliamentary Affairs*, vol. 54, no. 1, pp. 1–18.

Kerr, S, Gillett, J, Sandoz, N & Wilcox, W 2009, 'International financial reporting standards: impact on professional financial statement users', *Commercial Lending Review*, vol. 24, no. 5, pp. 3–9.

Leeson, PT & Dean, AM 2009, 'The democratic domino theory: an empirical investigation', *American Journal of Political Science*, vol. 53, no. 3, pp. 533–551.

Lindeberg, T 2007, 'The ambiguous identity of auditing', *Financial Accountability and Management*', vol. 23, no. 3, pp. 337–350.

MacDermott, K 2007, 'Whatever happened to frank and fearless? The systems of new public management and the ethos and behaviour of the Australian public service', *Discussion Paper 20/07*, Democratic Audit of Australia, Australian National University, Canberra.

Martinelli, A 1983, 'The ledger of Cristianus Lomellinus and Dominicus De Garibaldo, stewards of the city of Genoa (1340–41)', *Abacus*, vol. 19, no. 2, pp. 83–118.

Mayston, D 1993, 'Principals, agents and the economics of accountability in the new public sector', *Accounting, Auditing and Accountability Journal*, vol. 6, no. 3, pp. 68–96.

Meijer, AJ 2003, 'Transparent government: parliamentary and legal accountability in an information age', *Information Polity*, vol. 8, no. 1/2, pp. 67–78.

Meiksins Wood, E 1981, 'The separation of the economic and the political in capitalism', *New Left Review*, vol. I/127, pp. 66–95.

Mulgan, R 2004, 'Public sector reform in New Zealand: issues of public accountability', *Policy and Governance Discussion Paper 04–03*, Australian National University, Asia Pacific School of Economics and Government, Canberra.

National Audit Office (UK) 2001, 'Joining up to improve public services: report by the Comptroller and Auditor-General', HC 383 Session 2001–2002, 7 December.

Nonprofit Action 2015, 'Facts and stats about NGOs worldwide', viewed 25 January 2018, http://nonprofitaction.org/2015/09/facts-and-stats-about-ngos-worldwide/

Not-for-Profit Law n.d., 'Governance and legal duties of office holders', viewed 25 January 2018, www.nfplaw.org.au/governance

NZ Ministry for Culture and Heritage 2014, 'Dominion status', viewed 20 January 2018, https://nzhistory.govt.nz/culture/dominion-day

NZ Ministry for Culture and Heritage 2016, 'Political and constitutional timeline', viewed 20 January 2018, https://nzhistory.govt.nz/politics/milestones

Osborne, D 1999, 'Governance, partnership and development', in J Corkery (ed), *Governance: concepts and applications*, International Institute for Administrative Sciences, Brussels, pp. 37–65.

Pacioli, L 1494, *Summa de arithmetica*, Venice.

Pallot, J 1992, 'Elements of a theoretical framework for public sector accounting', *Accounting, Auditing and Accountability Journal*, vol. 5, no. 1, pp. 38–59.

Parliament of Australia 2012, *Australia's constitution: with overview and notes by the Australian government solicitor*, 9th edn, Commonwealth of Australia, Canberra.

Pilcher, R 2009, 'Deconstructing local government performance and infrastructure measurement', *Asian Review of Accounting*, vol. 17, no. 2, pp. 163–176.

Pilcher, R 2011, 'Implementing IFRS in local government – institutional isomorphism as NPM goes mad?' *Local Government Studies*, vol. 37, no. 4, pp. 367–389.

Pilcher, R 2014, 'Role of internal audit in Australian local government governance – a step in the right direction', *Financial Accountability and Management*, vol. 30, no. 2, pp. 207–238.

Pilcher, R & Dean, G 2009, 'Implementing IFRS in local government – value adding or additional pain?' *Qualitative Research in Accounting and Management*, vol. 6, no. 3, pp. 180–196.

Pilcher, R, Gilchrist, D, Singh, H & Singh, I 2013, 'The interface between internal and external audit in the Australian public sector', *Australian Accounting Review*, vol. 23, no. 4, pp. 330–340.

Pilcher, RA 2006a, 'Asset management in local authorities – financial fiction or management reality', in EL Lande & JC Scheid (eds), *Accounting reform in the public sector: mimicry, fad or necessity*, Experts Comptables Media, Paris, pp. 177–188.

Pilcher, RA 2006b, 'Examining the usefulness of transport infrastructure accounting in local authorities', Doctoral thesis, University of Sydney, Sydney.

Put, V & Turksema, R 2011, 'Selection of topics', in J Lonsdale, P Wilkins & T Ling (eds), *Performance auditing: contributing to accountability in democratic government*, Edward Elgar, Cheltenham, pp. 51–74.

PwC 2016, 'Fighting fraud in the public sector IV', extract from *Eighth PwC Global Economic Crime Survey*, July 2016, viewed 5 June 2017, www.pwc.com.au/publications/fraud-fighting-fraud-public-sector-iv.html

Reilly, A, Appleby, G, Grenfell, L & Lacey, W 2013, *Australian public law*, Oxford University Press, Oxford.

Revsine, L 1991, 'The selective financial misrepresentation hypothesis', *Accounting Horizons*, vol. 5, no. 4, pp. 16–27.

Rutherford, B 1990, 'Towards a conceptual framework for public sector financial reporting', *Public Money & Management*, vol. 10, no. 2, pp. 11–15.

Ryan, C, Guthrie, J & Day, R 2007, 'Politics of financial reporting and the consequences for the public sector', *Abacus*, vol. 43, no. 4, pp. 474–487.

Ryan, CM & Ng, C 2000, 'Public sector corporate governance disclosures: an examination of annual reporting practices in Queensland', *Australian Journal of Public Administration*, vol. 59, no. 2, pp. 11–23.

Seidman, G 2005, 'The origins of accountability: everything I know about the sovereigns' immunity, I learned from *King Henry III*', *Saint Louis University Law Journal*, vol. 49, no. 2, pp. 393–480.

Sterling, RR 1975, 'Toward a science of accounting', *Financial Analysts Journal*, vol. 31, no. 5, pp. 28–36.

Tooley, S & Hooks, J 2010, 'Public accountability: the perceived usefulness of school annual reports', *Australasian Accounting Business and Finance Journal*, vol. 4, no. 2, pp. 39–59.

Trewavas, K, Nives, BR, & Laswad, F 2012, 'The impact of IFRS adoption on public sector financial statements', *Australian Accounting Review*, vol. 22, no. 1, pp. 86–102.

United Kingdom Accounting Standards Board & European Financial Reporting Advisory Group (UKASB/EFRAG) 2012, *Considering the effects of accounting standards: position paper*, UKASB/EFRAG, Brussels, Belgium.

Walker, R, Clarke, F & Dean, G 1999, 'Reporting on the state of infrastructure by local government', *Accounting, Auditing and Accountability Journal*, vol. 12, no. 4, pp. 441–458.

Whitfield, T 2006, 'Parliamentary oversight: an auditor-general's perspective', *Australasian Parliamentary Review*, vol. 21, no. 1, pp. 88–93.

Wilkins, P 2002, 'Accountability and joined-up government', *Australian Journal of Public Administration*, vol. 61, no. 1, pp. 114–119.

Yamey, B 1994, 'Benedetto Cotrugli on bookkeeping (1458)', *Accounting, Business & Financial History*, vol. 4, no. 1, pp. 43–50.

Legislation

Constitution Act 1986 (NZ)

Corporate Law Economic Reform Program (Audit Reform and Corporate Disclosure) Act 2004 (Cwlth) (CLERP 9)

New Zealand Constitution Act 1852 (15 & 16 Vict., c. 72)

Public Finance Act 1989 (NZ)

Sarbanes-Oxley Act of 2002 (PL 107–204, 116 Stat. 745) (USC)

State-Owned Enterprises Act 1986 (NZ)

State Sector Act 1988 (NZ)

Statute of Westminster 1931 (22 Geo. 5, c. 4)

2 Differential reporting

What does it really mean for the public sector?

Robyn Pilcher[1] and David Gilchrist

Introduction

Zeff (1978, p. 63) claimed:

> What is abundantly clear is that we have entered an era in which economic and social consequences may no longer be ignored as a substantive issue in the setting of accounting standards. The profession must respond to the changing tenor of the times while continuing to perform its essential role in the areas in which it possesses undoubted expertise.

His ideas were thought to still be relevant today and were included at the beginning of the United Kingdom Accounting Standards Board and the European Financial Reporting Advisory Group (UKASB/EFRAG) (2011, p. n.p.) Discussion Paper, *Considering the Effects of Accounting Standards*. That very issue, in regards to standard setting for the public sector—specifically in this case the Australian public sector, is considered here. Australia and New Zealand (NZ) are leaders in adopting accounting standards early with both countries agreeing to adopt the International Financial Reporting Standards (IFRS) in 2003. These were known as A-IFRS and NZ IFRS respectively as they contained some minor amendments for the not-for-profit (NFP) and public sectors.

After its introduction, it was soon recognised that A-IFRS and NZ IFRS were too complex for many entities (see, for example, Pilcher & Dean 2009; Ryan, Guthrie & Day 2007), including small and medium entities (SMEs), NFPs and public sector organisations. Many of the disclosures, in particular, were seen to be too burdensome and using the cost-benefit analysis, it was decided, not only for the benefit of the public sector but also smaller businesses, that differential reporting would need to be introduced. In NZ, the NZ Financial Reporting Standards Board (NZ FRSB) established a Differential Reporting Framework in 2005 whilst in Australia, a Reduced Disclosure Requirements (RDR) regime was introduced by the Australian Accounting Standards Board (AASB) on 2 July 2010 (effective 1 July 2013 but with the option to early adopt). It was hoped that the RDR would enhance accountability by ensuring information was understandable, accessible and comparable (Bolivar & Galera 2012). RDR was made operational via AASB

1053 *Application of Tiers of Australian Accounting Standards* (AASB 2010e) and AASB 2010–2 *Amendments to Australian Accounting Standards Arising from Reduced Disclosure Requirements* (AASB 2010f). Remaining framed within Australia's transaction-neutral philosophy, RDR retains the decision-usefulness emphasis (as outlined in the International Accounting Standards Board's (IASB's), (2010) revised conceptual framework and earlier discussions mentioned previously) of the current Australian accounting standards.[2] Unfortunately, the regime was not tested prior to release as to its expected impact.

This chapter considers the potential impact of a differential reporting system on the public sector—something other countries could consider instead of IFRS for SMEs. The main reason this research was undertaken was to consider the process of reviewing the potential effects of a new/revised set of standards, prior to implementation, on public sector reporting. This is very much in line with the 'effect analysis' described in the USASB/EFRAG Position Paper released in 2012. Another reason was to determine possible efficiencies under RDR as well as identify other areas where the idea of an alternative differential reporting system may have merit. At all times the balance between cost and utility is considered as is the ultimate purpose of the reports themselves (for example, Carnegie 2005; Carnegie & Wolnizer 1995). However, other concepts are also contemplated in an attempt to ensure all bases are covered.

Findings support prior work suggesting it may be time to accept that transaction neutrality combined with decision-usefulness are outmoded as underlying concepts for financial reporting in the public sector (for example, Pilcher & Dean 2012). Even though the IFRS Foundation (Hoogervost 2015) has reintroduced accountability into its mission statement, according to Newberry (2015, p. 3), the term has been 'reinterpreted to fit the IASB's narrowed capital markets orientation'. As a result, any application of IFRS to governments (as part of the public sector) would be compromised (Newberry 2015). Perhaps if some type of due process was introduced—similar to that discussed in Europe and the United Kingdom (UKASB/EFRAG 2011)—then the development of differential standards could be evaluated in a timelier, and more effective, manner.

The next section reviews the background to the study. Then differential reporting is discussed along with information about the RDR. Subsequent to these, an outline of the proposed research design—effect analysis—is provided. The results are then presented whilst the penultimate section provides a discussion of these results. An overall conclusion with suggestions for future research appears at the end.

Background

Public sector reforms of the 1980s and 1990s saw the gap between the public and private sectors reduced (Hood 1995). The implementation of these reforms, in particular New Public Management (NPM), initially in Europe and the United Kingdom (UK) and later in Australia, was thought to enhance accountability and transparency of governments on the (debateable) basis that commercial models better achieved this outcome. As such, it was considered that government transparency and accountability required financial information that was more comparable, relevant and useful for decision-making. According to Bolivar and Galera (2007), IFRS could provide the framework for such reporting.

IFRS was introduced by the IASB with for-profit entities only in mind. There have been many papers written tracing the events leading up to both the adoption of accrual accounting and IFRS by various countries, including Australia (see, for example, Christensen & Parker 2010). In Australia, under the transaction-neutral philosophy, the Australian equivalents (A-IFRS) were implemented on 1 January 2005. As part of the convergence process, the AASB included Aus paragraphs in some standards to address private and public NFP accounting issues with public sector entities required, under legislation, to comply with these. It is said by its proponents that transaction neutrality 'provides a neutral financial management system which enhances accountability by allowing the production of impartial, representationally faithful and decision-useful financial reports' (Newberry 2003, p. 28). Regarding the public sector, the benefits are questionable as comparability within and between jurisdictions is not a high priority (Ryan, Guthrie & Day 2007).

The transition to A-IFRS was considered by many (for example, Haswell & McKinnon 2003; Palmer 2008) to be one of the most noteworthy events impacting on financial reporting in Australia for some time. Costs to companies in terms of time and resources in preparing for the change were highly significant (Ham 2002). For the public sector, in-depth research into the cost of change has not been conducted to the same degree. Yet, the public sector in Australia employs over 1,924,800 people (as at June 2016) (Australian Bureau of Statistics 2017) under the *Public Service Act 1999* (Cwlth) with agencies such as Centrelink, the Australian Tax Office and the Department of Defence amongst the largest tax-payer funded organisations in the country.

In addition to the huge compliance costs that came with the conversion to IFRS was the fact that many disclosures were totally irrelevant to certain users (Pilcher & Dean 2009). Hence, one of the reasons *IFRS for SMEs* and the RDR—differential reporting frameworks—were proposed was to simplify reporting for those organisations meeting the stated criteria (AASB 2010c). In Australia, while differential reporting was considered necessary, the adoption of the *IFRS for SMEs* was not considered appropriate given full IFRS had already been adopted (Institute of Chartered Accountants in Australia 2010). As well, the public sector still needed to meet the wider public accountability criteria (Newberry 2015) whereas SMEs did not have this same necessary condition. An alternative was proposed and so began the process that led to the adoption and implementation of the RDR in Australia.

Differential reporting

Differential reporting began to be discussed in countries such as the UK, the United States (US) and Australia back in the 1980s. According to Ceustermans,

Branson and Breesch (2012), differential reporting is simply the idea that there are different reporting requirements for different types of entities. The debate as to what 'types' of entities must meet relevant reporting standards is one that continues today. Interestingly, as many public sectors worldwide have yet to adopt accrual accounting—let alone IFRS—differential reporting has been occurring in an informal way for decades.

Europe, the UK, Ireland, the US and Africa are just some of the countries and continents considering differential reporting. For example, Accountancy Europe is considering the International Public Sector Accounting Standards; in the UK and Ireland differential reporting exists by way of IFRS for SMEs with FRS 102 *The Financial Reporting Standard Applicable in the UK and Republic of Ireland* (UK Financial Reporting Council 2015a) and FRS 105 *The Financial Reporting Standard applicable to the Micro-entities Regime* (UK Financial Reporting Council 2015b) recently released (refer to Chapter 12 for a more detailed discussion).

In Australia, according to Potter, Ravlic and Wright (2013), differential reporting guidelines were initially associated with the conceptual framework developed by the Australian Accounting Research Foundation in the mid-1980s. A comprehensive history of the development of differential reporting in Australia can be found in McCahey (1989) and Potter, Ravlic and Wright (2013).

Adoption of the IASB's *IFRS for SMEs* was expected to occur in Australia as it had for other countries (with some exceptions, such as the US). However, doubt was raised as it was considered a retrograde step in a country that had already adopted full IFRS recognition and measurement accounting policy options (Mackay 2008). Hence, the RDR was produced and implemented (in other words, IFRS with some exceptions).

One of the main areas of concern highlighted by the AASB was the difference between the recognition and measurement requirements of *IFRS for SMEs* compared to those contained in the full IFRS. The AASB's Chair also thought it important to address disclosure requirements at a principle level, not just an individual one (Stevenson 2012). Nevertheless, there were those who considered that, as *IFRS for SMEs* was used as a template for the RDR, the 'top-down' flaw they perceived in *IFRS for SMEs* was therefore incorporated into the RDR (BDO 2010, p. 2). In other words, the AASB started with full IFRS disclosures and then removed those it considered not applicable to the public sector.[3] Stevenson (2012 p. 3) claimed to have overcome this issue with the revised RDR and noted that:

> New Zealand has adopted a reduced disclosure version of NZ IFRS for its Tier 2 for-profit entities, which will align the disclosure concessions for these entities with the RDR for equivalent Australian entities.

In NZ, the FRSB agreed in 2002 to adopt IFRS with it being compulsory from 2007 (Bradbury & van Zijl 2007). Like Australia, transaction neutrality was applied with standards being adopted as such.

Reduced disclosure requirements

The RDR in Australia was expected to remove perceived inefficiencies occurring out of the application of full accounting standards by certain reporting entities, particularly under the transaction-neutral regime. Such entities have been identified as those for which the application of the full requirements for General Purpose Financial Statements (GPFS) is not efficient and for which a lesser reporting framework is considered sufficient in meeting the needs of users (AASB 2010e, para. BC10). The RDR is available to a wide range of entities in both the private and public sectors in preparing GPFS (refer AASB 2010e, para. 13).

In practical terms, the RDR has been implemented by the addition to standards of paragraphs indicating the specific requirements. Those entities that are entitled to adopt the RDR are identified via the creation of two tiers against which reporting requirements are assigned (AASB 2010e). If an organisation has public accountability, it is allocated to Tier 1 (adoption of full A-IFRS) in the case of private sector entities, while public sector entities can implement the RDR regime (i.e. Tier 2) provided they are not governments (AASB 2010e, para. 11/12). Public accountability is further defined (AASB 2010e, App. A, p. 12) as:

> accountability to those existing and potential resource providers and others external to the entity who make economic decisions but are not in a position to demand reports tailored to meet their particular information needs.

As BDO (2010) pointed out, this notion of accountability follows that included in the IASB's *IFRS for SMEs*. Newberry's (2015) concern, rightly, was that with public accountability referring to capital markets in *IFRS for SMEs*, accountability to others (such as discussed in Pilcher et al. 2013), is forgotten.

Nevertheless, in April 2017, the AASB and NZ Accounting Standards Board (NZASB) proposed changes to Tier 2 disclosure requirements. Several reasons were flagged with two—the maintenance of trans-Tasman harmonisation for Tier 2 NFP entities and with the benefits being seen to outweigh the costs—being the major focus. As a result, ED 277 *Reduced Disclosure Requirements for Tier 2 Entities* (AASB 2017) and ED NZASB 2017–1 *Amendments to RDR for Tier 2 For-profit Entities* (NZASB 2017) were released for comment. They were based on two rebuttable presumptions—the first being that the benefits of providing disclosures exceed costs; the second is where costs exceed benefits and so disclosures are not a *key disclosure*.

Clearly, the simpler the models used for financial reporting, the less cost involved in their preparation and audit. This aligns with the premise that government ministers require agencies to achieve their outcomes at the lowest cost possible (Guthrie, Parker & English 2003; Pilcher et al. 2013). As such, the RDR regime may not represent a complete solution to the difficulties of public sector reporting in the context of cost and utility (see, for example, BDO 2010). However, the adoption of the regime may be taken to represent an acceptance that the philosophies surrounding the creation of accounting standards—those of transaction neutrality and decision-usefulness—are not necessarily the best option, thereby giving permission for public sector regulators to consider alternative reporting regimes that might better suit their needs (Newberry 2003; Ryan, Guthrie & Day 2007). Given the public sector consists mainly of service organisations, then analysing RDR as is proposed here may be more suitable than any other type of cost/benefit type analysis. Alongside this, consideration should also be given to qualitative evaluations of reporting regimes such as proposed by Price and Wallace (2002) and Wiener (2006). UKASB/EFRAG (2012) tried to do this with its 'effect analysis' of alternatives to IFRS.

Effect analysis

The reason the UKASB and EFRAG wanted to integrate effect analysis into the standard setting due process was to strengthen that process and so enhance its transparency as well as the accountability and credibility of the standard setter. In other words, the consequences would be considered prior to full implementation of a new standard or major change to one (UKASB/EFRAG 2012, para. 3.4):

> The term "effects" rather than the term "costs and benefits", should be used to refer to the consequences of accounting standards rather than just a quantifiable cost benefit analysis.

This concept is what, in essence, drives the research behind this chapter which considers the prospects for gaining efficiencies in financial reporting in the Australian public sector with the RDR. An in-depth review of the applicable standards (available from the authors) was conducted to identify areas of reduced disclosure that may lead to preparation and audit efficiencies and/or clarity for users while still maintaining adequate transparency. This supports claims by Chan (2003) that increased information access (in this case through reduced complexity) is essential.

Initially, standards that contain RDR paragraphs were analysed to determine the extent to which the reductions provided by RDR were of value to the public sector. Value was interpreted as:

a   an efficiency where an observed opportunity for public sector reporting entities to reduce the disclosure burden by discontinuing compliance-only reporting (with a complementary reduction in audit costs); and/or

b   an improvement where an observed opportunity existed to enhance user value (i.e. utility) as a result of simplification of the reports developed under the RDR; and/or

c   an improvement in accountability/transparency because the financial reports being constructed with RDR focused on elements of significance to a parliamentary audience.

In other words, value in a public sector context relates to RDR's contribution toward simpler reports containing information relevant to accountability and transparency. One way to assess this is to consider the decision-usefulness of statements in terms of understandability, comparability and timeliness—something Bolivar and Galera (2012) did when analysing the fair value measurement basis. Efficiency is assumed to be created when the reporting regime requires less reporting or simplified elements. Like the UK 'effects analysis', this type of review would take place at various intervals throughout the due process phase (refer to UKASB/EFRAG 2012 for details of this timing).

Results

Many RDR reductions are not applicable to public sector needs. Rather, they focus on elements of reporting prevalent in the commercial sector. Further, because of the requirement for government agencies' reports to be consolidated into whole of government reports (prepared under A-IFRS), some of the potential RDR savings appeared to be unobtainable. To test potential effects of the RDR, the authors prepared a comprehensive analysis of the RDR for a sample of the standards.[4]

One of the reasons for the initial analysis was to determine whether RDR satisfied the decision-usefulness criterion for financial reporting, as well as accountability and transparency. To do this, the standards would need to improve efficiency, transparency and benchmarking (Bolivar & Galera 2007; Pilcher & Gilchrist 2012). Several significant reductions in reporting, as required under the RDR, were identified.

The RDR was implemented and then, in January 2017, the AASB released ED 277 *Reduced Disclosure Requirements for Tier 2 Entities* based on feedback from users (AASB 2017). According to the AASB (2017, p. 5) the revised standard is:

a) intended to result in a more robust approach to determining disclosure requirements for Tier 2 entities, with a clearer focus on user needs; and
b) being undertaken jointly with the NZASB to maintain trans-Tasman harmonisation for Tier 2 entities.

Several standards had been flagged for changed. One of these was AASB 7 *Financial Instruments: Disclosures* (AASB 2010a) which was also one of the standards selected by the authors as needing more consideration. The AASB has recommended that further reductions (specifics not yet available) be made to this standard's disclosures. From our analysis further reductions may not necessarily be a good thing. Originally, under RDR the key disclosures excluded were:

• Para 18 *Details of loan breaches during the period:* it would seem that this is an important disclosure in a public sector environment.
• Paras 27 and 27A *Fair value hierarchy disclosures:* i.e., the analysis for financial instruments measured at fair value into the hierarchy reflecting the significance of the inputs used in making the measurements (deleted August 2015).

- Para 31 *The disclosures of the risks:* arising from financial instruments and how they have been managed. Typically including credit risk, liquidity risk and market risk.
- Para 33 *Qualitative disclosures:* the exposures to risk and how they arise; its objectives, policies and processes for managing the risk and the methods used to measure the risk; and any changes from the previous period.
- Para 34 *Quantitative disclosures:* summary quantitative data about its exposure to that risk at the end of the reporting period.

Arguably, in a commercial sense, breaches of loans do not need to be reported. However, the application of this reduction in a public sector environment obviates against appropriate levels of transparency and could be a considerable issue for governments undertaking financing operations. The inclusion of paragraph RDR18.1 supports these assertions. With fair value, potentially significant transparency is lost here if entities are not required to report such information. This is especially so where disclosures relating to public sector specific reporting elements include those where the proportion of net assets, as a percentage of the whole, can be quite high. These assets include the value of land under roads, crown land and other public assets such as museum collections.

While private organisations would not necessarily need to report on those items excluded by RDR, it must be remembered that the public sector bears the onus of greater accountability and greater transparency (as explained earlier).

Another standard critical in the presentation of accounting information is AASB 107 *Statement of Cash Flows* (AASB 2010c). In the public sector context, it is undertaken in various forms such as the budget process, the forward estimates process and the whole of government reporting process, all of which provide transparency. Key disclosures excluded under the RDR are:

- Reconciliation of cash flows from operating activities (when an entity uses the direct method).
- Disclosure cash received or paid from subsidiaries and other businesses in respect of both obtaining and losing control of subsidiaries or other businesses. Arguably, this element should continue to be disclosed.
- Disclosure of the amount of the cash flows arising from the operating, investing and financing activities of each reportable segment.

Under ED 277, the AASB is not proposing to make any changes to this standard (AASB 2017). Perhaps this decision needs to be reassessed as, for example, public sector entities need to report all sales relating to the second dot point as a matter of transparency.

These are just two examples of standards where differential reporting can have an impact on the public sector. There are many other standards (such as AASB 2007, 2010b, 2010d, 101, 108 and 1052) that appear to have been ignored in any review process.

Further discussion

For public sector entities other than the federal, state, territory and local governments currently preparing GPFSs, there is potentially some benefit resulting from RDR. The challenge is to determine whether *all* Australian Tier 2 entities can implement these or if entities will need to be identified on an agency by agency, state by state basis. Most agencies would need to report transactions that are of qualitative interest to various audiences (for future research).

As such, there are three major policy challenges facing public sector regulators in relation to RDR. First, there is the issue of consolidation of financial statements from entity level into the whole of government reports. While individual public sector agencies are, in theory, allowed to adopt RDR, governments (and hence consolidated whole of government reports) are not entitled to (AASB 1053, para 13(c)). Therefore, there is a potential need for significant additional disclosures in individual agency reports in order to bridge the gap between RDR and A-IFRS. As a result, there is minimal advantage in adopting the RDR at the agency level as savings would be lost once consolidation is required. Secondly, a challenge exists for state and Commonwealth Treasuries to allow the application of RDR across the bulk of the sector whilst still ensuring those few agencies with substantive reporting obligations (for example, financial service agencies) report information that allows for effective and meaningful accountability, transparency and for consolidation. Treasuries may consider varied adoption. However, such an approach will increase complexity and the costs of reporting because additional financial reporting models would need to be developed. As well, it needs to be conducted within the context of other related financial management reforms—a concept suggested by Carlin (2005) in relation to accrual accounting but applicable here.

Given the RDR project is linked to the state and Commonwealth's aim to reduce costs associated with financial reporting, differential reporting may be just the beginning. This leads to the third, and perhaps more significant policy level challenge, being Treasuries considering the outcomes associated with the reporting of financial information, performance commentary and the unaligned requirements of the A-IFRS, RDR, Government Finance Statistics and other regulations applicable to certain agencies. Reporting, as well as the consideration of efficiencies, might be found in a more subtle application of the standards themselves.[5]

While Treasuries may consider varied reporting requirements across the public sector, auditors-general are likely to baulk at the increased complexity that may require additional time to complete the audit process. This complexity would relate to the need for additional disclosure information to be provided outside of financial statements deploying RDR which must then be audited as part of the whole of government audit process. Although auditors-general do not make an overt case for or against RDR, efficiencies gained in the audit of individual agencies are likely to be lost in auditing additional disclosures.

Conclusion and future research

There has been some debate concerning the applicability of IFRS to the public sector (see, for example, Pilcher & Dean 2012). However, with more and more countries moving in this direction and with Australia and NZ working closely on RDR, it appears to be here to stay. Hence, how can we make it more relevant and ensure in the future that some type of effect analysis is considered in the due process of any further major changes? Initially the research detailed in this chapter examined the potential impact of RDR and found it is likely to only bring marginal benefits unless:

- Specific deviations from reporting requirements are established by Treasury for specific agencies in order to facilitate the consolidation process;
- Other potential elements of reduced disclosure, not currently incorporated into the RDR, are considered by public sector regulators with a view to seeking more appropriate efficiencies. This process will likely need more focused efforts in order to identify the audience(s) and to establish that audience's requirements.

Future research will examine the revised RDR requirements in each accounting standard and compare it with the requirements of each Australian state and territory model template. Qualitative materiality also requires further research.[6] Given the political environment associated with the public sector (for example, Pilcher & Dean 2009; Newberry 2015), qualitative materiality becomes extremely important as both primary and secondary users want to ensure the utmost propriety is applied. Therefore, when examining the materiality of transactions and balances for reporting purposes, public sector preparers must consider both quantitative (i.e. financial/technical) and qualitative materiality. With public accountability linked very closely to fiduciary capacity (Newberry 2015), qualitative materiality becomes even more important (Price & Wallace 2002). While some reductions are logical for Tier 2 commercial organisations, qualitative materiality may mean that public sector organisations should still report items considered immaterial in a monetary sense.

This chapter details the pros and cons of differential reporting for the public sector. It also provides reasons for other countries to encourage standard setters to conduct some type of due process (such as 'effect analysis' or the post-analysis review by the AASB) prior to implementing any major, costly, changes.

Notes

1 Curtin University, Perth WA, Australia (r.pilcher@curtin.edu.au).
2 'The AASB makes accounting standards with a view to requiring like transactions and events to be accounted for in a like manner for all types of entities. This is referred to as "transaction neutrality"' (AASB 2011, para 39).
3 Obviously it was far more complex than this. See Potter, Ravlic and Wright (2013) for more details. The AASB are currently revising the RDR framework and, in particular, the minimum disclosures required of all Tier 2 entities (AASB 2015a Action Alert No. 173).

4 A detailed analysis of these five standards in tabular format is available from the authors.

5 August 2015 the AASB released *ED 270 Reporting Service Performance Information* in an attempt to 'establish principles and requirements for an entity to report service performance information useful for accountability and decision-making purposes' (AASB 2015b, p. 6).

6 Here the term qualitative materiality refers to those instances where financial reporting using the litmus test of quantitative materiality is insufficient for appropriate levels of disclosure regarding the nature and effectiveness of the allocation and consumption of public resources.

References

Australian Accounting Standards Board (AASB) 2007, 'AASB 1052 Disaggregated disclosures', AASB, Melbourne, viewed 30 July 2015, [updated June 2014], www.aasb. gov.au/admin/file/content102/c3/AASB1052_12-07_ERDRjun10_07-09.pdf

Australian Accounting Standards Board (AASB) 2010a, 'AASB 7 Financial instruments disclosures', AASB, Melbourne, viewed 30 July 2015, [updated August 2015], www. aasb.gov.au/admin/file/content105/c9/aasb7_08-05_compdec08_07-08.pdf

Australian Accounting Standards Board (AASB) 2010b, 'AASB 101 Presentation of financial statements', AASB, Melbourne, viewed 30 July 2015, [updated July 2015], www. aasb.gov.au/admin/file/content105/c9/AASB101_07-04_COMPsep05_01-06.pdf

Australian Accounting Standards Board (AASB) 2010c, 'AASB 107 Statement of cash flows', AASB, Melbourne, viewed 8 September 2016, [updated August 2015], www. aasb.gov.au/admin/file/content105/c9/AASB107_07-04_COMPjul07_07-07.pdf

Australian Accounting Standards Board (AASB) 2010d, 'AASB 108 Accounting policies, changes in accounting estimates and errors', AASB, Melbourne, viewed 8 September 2016, [updated August 2015], www.aasb.gov.au/admin/file/content105/c9/ AASB108_07-04_COMPmay11_07-11.pdf

Australian Accounting Standards Board (AASB) 2010e, 'AASB 1053 Application of tiers of Australian accounting standards', AASB, Melbourne, viewed 8 September 2016, [updated January 2015], www.aasb.gov.au/admin/file/content105/c9/AASB1053_06-10.pdf

Australian Accounting Standards Board (AASB) 2010f, 'AASB 2010–2 Amendments to Australian accounting standards arising from reduced disclosure requirements', AASB, Melbourne, viewed 8 September 2016, www.aasb.gov.au/admin/file/content105/c9/ AASB2010-2_06-10.pdf

Australian Accounting Standards Board (AASB) 2011, 'AASB policies and processes', AASB, Melbourne, viewed 3 September 2016, www.aasb.gov.au/admin/file/content102/ c3/Policy_Statement_03-11.pdf

Australian Accounting Standards Board (AASB) 2015a, 'AASB Action Alert Issue No. 173, 9 July 2015', viewed 3 September 2016, www.aasb.gov.au/admin/file/content102/ c3/M146_Action_Alert_July_2015.pdf

Australian Accounting Standards Board (AASB) 2015b, 'AASB Exposure Draft (ED) 270 Reporting Service Performance Information', AASB, Melbourne, viewed 12 March 2017, www.aasb.gov.au/admin/file/content105/c9/ACCED270_08-15.pdf

Australian Accounting Standards Board (AASB) 2017, 'AASB Exposure Draft (ED) 277 Reduced Disclosure Requirements for Tier 2 Entities', AASB, Melbourne, viewed 30 September 2017, www.aasb.gov.au/admin/file/content105/c9/ACCED277_01-17.pdf

Australian Bureau of Statistics 2017, '6248.0.55.002 – Employment and earnings, public sector, Australia, 2016–17', viewed 13 February 2017, www.abs.gov.au/ausstats/abs@. nsf/mf/6248.0.55.002/

BDO 2010, 'Response to call for comment on ED192 revised differential reporting framework', 23 April 2010 (Submission 24), viewed 13 February 2017, www.aasb.gov.au/admin/file/content106/c2/ED192_sub_24.pdf

Bolivar, M & Galera, A 2007, 'Could fair value accounting be useful, under NPM models, for users of financial information?' *International Review of Administrative Sciences*, vol. 73, no. 3, pp. 473–502.

Bolivar, M & Galera, A 2012, 'The role of fair value accounting in promoting government accountability', *ABACUS*, vol. 48, no. 3, pp. 348–386.

Bradbury, M & van Zijl, T 2007, 'International financial reporting standards and New Zealand: loss of sector neutrality', *Research in Accounting Regulation*, vol. 19, pp. 35–51.

Carlin, T 2005, 'Debating the impact of accrual accounting and reporting in the public sector', *Financial Accountability and Management*, vol. 21, no. 3, pp. 309–336.

Carnegie, GD 2005, 'Promoting accountability in municipalities', *Australian Journal of Public Administration*, vol. 64, no. 3, pp. 78–87.

Carnegie, GD & Wolnizer, PW 1995, 'The financial value of cultural, heritage and scientific collections: an accounting fiction', *Australian Accounting Review*, vol. 5, no. 1, pp. 31–47.

Ceustermans, S, Branson, J & Breesch, D 2012, 'Differential financial reporting requirements: developing a framework using a multi-actor multi-criteria analysis', *SSRN Electronic Journal*, https://ssrn.com/abstract=2005053.

Chan, J 2003, 'Government accounting: an assessment of theory, purposes and standards', *Public Money and Management*, vol. 23, no 1, pp. 13–20.

Christensen, M & Parker, L 2010, 'Using ideas to advance professions: public sector accrual accounting', *Financial Management and Accountability*, vol. 26, no. 3, pp. 246–266.

Financial Accounting Foundation n.d, 'Accounting standards', viewed 15 September 2017, www.accountingfoundation.org/jsp/Foundation/Page/FAFSectionPage&cid=1351027541272

Financial Reporting Council (UK) 2015a, *FRS 102 The financial reporting standard applicable in the UK and Republic of Ireland*, Financial Reporting Council, London.

Financial Reporting Council (UK) 2015b, *FRS 105 The financial reporting standard applicable to the micro-entities regime*, Financial Reporting Council, London.

Guthrie, J, Parker, L & English, L 2003, 'A review of new public financial management change in Australia', *Australian Accounting Review*, vol. 13, no. 2, pp. 3–9.

Ham, P 2002, 'Peace, love and accounting', *CA Charter*, vol. 73, pp. 39–40.

Haswell, S & McKinnon, J 2003, 'IASB standards for Australia by 2005: catapult or Trojan horse?' *Australian Accounting Review*, vol. 13, no. 29, pp. 8–16.

Hood, C 1995, 'The new public management in the 1980s: variations on a theme', *Accounting, Organizations and Society*, vol. 20, no. 2/3, pp. 93–110.

Hoogervost, H 2015, 'Financial reporting standards for the world economy', speech presented for the IASB at the *International Financial Reporting Standards (IFRS) Foundation Conference*, 15 April 2015, Toronto, Canada, viewed 30 August 2016, www.ifrs.org/Alerts/Conference/Documents/2015/Speech-Hans-Hoogervorst-mission-statement-April-2015.pdf

Institute of Chartered Accountants in Australia (ICAA) 2010, 'Reduced disclosure regime', viewed 1 March 2011, www.charteredaccountants.com.au/Industry-Topics/Reporting/Current-issues/Reduced-disclosure-regime/News-and-updates/Reduced-disclosure-regime.aspx

International Accounting Standards Board (IASB) 2009, 'International financial reporting standard for small and medium-sized entities (IFRS for SMEs)', viewed 30 August 2015, http://ifrs.org

International Accounting Standards Board (IASB) 2010, 'Conceptual framework for financial reporting 2010', viewed 30 August 2015, http://eifrs.ifrs.org/eifrs/files/234/conceptualframeworksep2010_151.pdf

MacKay, R 2008, 'Is IFRS for SMEs a friend or a foe?' *Charter* April 2008, pp. 68–69.

McCahey, J 1989, 'Differential reporting', *Australian Accountant*, vol. 59, no. 6, pp. 83–87.

New Zealand Accounting Standards Board (NZASB) 2017, 'ED NZASB 2017-1 Amendments to RDR for Tier 2 For-profit Entities', April.

Newberry, S 2003, ' "Sector neutrality" and NPM incentives: their use in eroding the public sector', *Australian Accounting Review*, vol. 13, no. 2, pp. 28–34.

Newberry, S 2015, 'Public sector accounting: shifting concepts of accountability', *Public Money and Management*, vol. 35, no. 5, pp. 371–376.

Palmer, PD 2008, 'Disclosure of the impacts of adopting Australian equivalents of international financial reporting standards', *Accounting and Finance*, vol. 48, no. 5, pp. 847–870.

Pilcher, R & Dean, G 2009, 'Consequences and costs of compliance of financial reporting for local government', *European Accounting Review*, vol. 18, no. 4, pp. 725–744.

Pilcher, R & Dean, G 2012, 'The consequence of accrual reporting on local government risk – Australian evidence', in F. Capalbo (ed), *L'applicazione della contabilità economica nel settore pubblico: aspettative, risultati e criticità*, Giappichelli, Torino, pp. 27–48.

Pilcher, R & Gilchrist, D 2012, 'Reduced disclosure – the finer points', *Public Accountant*, vol. 28, no. 1, February/March, pp. 44–45.

Pilcher, R, Gilchrist, D, Singh, H & Singh, I 2013, 'The interface between internal and external audit in the Australian public sector', *Australian Accounting Review*, vol. 23, no. 4, pp. 330–340.

Potter, B, Ravlic, T & Wright, S 2013, 'Developing accounting regulations that reflect public viewpoints: the Australian solution to differential reporting', *Australian Accounting Review*, vol. 23, no. 1, pp. 18–28.

Price, R & Wallace, W 2002, 'An international comparison of materiality guidance for governments, public services and charities', *Financial Accountability and Management*, vol. 18, no. 3, pp. 291–308.

Ryan, C, Guthrie, J & Day, R 2007, 'Politics of financial reporting and the consequences for the public sector', *ABACUS*, vol. 43, no. 4, pp. 474–487.

Stevenson, KM 2012, 'Comments on the IASB's request for information: comprehensive review of IFRS for SMEs', Australian Accounting Standards Board, viewed 13 February 2018, www.aasb.gov.au/admin/file/content102/c3/AASB_Letter_IASB_Review_for_SMEs_11-12.pdf

United Kingdom Accounting Standards Board & European Financial Reporting Advisory Group (UKASB/EFRAG) 2011, 'Considering the effects of accounting standards', *Discussion Paper*, January.

United Kingdom Accounting Standards Board & European Financial Reporting Advisory Group (UKASB/EFRAG) 2012, 'Considering the Effects of Accounting Standards', *Position Paper*, June.

Wiener, J 2006, 'Better regulation in Europe', *Duke Law School Faculty Scholarship Series*, October.

Yamey, BS 1994, 'Benedetto Cotrugli on bookkeeping 1458', *Accounting, Business & Financial History*, vol. 4, no. 1, pp. 43–50.

Zeff, SA 1978, 'The rise of "economic consequences"', *The Journal of Accountancy*, vol. 146, no. 6, pp. 56–63 as sited in UKASB/EFRAG *Considering the Effects of Accounting Standards*, Discussion Paper, January 2011.

3 Depreciation in local government—still the problems continue

Robyn Pilcher[1]

Introduction

As part of the overall public sector reforms of the 1980s, the *Local Government Amendment Act 1989* (New Zealand (NZ)) was introduced to change cash accounting to accrual reporting. Interestingly, this coincided with the NZ Local Government Commission reducing the number of councils from over 800 to 87 (McKinlay Douglas Ltd 1998). Four years later, Australia followed suit with the release of Australian Accounting Standard (AAS) 27 *Financial Reporting by Local Government* by the Australian Accounting Research Foundation (AARF 1993). This entailed the first-time recognition of infrastructure assets and an additional expense—depreciation—being included in the profit and loss statement of local councils. At the same time, legislation for local government authorities (LGAs) was enacted in each Australian state and one territory providing 'the legal framework for an effective, efficient, environmentally responsible and open system of local government' (*Local Government Act 1993* (NSW), s. 7(a)).[2] Then, in 2006, local governments in both Australia and NZ had to produce their first set of financial reports to comply with the International Financial Reporting Standards (IFRS) (Pilcher & Dean 2009).

The local government reforms were meant to produce many benefits, including improved asset management through the development of asset management plans. However, valuation and depreciation of roads is still, after all these years, causing problems for both council engineers and accountants alike. For example, Ditchburn (2017, p. 16) claimed:

> Road asset data is an essential component of a road manager's tool kit. However, this data 'language' varies across road and government agencies—and often within organisations—making comparisons difficult and stymying innovation.

Early work by Pilcher (2005, 2009), Goldsmith (2002) and others found that communication between engineers (responsible for reporting the physical condition of infrastructure) and accountants (responsible for all financial aspects, including depreciation) was basically non-existent. Interestingly, a recent article in the

Institute of Public Works Engineering Australasia's (IPWEA's 2017) *Inspire* magazine, detailed findings from a round table held to discuss the challenges facing local government and engineers communicating with accounting staff. On that panel, Peter Way (Chair of the Australian arm of the IPWEA National Asset Management Strategy Council) (2017, p. 32) began the discussion with the following:

> There's still very much a silo mentality within a lot of council organisations, with the various departments driven by their own needs and objectives, hence [there is] a lack of collaboration and communication between them.

There are three aims for this particular chapter. The first outcome will be to bring to the attention of academics, once again, the problems associated with asset management and depreciation by examining the past, the present and the future. The second goal is to raise the various issues still in need of research and the final aim is to raise yet another question—can a recycled idea like depreciation ever be resolved (Sterling 1975)? This chapter is only the tip of the iceberg when it comes to the amount of research still to be undertaken.

To begin, this chapter presents a brief background to local government in Australia and NZ. Then, an outline of asset management and depreciation theories and practices over the years, and their importance within local government reforms, is advanced. Within this section is a brief review of discussion forums—an area not commonly used in accounting research but one that can reveal current issues in asset management as well as be a catalyst for future research.[3] For the purposes of our research, the discussion forum we are using will be referred to as Accounting and Engineering (XAE) Public Forum.[4] The penultimate section considers the results of the review with the conclusion summarising the research and providing suggestions for future research. This future research—potentially the most important aim of the chapter—provides an exciting and unique opportunity to explore not only accounting concepts, but also the use of social media in the research of these concepts.

Background to local government in Australia and New Zealand

In Australia, there are three levels of government—federal, state and local. In 2017 in Australia there were 560 LGAs (also known as councils) (Australian Local Government Association (ALGA 2017). Councils manage a significant number of infrastructure assets, including buildings, parks and gardens, roads, bridges, council land and drainage networks. These assets, in turn, support services such as home and community care, maternal and child health care, recreation and leisure facilities, waste and environment management, transport and economic development (Victorian Auditor-General's Office 2014). Hence, it is essential that this infrastructure should be of a satisfactory standard in terms of providing services in a relevant, functional, safe, reliable and cost-efficient manner.

NZ is represented by 78 LGAs. As in Australia, these councils are responsible for managing different infrastructure assets designed to support the NZ community. In 2015, fixed assets were valued at $NZ107.9 billion whilst in Australia the gross replacement value of local government infrastructure was $A438 billion (ALGA 2015). Maintaining these assets in a 'satisfactory' condition is no small achievement.

Accounting standards impact on valuation, depreciation, revaluation, impairment and so on regarding a council's assets. In other words, information related to asset management.

Asset management from Domesday to now

Asset management is a topic that one could spend hundreds of hours exploring. If we go as far back as the Domesday Book (compiled in England in 1086), we can see assets such as land and livestock were recorded. For what purpose? This is still being debated but one possibility greatly favoured was that it was used for taxation purposes (BBC 2014; *The Domesday Book Online* n.d.). Four hundred years on, in the accounting for United Kingdom (UK) parishes, we see that accounting for assets (inventory) was very inconsistent. Several historians have analysed the accounts of the churchwardens in various parishes (for example, Cox 1913; Kitto 1901). In many parishes (and Jones 1994 uses the examples of Bodicote, Hooton, Pagnell and St Nicholas) there was no mention whatsoever of inventories. However, others (such as Ashburton) did include physical items in the main accounts. Then, from 1509, physical inventories were given values and were regular entries under 'valuations' (Jones 1994). So, for example, prior to 1509, the accounts might have included a 'silver spoon, a plate and a cover' (Jones 1994, p. 386). Then, from 1509/1510 they would appear as: '$2^{1/2}$ oz. of silver worth 7s. 11d. and 14s. in wax' (Jones 1994, p. 386). These valuations appeared until 1557 when accounts reverted back to being entirely cash-based.

Although the county and the parish may be older, when considering local councils, it has been argued that 'the local government accounting profession came from the boroughs' (Jones 1994, p. 388). Like today, there was a local government act (*Municipal Corporations Act 1835* (5 & 6 Wm. IV., c. 76) (UK)) and management were directly accountable to the ratepayers. It was several decades on before the cash-based system gave way to accrual accounting in local government.

Today, LGA infrastructure represents a major investment which, in developed countries, has been built up progressively over many centuries and which requires detailed asset management. The Australia/NZ International Infrastructure Manual (Ingenium 2002, p. 1.3) claims the goal of infrastructure asset management is:

> to meet a required level of service in the most cost-effective way through the creation, acquisition, maintenance, operation, rehabilitation and disposal of assets to provide for present and future customers.

So, we can see that asset management is influenced by both physical and financial factors. Unfortunately, failure to manage assets properly can be due to aspects that affect one or both of these factors. It can be due to a lack of resources, engineering or accounting creativity, financial or even political pressures that impact on the accounting system in place at the time (Pilcher 2006). Revsine (1991, p. 16) stated that 'financial reporting rules are often arbitrary, complicated and misleading'—providing opportunity for manipulation of financial figures so as selectively to misrepresent economic reality when deemed necessary by management. This is cause for concern if one considers the impact failing infrastructure can have on the community. Engineers may provide advice that council accountants, due to lack of resources or loose interpretation of the accounting standards, ignore. An example of an actual infrastructure failure is a bridge collapse in February 2017 in South Australia. Bridges rated by engineers as 'poor' are still being used, as maintenance and depreciation rates are calculated based on a variety of factors, not always engineering based. Rod Hook, a former Department of Transport and Infrastructure chief executive, had this to say about the rating system: 'what it does is measure the value of the bridge compared to its value when it was built and gives an indication of when maintenance and resourcing needs to increase' (in Lagenberg 2017 n.p.).

Very similar results can be found worldwide. In the UK, a study carried out by the Royal Automobile Club (RAC) found that 'thousands of council-maintained road bridges are substandard and not fit to bear the weight of the heaviest lorries' (Lancefield 2017). In Canada in 2016, 35% of assets (including roads) were found to be in a poor condition, and declining (Canada Infrastructure 2016). In the United States (US) in 2005 The American Society of Civil Engineers (ASCE) gave America a D rating after assessing 12 categories of infrastructure ranging from rails and roads to wastewater treatment and dams (ASCE 2005). In a 2013 report on the nation's infrastructure by the ASCE it was claimed that 'although one out of every nine bridges was structurally deficient, the bridges (and connecting roads) were vital to motorists, who take 210 million trips daily across a deficient bridge' (Bello 2013). The same stories of funding shortages, lack of resources available to repair infrastructure when needed and potential mis-reporting of actual costs could all contribute to the many potential or actual disasters.

It is obvious from this information that asset management and infrastructure condition are connected. In 2010, Engineers Australia released their *Infrastructure Report Card* (none has been released since), providing a C+ ranking across the country. Local government roads were given an overall rating of D+, indicating they were in very poor condition. Given LGAs are responsible for around 660,000 km of roads (Roads Australia 2017), this is a major concern.

NZ has a good reputation regarding asset management (NZ Office of the Controller and Auditor-General 2014). Although NZ LGAs are responsible for far less roads than Australia, they still need to maintain around 80,000 km. To date there has been an under-investment in their maintenance which they are looking to address (NZ Ministry of Transport 2015).

Again, looking overseas, in the UK, of the total road length (396,703 km), 97% is managed by local authorities. In 2010–2011 nearly 60% of roads were in a poor condition in need of some type of maintenance. According to the UK Government Department for Transport (2017), this has been reduced to around 20%. In the US in 2010, on average 45% of all roads were in 'significantly poor condition' (The Council of State Governments 2010, p. 1). However, looking at individual states provides an even worse scenario. For example, in California 75% of roads were considered to be in a poor condition, in Connecticut 74% and in the District of Columbia it was 100%. In 2016 and 2017, a similar finding was reported (although with the District of Columbia statistics missing) with an average of 49% of roads in 'poor/mediocre condition' (US Government Department for Transportation 2016, n.p.; ASCE 2017, p. 5).

From these examples (and from the wording of the current accounting standards allowing individual judgement) we can see that human intervention by way of determining 'value', 'depreciation' (to get a book value) and 'maintenance' is apparent. The word 'measure', in itself, opens a can of worms (for example, see Miller & Loftus 2000). Issues related to measurement provide a conundrum and in the 21st century continue to confuse both preparers and users of financial statements (Pilcher 2009). There is no doubt this confusion will continue. Examining the various uses in the literature of 'measurement', 'value' and 'cost' it would seem that 'some interpretations suffer from 'catachresis'—or are conditioned by what Whitehead (1929) described as recourse to 'misplaced concreteness' (in Pilcher 2009, p. 167).[5]

Historical analysis of asset valuations is beyond the scope of this chapter, but issues apparent in modern day local government reporting—political influence; use of estimations; personal judgements; depreciation manipulation—were just as common then as they are now (as detailed previously). Today, asset valuations are still providing challenges for preparers. One way of discovering this is to consider, as I did for this chapter, joining a discussion forum or weblog (blog) relevant to the topic under consideration.

Blogs are set up with public or semi-public profiles, target people rather than topics and are structured as personal networks (Rettberg 2009). Discussion forums, in comparison, involve a relatively smaller number of participants; the messages are relevant to this smaller group; there is mutual consideration and involvement by participants and 'some kind of cognitive and affective engrossment in it' (Goffman 1963, p. 36).

One way of analysing discussion forums is with content analysis. Although word limits mean this chapter can't go into detail, Marra, Moore and Klimezak (2004) provided a great starting point for those considering content analysis of forums or blogs.

Valuation issues, something raised in discussion forums, not only have multiple consequences for local councils today, but will impact on all associated aspects of asset management in the future. For example, there is *still* a difference in Australia between jurisdictions in the methods each uses.

> Note that there is a difference [between Australian states as] in Victoria Councils are required to report at greenfield values [as say, compared to current replacement cost]. The greenfield method meets financial reporting requirements, but for councils' practical asset management purposes, may significantly underestimate the actual cost of renewing the infrastructure.
>
> (XAE Public Forum, Council B, SA Accountant, June 2014)

This method of reporting has many consequences, not least of which is its impact on depreciation.

Depreciation through the years

In his discussion on depreciation, Sterling (1975, p. 28) claimed the topic and its related problems have been debated, pushed aside and debated again and would continue to be so in the future—'recycled ideas without resolving issues'. Another controversial notion appearing in his 1975 work, as well as others, was his view of depreciation as an arbitrary convention, subject to the imagination (or, in the words of the current accounting standards, 'approximation methods') of the pre-parer (AASB 116 2015, para. 46).

Chandler and Edwards (1996) provided another example of 'recycled ideas' with their discussion of 'recurring issues' which concerned auditing practitioners more than 100 years ago. It is interesting to note Chandler and Edwards's (1996, p. 22) comment: 'The events and discussion of one century ago may seem remote indeed, yet in reading the material, the immediate impression is one of familiarity with the issues under discussion'. Perhaps readers will form the same opinion upon reading the rest of this chapter.

Today one can select any accounting book and find the definition of depreciation. In general, the purpose of depreciation is to match the net cost of a fixed (or non-current) asset to revenue arising during each accounting period (for example, Cavinato 1991). Earlier definitions of depreciation were not so clearly enunciated.

Possibly the earliest theory of depreciation, that of falling price, was expressed by the Roman Vitruvius who described annual depreciation as 'the price of passing of each year' (Chatfield 1977, p. 96). Vitruvius set the rule that in valuing a masonry wall, one-eighteenth of its cost should be deducted each year it had stood. Other early examples are that of John Mellis (1588), who showed 10 guineas written off for the 'decay' of household implements and Stephen Monteage (1683), who wrote six pounds off the opening value of the stock of horses 'for their use and impairing' (Littleton 1933, pp. 223–224).

However, it was not until the advent of industrialisation in the 18th century and an increase in expenditure on fixed assets that the practice of depreciation became more common. Innovations such as Kaye's 'Flying Shuttle' in the 1730s, Hargreave's 'Spinning Jenny' (1765), Arkwright's water-powered spinning frame (1769) and Cartwright's power loom (1784) led businesses to pay more attention to accounting for the requisite capital expenditure (Edwards 1989).

Valuation methods of depreciation, as used in the 16th, 17th and 18th centuries, were difficult to standardise. Even by the 19th century, the idea of depreciation was not clearly established and many thought it should not be used at all. In 1878, the US Supreme Court criticised the practice of reducing operating expenses by depreciation and would only allow expenditure actually incurred to be deducted from overall gross earnings (*US v Kansas Pacific Railway Company*, [1878] 99 US 455). Pitts's (1998) study of British coal companies 1864–1914, found that a large variety of depreciation policy and disclosure policy existed and that the practice for depreciation varied from company to company and within a company over time.

One line of thought was that the lack of a clear definition of depreciation was indicative of the confusion surrounding the concept at the time (Chatfield 1977). Whether it is depreciation in general, useful life or residual value, inconsistency continues even now. There are those who consider with regular maintenance, residual value is not needed (nor is depreciation) as roads would have an unlimited life (Goldberg 1960; Pilcher 2005; Woodward 1956). On the other hand, Jeff Roorda and Associates (2010) claimed roads did deteriorate no matter how often maintenance occurred. One of the main issues identified by engineers and accountants is how residual value and useful lives are calculated:

> Residual values are best guess. . . . Different organisations—have different calculations and culture.
>   (XAE Public Forum, Council C, Accountant SA, July 2013)

> How are others dealing with the sensitivity of depreciation to useful life (and remaining life) in deriving a realistic valuation representing Council's financial position?
>   (XAE Public Forum, Council D, Engineer WA, March 2016)

According to International Accounting Standard (IAS) 16 *Property, Plant & Equipment* (2004, para. 53), 'The depreciable amount of an asset is determined after deducting its residual value'. The definition of residual value refers to the estimated amount that an entity would currently obtain from disposal of the asset at the end of its useful life to the entity. 'The estimation of the useful life of the asset is a matter of judgement' (IAS 16 2004, para. 57). Hence, 'best guess' estimates play havoc with any comparative ratios and also allow for manipulation of figures to occur. This thinking is in line with others, such as Pitts (1998) and Edwards (1989) who, for example, believed that the existence of ulterior motives may have been the cause of inconsistencies and errors in the past. Where directors wished to increase the dividend, a common ploy was to reduce or altogether omit the depreciation charge when calculating reported profit, thereby publishing a figure which *The Accountant* described as 'absolutely false, misleading and mischievous' (23 March 1889, p. 149, quoted in Edwards 1989, p. 185).

Pitts (1998, p. 39) claimed that analysis of company archives (1864–1914) confirmed that reported profits were often determined with planned dividends in mind:

> The lack of a legal requirement of how profit was to be determined, and in particular the freedom of choice on depreciation, even omitting it altogether, led to great flexibility in determining the profit figure . . . leaving depreciation to vary in order to pick up the slack between operating cash surplus and dividend.

Even the English Courts were indecisive in their rulings on depreciation. *Lindley. J.* in *Lee v Neuchatel Asphalte Co. [1889] 41 Ch D 1* ruled that depreciation did not have to be included in the profit figure when taking into account dividend distribution. Whereas, in *re Ebbw Vale Steel, Iron and Coal Co. Ltd [1877] 4 Ch D 827*, the court ruled in favour of including depreciation.

Regarding local government, Jones (1985) claimed that in the report by the Departmental Committee on the Accounts of Local Authorities (1907), depreciation formed the first real controversy in relation to accounts of the private sector versus those of the municipalities. When it came to capital assets the report committee claimed, 'We are strongly of opinion that original cost, when known, is the only satisfactory basis for the statement of the values of assets on the balance sheets' (Departmental Committee on the Accounts of Local Authorities, 1907, para 61, p. 16).

Spencer (1996, p. 49), considered the most 'unfortunate' aspect of the depreciation charge was that if councils devoted resources to infrastructure maintenance, higher asset values would mean higher depreciation charges which, when coupled with maintenance expenses, would lead to a bottom-line deficit (or smaller surplus). As mentioned earlier, maintenance is reliant upon the condition of an asset. More inconsistencies and differences between engineering and accounting methods exist in relation to rating the condition of roads. For example, different scales may be used and externalities that impact on accounting figures may affect what the engineers determine to be an accurate reflection of an asset's condition.

> I do get to meet with a wide range of organisations both in Australia and New Zealand and the only thing I have found that is consistent is the inconsistency between organisations and in some cases within the same organisation . . . the two most common scales I have seen are the 0–10 and the 0–5 however even in those there can be variation on what people define each level at. . . . If [different] organisations are using different scales with different condition definitions then that makes it very hard to compare.
>
> (XAE Public Forum, Financial Industry, Accountant Vic, Nov 2014)

Figures, such as depreciation, and the way in which it is calculated can have an enormous impact on service potential, funding, decision-making and performance indicators (Akbar, Pilcher & Perrin 2012; Walker, Clarke & Dean 2000). Concern over the effect large depreciation expenses have on the 'bottom-line' of the operating statement has, for some, shifted emphasis from asset management to compliance reporting (Pilcher & Dean 2009).

For most local councils in Australia and NZ, depreciation is the second largest expense after employee costs (Edgerton 2009). Unfortunately, it is reliant upon value judgements and estimations of its various components (Lapsley 1980; Arcas & Marti 2016). Even though depreciation of infrastructure assets has been considered in various forms throughout the history of local government accounting, it *still* has not been resolved.

Conclusion and future research

Asset management and depreciation will continue to create difficulties for local councils and to provide academics with a rich source of data for many more years to come. The root of the problems can be traced back many hundreds of years and could, potentially, continue to evolve over many hundreds more. As Edgerton (2013, p. 8) commented, 'The valuation of specialised public sector assets is a highly specialised field often requiring detailed accounting, engineering and valuation knowledge'.

The need to have good communication paths between engineers and accountants is one issue recognised as vital. In today's world, communication via discussion on issues relevant to the theme of this chapter can be found by reviewing public forum blogs or discussion boards. These issues will be the subject of future research and writings by the author. For those interested in doing their own research of blogs or discussion forums, an examination of available literature indicated there is very little written on this topic. In particular, very little information exists on how blogs or discussion forums are used in an everyday context (Savolainen 2011). Interestingly, specific research looking at discussion forums and accounting issues are, to the best of my current knowledge, almost non-existent. So the field is ripe for further research.

Valuation methodologies, decisions based on a person's individual judgement, problems with residual values, useful lives and so on, continue to plague local councils even now—over 300 years on from some of the first documented cases. In 1975, Sterling claimed that accountants do not resolve issues, instead they abandon and then recycle them—he may well have been right. Future analysis will expand this considerably by applying the knowledge gained here to help determine other important factors such as: overall reporting usefulness; communication between engineers and accountants; consistency of policies and procedures; and many others that need to be explored further.

Notes

1 Curtin University, Perth WA, Australia (r.pilcher@curtin.edu.au).
2 Australia consists of six states and two territories. However, one territory—the Australian Capital Territory—does not have local government.
3 For those of us who are grammar pedants, whether to use 'forums' or 'fora' can be confusing. However, apart from the *Oxford Dictionary of English* (Stevenson 2010) indicating that the plural fora (as in the original Latin) is mainly used when referencing ancient Roman public squares, 'forums' is the way the word appears in relation to 'discussion forums'.
4 For the purposes of this chapter only, the discussion forum reviewed, although a public one, will be referred to as XAE. Further information available from the author.
5 '"Catachresis' for grammarians" refers to when a word is used in a wrong sense' (Gowers 1954, p. 75)
6 For the purposes of this chapter only, the discussion forum reviewed, although a public one, will be referred to as XAE. Further information available from the author.

References

Accounting and Engineering (XAE) 2013, 'Public Forum', July 2013.[6]
Akbar, R, Pilcher, R & Perrin, B 2012, 'Performance measurement in Indonesia: the case of local government', *Pacific Accounting Review*, vol. 24, no. 3, pp. 262–291.

The American Society of Civil Engineers (ASCE) 2005, 'Report card for America's infrastructure', viewed 30 November 2017, www.asce.org/reportcard

The American Society of Civil Engineers (ASCE) 2017, 'Infrastructure report card', viewed 30 November 2017, www.infrastructurereportcard.org/

Arcas, MJ & Marti, C 2016, 'Financial performance adjustments in English local government', *Australian Accounting Review*, vol. 26, no. 2, pp. 141–152.

Australian Accounting Research Foundation (AARF) 1993, 'Australian accounting standard (AAS) 27 financial reporting by local governments', AARF, Melbourne.

Australian Local Government Association (ALGA) 2015, 'National state of the assets 2015', Roads and Community Infrastructure Report, November.

Australian Local Government Association (ALGA), viewed 6 January 2017, http://alga.asn.au/

Australian Accounting Standards Board (AASB) 2015, 'AASB 116 Property, plant and equipment', AASB, Melbourne.

Awty, A 2002, 'Time for debate', *Australian CPA*, vol. 17, no. 3, pp. 40–41.

Barnes, K & Lord, B 2017, 'Intergenerational equity: treatment of infrastructure in New Zealand local government financial planning', *Financial Accountability and Management*, vol. 33, no. 2, pp. 127–145.

BBC 2014, 'British history: the Domesday Book, UK', viewed 29 June 2017, www.bbc.co.uk/history/british/normans/doomsday_01.shtml

Bello, M 2013, 'Bridge collapse shines light on aging infrastructure', *USA Today*, 24 May, viewed 23 May 2017, www.usatoday.com/story/news/nation/2013/05/24/washington-bridge-collapse-nations-bridges-deficient/2358419/

Brief, RP 1967, 'A late nineteenth century contribution to the theory of depreciation', *Journal of Accounting Research*, vol. 5, no. 1, pp. 27–38.

Canada Infrastructure 2016, 'Canadian infrastructure report card: informing the future', viewed 1 November 2017, www.canadainfrastructure.ca/downloads/Canadian_Infrastructure_Report_Card_Key_Messages_2016.pdf

Cavinato, J 1991, 'An appreciation for depreciation', *Chilton's Distribution*, vol. 19, no. 4, pp. 66–70.

Chandler, R & Edwards, JR 1996, 'Recurring issues in auditing: back to the future?' *Accounting, Auditing and Accountability Journal*, vol. 9, no. 2, pp. 4–29.

Chatfield, M 1977, *A history of accounting thought*, Robert E Krieger Publishing Company, New York.

Council A Asset Manager, NSW 2013, 'XAE public forum', post July, viewed 1 March 2017.

Council B Accountant, SA 2014, 'XAE public forum', post June, viewed 1 March 2017.

Council C Accountant, SA 2013, 'XAE public forum', post July, viewed 1 March 2017.

Council D Engineer, WA 2016, 'XAE public forum', post March, viewed 1 March 2017.

The Council of State Governments 2010, 'Condition of U.S. roads and bridges', *Capitol Facts and Figures*, 30 August, viewed 1 May 2017, http://knowledgecenter.csg.org/kc/content/condition-us-roads-bridges

Cox, JC 1913, *Churchwardens' accounts from the fourteenth century to the close of the seventeenth century*, Methuen, London.

Departmental Committee on the Accounts of Local Authorities 1907, 'Report of the Departmental Committee appointed to inquire into the accounts of local authorities', vol. 1, Cmd 3614, Wyman & Sons Ltd for HMSO, London.

Ditchburn, E 2017, 'Paving the way', IPWEA *Inspire*, Issue 4, April, pp. 16–17.

The Domesday Book Online n.d., viewed 29 June 2017, www.domesdaybook.co.uk/

Edgerton, D 2009, 'Depreciation of infrastructure assets: South Australia local government technical information paper', APV Valuers and Asset Management, Brisbane, Queensland.

Edgerton, D (APV) 2013, *Valuation and depreciation: a guide for the not-for-profit and public sector under accrual based accounting standards*, CPA Australia, Sydney.

Edwards, JR 1989, *A history of financial accounting*, Routledge, London.

Engineers Australia 2010, 'Infrastructure report card Australia 2010', viewed 4 April 2016, www.engineersaustralia.org.au/resource-centre/resource/infrastructure-report-card-2010

Financial Industry Accountant, Vic 2014, 'XAE public forum', post November, viewed 1 March 2017.

Goffman, E 1963, *Behaviour in public places: notes of the social organizations of gatherings*, Free Press, New York.

Goldberg, L 1960, *Concepts of depreciation*, Law Book Co., Sydney.

Goldsmith, T 2002, 'Resources and reserves – their impact on financial reporting, valuation and the expectations gap', *Proceedings of CMMI Congress*, 28 May, Cairns, Australia.

Gowers, E 1954, 'The complete plain words: a guide to the use of English', viewed 4 December 2016, www.ourcivilisation.com/smartboard/shop/gowerse/complete/index.htm

Ingenium 2002, *International infrastructure management manual, Australia/New Zealand version*, IPWEA, Wellington, New Zealand.

International Accounting Standards (IAS) Committee 2004, IAS 16 *Property, plant and equipment*, 9 December.

Institute of Public Works Engineering Australasia (IPWEA) 2017, *Inspire*, Issue 4, April, IPWEA, NZ.

Jeff Roorda and Associates 2010, 'The local roads funding gap: study of local roads funding in Australia 1999–2000 to 2019–2020', Australian Local Government Association, viewed 12 October 2017, https://alga.asn.au/site/misc/alga/downloads/transport/Local-RoadsFunding.pdf

Jones, RH 1985, 'Accruals accounting in UK local government: a historical context for continuing controversies', *Financial Accountability & Management*, vol. 1, no. 2, pp. 145–160.

Jones, RH 1994, 'Accounting in English local government from the Middle Ages to c1835', in RH Parker & BS Yamey (eds), *Accounting history some British contributions*, Clarendon Press, Oxford.

Kitto, JV 1901, *St Martin-in-the-fields: the accounts of the churchwardens, 1525–1603*, Simpkin, Marshall, Kent, Hamilton & Co, London.

Lagenberg, A 2017, 'South Road bridge collapse raise safety fears as figures show half of state's bridges ranked as "poor"', *The Advertiser*, 1 February, viewed 23 May 2017, www.adelaidenow.com.au/news/south-australia/south-rd-bridge-collapse-raise-safety-fears-as-figures-show-half-of-states-bridges-ranked-as-poor/news-story/679424adb374 4997532f9cfc38f0936a

Lancefield, N 2017, 'Thousands of UK bridges at risk of collapse, warns RAC', *Independent*, 10 March 2017, viewed 23 May 2017, www.independent.co.uk/news/uk/home-news/thousands-uk-bridges-substandard-at-risk-of-collapse-not-fit-to-take-weight-lorries-hgvs-a7621661.html

Lapsley, I 1980, 'Towards public sector capital maintenance', *Public Finance and Accountancy*, October 1980.

Littleton, AC 1933, *Accounting evolution to 1900*, Russell & Russell, New York.

Marra, RM, Moore, JL & Klimezak, AK 2004, 'Content analysis of online discussion forums: a comparative analysis of protocols', *Educational Technology Research and Development*, vol. 52, no. 2, pp. 23–40.

Marsh TM & Fischer M 2013, 'Accounting for agricultural products: US versus IFRS GAAP', *Journal of Business & Economics Research*, vol. 11, no. 2, pp. 79–87.

McKinlay Douglas Ltd 1998, 'The 1990s local government reforms in New Zealand: what was ordered and what was delivered', *A paper prepared for local government New Zealand*, viewed 15 July 2017, www.mdl.co.nz/site/mckinley/LocalGovernmentReformNZ1990s.pdf

Miller, MC & Loftus, JA 2000, 'Measurement entering the 21st century: a clear or blocked road ahead', *Australian Accounting Review*, vol. 11, no. 2, pp. 4–18.

NZ Ministry of Transport 2015, 'Connecting New Zealand – state of our infrastructure', viewed 5 July 2017, www.transport.govt.nz/ourwork/keystrategiesandplans/connectingnewzealand/cnzstateofinfrastructure/

NZ Office of the Controller and Auditor-General 2014, 'Water and roads: funding and management challenges', NZ Parliament, November, viewed 5 July 2016, www.oag.govt.nz/2014/assets

Pilcher R 2005, 'Financial reporting and local government reform – a (mis)match?' *Qualitative Research in Accounting & Management*, vol. 2, no. 2, pp. 171–192.

Pilcher, R 2006, 'Asset management in local authorities – financial fiction or management reality', in EL Lande & J-C Scheid (eds), *Accounting reform in the public sector: mimicry, fad or necessity*, Experts Comptables Media, Paris, pp. 177–188.

Pilcher R 2009, 'Deconstructing local government performance and infrastructure measurement', *Asian Review of Accounting*, vol. 17, no. 2, pp. 163–176.

Pilcher R & Dean, G 2009, 'Implementing IFRS in local government: value adding or additional pain?' *Qualitative Research in Accounting & Management*, vol. 6, no. 3, pp. 180–196.

Pitts, MV 1998, 'Did dividends dictate depreciation in British coal companies 1864–1914?' *Accounting History*, vol. 3, no. 2, pp. 37–67.

Pryor C 2013, 'Local governments and the modified approach to reporting the cost of infrastructure', *The Journal of Government Financial Management*, vol. 62, no. 1, pp. 43–49.

Rettberg, JW 2009, *Blogging*, Polity Press, Cambridge.

Revsine, L 1991 'The selective financial misrepresentation hypothesis', *Accounting Horizons*, vol. 5, no. 4, pp. 16–27.

Roads Australia 2017, viewed 5 July 2017, www.roads.org.au/

Savolainen R 2011, 'Requesting and providing information in blogs and internet discussion forums', *Journal of Documentation*, vol. 67, no. 5, pp. 883–886.

Spencer, J 1996, 'Local government issues in publicly owned assets', *Proceedings of the Seminar on Asset Valuation in the Public Sector, Public Accounts Committee*, Sydney, April, pp. 43–52.

Sterling, RR 1975, 'Toward a science of accounting', *Financial Analysts Journal*, vol. 31, no. 5, pp. 28–36.

Stevenson, A (ed) 2010, *Oxford dictionary of English*, 3rd edn, Oxford University Press, Oxford.

UK Government Department for Transport 2017, 'Road conditions in England 2016', 23 March, viewed 5 May 2017, www.gov.uk/government/statistics/road-conditions-in-england-2016

USA Government Department for Transportation 2016, 'Road and bridge data by state', 13 October, viewed 1 May 2017, www.transportation.gov/policy-initiatives/grow-america/road-and-bridge-data-state

Victorian Auditor-General's Office 2014, 'Asset management and maintenance by councils', Parliamentary Paper, no. 298, Melbourne.

Walker, RG, Clarke, FL & Dean, GW 2000, 'Options for infrastructure reporting', *ABACUS*, vol. 36, no. 2, pp. 123–159.

Way, P 2017, 'What are the greatest challenges to aligning asset and financial management within local government', IPWEA *Inspire*, Issue 4, p. 32.

Whitehead, AN 1929, *Process and reality*, Harper, New York.

Woodward, PD 1956, 'Depreciation – the development of an accounting concept', *The Accounting Review*, vol. 31, no. 1, pp. 71–76.

Legislation

Local Government Amendment Act 1989 (NZ), viewed 20 December 2016, www.legisla tion.govt.nz/act/public/1989/0001/latest/DLM142035.html

Local Government Act 1993 (NSW), NSW Government Press, Sydney.

Municipal Corporations Act 1835 (5 & 6 Wm. IV., c. 76) (UK), Parliament of the United Kingdom, viewed 2 March 2004, www.lincolnwaites.org.uk/municipalreform.shtml

Cases

Lee v Neuchatel Asphalte Co. and Others, English Court of Appeal; [1889]; 947, (41 Ch D 1; 58 L.J. Ch. 408; 61 L.T. 11; 37 W.R. 321; 5 T.L.R. 260; 1 Meg. 140).

re Ebbw Vale Steel, Iron and Coal Co. Ltd [1987] 4 Ch D 827, reported in Edwards, JR 1989, *A history of financial accounting*, Routledge, London, p. 179.

US v Kansas Pacific Railway Company, US Supreme Court [1878] 99 US 455.

4 The consequences of the current public sector reporting framework for government accountability and decision making

Janet Mack[1]

Introduction

In this chapter, the changes that have occurred in the Australian government's (Commonwealth) accounting systems and its reporting/disclosure regimes over the last 30 years and the consequential effects on accountability will be considered. Many of these changes result from a combination of several factors (Broadbent & Guthrie 1992; Ryan 1995). One of the factors proposed as being a catalyst for the changes is the emergence of the 'new right' and its promotion of market solutions to public sector resourcing problems (Hood 1991). Whilst the focus here is on the Australian Commonwealth government, it is also relevant to the various state governments within Australia that have adopted similar changes and to international jurisdictions since these changes have also occurred in other western democracies. As an example, accrual accounting, badged as resource accounting, was introduced in the United Kingdom (UK) in 2001 (Connolly & Hyndman 2006). There were in the UK, as there had been in Australia, concerns about the ability of accrual accounting to deliver effective accountability mechanisms (Carlin 2005).

While, as noted, there have been considerable changes in the way in which the Commonwealth government both provides and discloses planned future expenditure and reports on its performance, the emphasis here will be on the big picture changes that have occurred and the effects that they have had rather than on the fine detail. As Barton (2011, p. 435) stated:

> the adoption of an accounting system by the Australian government appropriate for its information needs has been a long and arduous task involving many conflicts and differences of opinion over almost 30 years.

The aim of this chapter is to highlight some of the more significant changes and the effect that they have had on accountability. In particular, the role of budget documents as an accountability mechanism will be the focus of attention. The effects will be demonstrated by examining the relevant budget statements and annual reports of the Commonwealth Department of Transport and Regional

Development (variously titled) for 1996–1997 and 2016–2017. The disclosure of information and how it is disclosed are not trivial matters in the context of accountability. The budget disclosures made by government can be used to assess their commitment to policy by operationalising (providing funds) for their policies. The next section of this chapter will briefly explore accountability in the public sector. This will be followed by an explanation of the development of financial accounting and accountability for the Australian Commonwealth government. The effects of these changes will be demonstrated and a critique of the changes will conclude the chapter.

Accountability

Accountability is a term used in many contexts—social, political and business—and it is regarded as an important tenet in all of these arenas (Cummings & Anton 1990; Ferris et al. 1995). Taylor and Rosair (2000) provided a selection of definitions of accountability in a public sector context as provided by prior literature. They noted that intrinsic to the definitions is the idea that there is a right by particular parties to call on other parties to provide information on issues of compliance and performance. Taylor and Rosair (2000) also suggested that the traditional model of accountability in the public sector—fiduciary accountability, which focused on accountability for allocated funds—has been expanded to include a managerial accountability in which the entity is also accountable for the efficiency and effectiveness with which it uses those funds. However, arguments were presented that this emphasis on performance is problematic in the public sector where there is no universal or ultimate performance indicator such as that which exists in the private sector (Taylor & Rosair 2000). Sendt (2000), the then-New South Wales (NSW) Auditor-General, also acknowledged the importance of the notion of accountability for performance. He argued that simple bottom line measures of performance do not have much meaning for many of the activities that governments are engaged in and that information on the effectiveness of the operations of government would be more useful.

In a political context, Mulgan and Uhr (2000, p. 2) stated that:

> The term "public accountability" refers to an important range of accountability practices, covering all those types of accountability which are for important reasons of democratic legitimacy, acted out in public with the aim of generating a public record of performance open to community examination and debate.

A common feature of all of these comments on or views of public accountability is that public accountability encompasses more than merely accounting for, and reporting on, financial stewardship. Public accountability also requires a focus for the way in resources have been managed from both an administrative and political perspective. This importance of administrative processes as an essential element of public accountability was argued by Barrett (2003), who contended that conformity with the administrative processes that delegate authority for action also provide a framework against which reporting and auditing can ensue. Public accountability includes accountability for policy, process and equity (Jubb & Kelso 1998). It has been argued that the current focus on financial accountability in the public sector will result in an erosion of public accountability, as the information provided to meet financial accountability purposes does not provide information about such issues as fairness, equity and process (Coy, Fischer & Gordon 2001; Jubb & Kelso 1998; Parker & Gould 1999). The importance of the choice of a reporting framework that adequately discharges the accountability obligations of the public sector is considered in the next section.

The development of Australian Commonwealth Government accounting, accountability and reporting

The Australian political system is based on the Westminster system of 'responsible government' that originated and was operating in the UK at the time Australia became an independent nation (Stewart & Ward 1996). This doctrine of responsible government holds a key assumption that Parliament is the central body in a chain of accountability that allows the electorate to hold those who govern accountable for their actions. Thus, as the central player in the chain of accountability, Parliament is accountable to the public (Davis et al. 1993). One of the functions of parliament is that of controlling government expenditure by evaluating financial proposals and subsequently ensuring that government funds have been expended appropriately. In practice, the task of scrutiny of the appropriate dispersion of funds usually falls to the auditor-general who then reports to parliament.

The audit function can be seen as fundamental to accountability as it offers independent verification of the account presented to discharge accountability. The notion of audit was alluded to in the constitution of NSW as adopted in 1855 (*New South Wales Constitution Act 1855* (UK)). That document also enshrined the tradition that all government revenues should be held in a single consolidated fund and that appropriation from that fund could only be made by Parliament. However, that Act provided no indication of precisely what an 'audit' might mean or who would conduct it. At the formation of the Commonwealth of Australia in 1901, the Australian Constitution in Sections 81 and 83 asserted (as had the NSW Constitution before it) that all revenues raised shall be held in one consolidated Revenue Fund and that money could only be withdrawn from that fund as a result of 'appropriation made by law' (*Commonwealth of Australia Constitution Act 1900* (UK), s. 83 (hereafter the Australian Constitution)). The role of audit was explicated in the *Audit Act 1901* (Cwlth). This Act provided for the appointment of an auditor-general by the Governor General as well as providing for the role's independence from government. The *Audit Act* also provided considerable detail of the work of the auditor-general. Section 40 of the *Audit Act* required the treasurer to keep a cash book that was to be examined by the auditor-general and, in particular, noted in Section 41 (f) that the auditor-general was to 'ascertain whether such moneys were legally available for and applicable to the service or purpose to which the same shall have been applied or charged'. In other words, was the expenditure in line with the appropriation (see also s. 31 (2) of the *Audit Act*).

The result of these arrangements in both the Australian Constitution and the *Audit Act* was that the budget document, which provides the basis for the appropriation bills to provide funds for the operation of government, became a central pillar in the discharge of government accountability in so far as the auditor-general's examination of the revenues and expenditures of government is made in the context of that appropriation. Willoughby (1918) noted that budgets have the capacity to not only indicate future direction but also assess past performance. That budgets are an important accountability mechanism for governments has been recognised by a number of researchers. Wines and Scarborough (2006) identified the importance of budgets as a monitoring mechanism between the government and the electorate. Wanna, Kelly and Forster (2000) identified the importance of budgets in the context of political power and the effect that they have on members of the community. Ma and Hou (2009) also observed that budgets play a twin role, in being both mechanisms for bureaucratic accountability whereby bureaucrats are held accountable to the chief executive and also for a form of horizontal accountability that holds government accountable to the electorate through parliament.

The first substantive movements for change from this system came in 1976 with the establishment of the Royal Commission on Australian Government Administration (RCAGA), commonly referred to as the Coombs Report. The Commonwealth Auditor-General at the time, Duncan Steele Craik, made two submissions to the Commission suggesting that the auditor-general's role could expand its audit function beyond compliance to also encompass efficiency audits. He argued that the scrutiny of agencies by parliament would be significantly improved if the auditor-general was able to report on the economy and efficiency realised by the administrative processes. In the context that the RCAGA proposed (that public sector managers should be given clearer responsibility for their roles and as well increased discretion in performing those roles), they also recommended that efficiency audits should be introduced to assess the performance of departments. After consideration of several options, including the creation of a new agency, the RCAGA (in Coombs 1976, p. 49, para. 3.6.17) determined that the auditor-general would be the most appropriate agency to carry out this new role on the basis that:

> The Auditor-General has . . . a traditional independence and a link with the legislative and historical authority of Parliament that is essential to one whose task is to assess the performance of the executive arm of government.

While the government treasury was not in favour of this course of action, Steele Craik received support from within government (most notably the Head of the Department of Prime Minister and Cabinet) and, as a consequence, the recommendation was accepted (Wanna, Ryan & Ng 2001). This inclusion of efficiency audits in the auditor-general's mandate was a significant development since it marked a move away from accountability just for financial compliance to include accountability for performance.

The next significant change was the move to accrual accounting. There were two discrete phases in the move towards accrual accounting. In the first phase, a financial management improvement plan evolved between 1984 and 1990. This plan was formulated to encourage public sector managers to be concerned more with results and less with compliance and inputs. Consequently, it gave managers more discretion within the budget structure. A key component of the plan was the introduction of programme management and budgeting. Under programme management and budgeting, departments were required to report their activities under programmes rather than input categories. In this way it was expected that funding would be aligned with programmes and objectives rather than inputs. The budget and financial accounting and reporting were, however, still cash based.

The use of cash budgeting and accounting was questioned from the late 1980s onwards. Cash budgets focus on inputs, not output. There was a growing concern that, with the increased size and nature of government and the influence of New Public Management, cash accounting was unable to determine the full cost of the provision of government services and thus was not able to inform government agencies about the potential for efficiencies in their use of resources. This led to the endorsement of accrual accounting for use within the 'new' public sector as the vehicle by which agencies would improve their accountability and manage their finances more efficiently (Guthrie 1998; Ryan 1998). However, it was also argued that accrual accounting and the natural extension of the presentation of a private sector general purpose financial reporting model were inappropriate for the public sector given its complex mix of operating structures, sources of financing, operating motives and accountability obligations (see, for example, Carnegie & Wolnizer 1995; English 1999, 2003; Guthrie 1998; Walker 1989). Despite these concerns the Commonwealth government announced the introduction of accrual accounting in 1992 and by 1994 it had been adopted by all departments (Barton 2009). The enactment of a suite of four pieces of legislation crystallised the government reform agenda. The *Financial Management and Accountability Act 1997* (Cwlth) and the *Commonwealth Authorities and Companies (CAC) Act 1997* (Cwlth) provided parameters for the use of Commonwealth resources as well as a reporting and accountability framework. The emphasis in this legislation moved from programme reporting to an outcomes and outputs framework and, importantly, required financial statements to be prepared using accrual accounting. The *Auditor-General Act 1997* (Cwlth) provided more independence for the auditor-general as well as empowering Parliament with a greater say in its audit priorities. Associated with these reforms was the enactment of the *Charter of Budget Honesty Act 1998* (Cwlth). This Act required regular reports setting out fiscal strategy to be provided and an intergenerational report to be provided at a minimum of five-yearly intervals. There was also a focus on information that would be available to the electorate with the Act providing for a pre-election economic and fiscal outlook report, and the costing of election commitments. The move to accrual budgeting, however, lagged behind the adoption of accrual accounting for reporting purposes. The first full federal budget developed on an accrual basis and using an outcomes and outputs framework was in 1999–2000.

The final step in the development of accounting and reporting was the introduction of Australian Accounting Standards Board (AASB) 1049 *Whole of government and general government sector financial reporting* (AASB 2012) to apply for accounting periods beginning on or after July 2012 but before January 2013. The purpose of this standard was to harmonise generally accepted accounting principles and Government Finance Statistics (GFS)-based financial statements. GFS are compiled by the Australian Bureau of Statistics (ABS) and measure the financial activities of government and in particular measure the impact of those activities on other sectors of the economy (ABS 2003). They are derived from the *Government Statistics Manual* (International Monetary Fund 2001) and ensure that statistics produced by the ABS are comparable with those of other countries also using the standards. It also enables the ABS to fulfil reporting requirements by providing statistics to international agencies on the required basis. Until the release of AASB 1049, GFS ran alongside the reporting requirements of the various audit and financial accountability legislation as another form of reporting on the financial activity of government. AASB 1049 also required budgetary reporting.

This brief and somewhat selective discussion of the changes that have occurred in Commonwealth government reporting over the last 30 years reveals that there has been substantial change from a cash based budget reporting system (with the budget being the sole reporting document) to an accrual based budgeting and reporting system that includes the preparation of general purpose financial statements much as you would expect to see in the private sector. In the next section, the budget documents and the annual reports of the Department of Transport and Regional Development will be examined as a case study to illustrate the effect of these changes on the accountability of the department.

Disclosure case study—Department of Transport and Regional Development

In this section the contents of the portfolio budget statements and annual reports of the department are compared to illustrate the changes that have occurred in these accountability documents subsequent to the adoption of accrual accounting and budgeting in the Commonwealth government. In order to clearly demonstrate the totality of the changes that have occurred with respect to accountability, year by year analysis was not undertaken. Rather, a comparison was made for the time frame that encompassed the substantive changes to the budgeting and reporting frameworks. To a large extent, since all departments are subject to the same regulation, which department analysed was not significant. However, two criteria were identified. These were the availability of the data on the department's website and whether there had been changes to the department's title or function. The first criterion required the portfolio budget statements for 1996–1997 and 2016–2017 to be available and the annual reports for the years 1996–1997 and 2015–2016 also to be available (the difference in years reflects the timing of the release of the reports). These dates were chosen as they covered the period of the substantial changes to the budgeting and reporting frameworks. The only department that met this criterion was the Department of Transport and Regional Development. Consequently, the second criterion was not considered.

Portfolio budget statements

Portfolio budget statements explain the government-agreed outcomes of government agencies and explain the appropriation bills. They provide senators and members of the House of Representatives with information to enable them to assess the relevant appropriation bills. In 1996–1997, the portfolio budget statements for this Commonwealth department were prepared on a programme basis and were cash based. By 2016–2017, the portfolio budget statements were prepared on a full accrual basis.

In the portfolio budget statements for 1996–1997, the statements set out the links between sub-programme objectives, performance reports and forecasts, and resources for all sub-programs in the portfolio (Transport and Regional Development 1996). The statement comprised both textual and financial information about the activities of the portfolio. The financial information included outlay comparisons with the previous year (both budget and actual) and estimates for the following three years, details of programme and sub-programme resources compared to the budget and actual expenditure of the previous year, and reconciliations of expenditure from appropriations to programmes for the current year.

The portfolio budget statements for 2016–2017 reflected the move to the outputs and outcomes framework (Transport and Regional Development 2016b). Again the statement comprised both textual and financial information about the activities of the portfolio but also included a much larger range of statements and schedules. The following financial information was provided. An entity resource statement showing the total funding available to the department in pursuit of its programmes and services provided the 2015–2016 estimated actual and the 2016–2017 estimate. Budgeted expenses for each outcome provided information about how the resources would be used in pursuit of departmental outcomes. For each of these statements, as well as the 2015–2016 estimated actual numbers and 2016–2017 budget numbers, forward estimates numbers for the next three years were also provided. The budgeted financial statements and capital budget statement also provided the 2015–2016 estimated actual numbers and 2016–2017 budget numbers and forward estimates numbers for the next three years. The remaining two statements provided were the Budget Measures table, which detailed any changes made since the mid-year economic and fiscal outlook for budget periods from 2016–2017 to 2019–2020, and the statement of asset movements for the budget year 2016–2017.

There are three major differences between the two portfolio budget statements. First, while the 1996–1997 statements provided budget and actual figures, the 2016–2017 statements did not. The provision of budget to actual comparatives is an important accountability mechanism. Second, there was no reconciliation from appropriation to expenditure. This breaks the direct link between the portfolio budget statements and the appropriation bills. Third, the 2016–2017 statements included budgeted financial statements. The last two differences reflect the move to accrual accounting and the adoption of the general purpose financial reporting framework.

Annual reports and financial statements

The 1996–1997 annual report for the department comprised five sections: secretary's overview, programme performance reporting, financial statements, appendices and aid to access (Department of Transport and Regional Development 1997). The following financial information was provided. The Programme Performance Report provided a financial resources summary at a highly aggregated level that offered information on the resources available to the department. It included 1995–1996 actual figures, 1996–1997 budget figures and 1996–1997 actual figures. For each programme and sub-programme, a financial summary was provided as well as a detailed resource table and offered information with respect to 1995–1996 actual figures, 1996–1997 budget figures and 1996–1997 actual figures. The financial statements included statements of: revenue and expenses; assets and liabilities; revenue and expenses by programme; assets and liabilities by programme; and cash flows. Schedules of commitments and contingencies were provided along with a statement of transaction by fund and notes to the accounts. With the exception of fund transaction information which provided 1996–1997 budget figures, 1996–1997 actual figures and 1995–1996 actual figures, all of the other statements and notes reported current and prior year actual figures.

The 2015–2016 annual report for the department comprised seven chapters, six appendixes, the financial statements and key terms and index (Transport and Regional Development 2016a). The following financial information was provided. In the Year in Review, a five-year summary of the department's financial performance and position was provided along with the change from last year. In the appendix, entity resource statements and expenses for outcomes were provided which reconciled the department's use of resources in cash terms. For revenues, the headings actual available appropriation, payments made and balance remaining were used, while for expenses the headings were budget, actual expenses and variation. For expenses, this information was provided for each output.

The financial statements were as to be expected in a set of general purpose financial statements. These included a: statement of comprehensive income; statement of financial position; statement of changes in equity; cash flow statement; and notes to the accounts. These statements all included (along with the current and previous year's figures) the budgeted figures for the year of the report. There was also a statement explaining the major budget variance. These are both requirements of AASB 1049. None of the notes included budget information.

The most obvious difference between the two annual reports was that the 2015–2016 report looked much more like a private sector annual report. However, beyond this superficial change, there were more substantive differences. The inclusion of budgetary information in the financial statements and the accompanying explanation with respect to the major variances was the most evident difference. The other particular disparity was the placement of the information regarding resource summaries and statements. In 1996–1997 this information was positioned in the Programme Performance reporting section which, on the face of it, was a logical placement. However, in the 2015–2016 annual report, it was situated in the Appendices chapter before the financial statements.

Conclusion

What is apparent from the case study described above is that accounting reforms have introduced uncertainty and, more particularly, confusion in government reporting both in terms of what is reported and where it is reported. There is now detailed information presented in a variety of formats and reports, resulting in a lack of clarity. This clearly affects the use of the various reporting mechanisms as accountability mechanisms. The portfolio budget statements are diminished in their capacity to perform an accountability function since they no longer include the capacity to compare budget to actual figures. One of the fundamental purposes of a budget (along with planning for the future) is to provide a benchmark for comparing future performance. This purpose is not now directly achievable, although by looking at the budget in conjunction with the Appendix in the annual report it is still possible to achieve it. This presupposes, though, that the person interested in the information knows both what to look for and where to find it—accountability from a budget perspective has become fragmented.

With respect to the inclusion of budget information and the explanation of variances in the financial statements, the most obvious question is why? There are effectively now two sets of budget to actual figures: which ones are appropriate and in which circumstances? It seems that what has occurred is an obfuscation of the accountability function of both documents—the portfolio budget statements and the financial statements. It also appears that the current framework gives primacy to the general purpose financial reports over the budget process. Since the primary objective of general purpose financial reports is to assist statement users to make resource allocation decisions rather than to meet accountability needs, the current framework also seems to be giving primacy to decision-usefulness over accountability despite the concerns expressed about the inadequacy of the private sector-based general purpose financial reporting model to deliver on accountability in the public sector.

In short, accountability has gone from being uncomplicated to now being very complicated. In order to assess performance against budget it is now necessary to look at both the portfolio budget statements and the annual report. From an accountability perspective this is not ideal. The analysis presented here supports the view of Likierman (1992, p. 23) that cash accounts 'despite their crudeness have a degree of transparency that accrual accounts cannot give'. This begs the question, then, as to whether the adoption of a private sector accounting and reporting framework to address the perceived inadequacies of the cash accounting regime has enhanced accountability in the Australian public sector. It may have been more appropriate and more reflective of the public sector context (given the restrictions of the Constitution and the willingness of the Commonwealth Auditor-General in 1976 to perform efficiency/performance audits) to promote efficiency and effectiveness in the public sector via an approach that utilised the existing cash framework and included performance reports. The results of this study with respect to the loss of clarity and the fragmentation of accountability information will be of interest to other Australian and international jurisdictions that operate under a Westminster-style government and have adopted accrual accounting.

Note

1   Queensland University of Technology, Brisbane Qld, Australia (j.mack@qut.edu.au).

References

Australian Accounting Standards Board (AASB) 2012, *AASB 1049 Whole of government and general government sector financial reporting*, AASB, Canberra.

Australian Bureau of Statistics (ABS) 2003, *Australian system of government finance statistics: Concepts, sources and methods*, cat. no. 5514.0.55.001, ABS, Canberra.

Barrett, P 2003, 'Government sector accountability – the impact of service charters in the Australian public sector', *Queensland Commonwealth Regional Heads Forum, 15th Annual Government Business Conference*, 22 May, Australian National Audit Office,, Queensland, pp. 1–63.

Barton, A 2009, 'The use and abuse of accounting in the public sector financial management reform program in Australia', *ABACUS*, vol. 45, no. 2, pp. 221–248.

Barton, A 2011, 'Why governments should use the government finance statistics accounting system', *ABACUS*, vol. 47, no. 4, pp. 411–445.

Broadbent, J & Guthrie J 1992, 'Changes in the public sector: A review of recent "alternative" accounting research', *Accounting Auditing and Accountability Journal*, vol. 5, no. 2, pp. 3–31.

Carlin, T 2005, 'Debating the impact of accrual accounting and reporting in the public sector', *Financial Accountability and Management,* vol. 21, no. 3, pp. 309–336.

Carnegie, G & Wolnizer P 1995, 'The financial value of cultural, heritage and scientific collections: an accounting fiction', *Australian Accounting Review*, vol. 5, no. 1, pp. 31–47.

Connolly, C & Hyndman, N 2006, 'The actual implementation of accruals accounting: caveats from a case within the UK public sector', *Accounting, Auditing and Accountability Journal*, vol. 19, no. 2, pp. 272–290.

Coombs, R 1976, *Royal commission on Australian government administration: report*, Australian Government Publishing Service, Canberra.

Coy, D, Fischer, M & Gordon, T 2001, 'Public accountability: a new paradigm for college and university annual reports', *Critical Perspectives on Accounting*, vol. 12, no. 1, pp. 1–31.

Cummings, L & Anton, R 1990 'The logic and appreciation dimensions of accountability', in S Srivastva & D Cooperrider (eds), *Appreciative management and leadership*, Jossey-Bass, San Francisco, pp. 257–286.

Davis, G, Wanna, J, Warhurst, J & Weller, P 1993, *Public policy in Australia*, 2nd edn, Allen & Unwin, St Leonards, NSW.

Department of Transport and Regional Development 1996, *Portfolio budget statements 1996–1997*, Australian Government Publishing Service, Canberra.

Department of Transport and Regional Development 1997, *Annual report 1996–1997*, Australian Government Publishing Service, Canberra.

Department of Transport and Regional Development 2016a, *Annual report 2015–2016*, Australian Government Publishing Service, Canberra.

Department of Transport and Regional Development 2016b, *Portfolio budget statements 2016–2017*, Australian Government Publishing Service, Canberra.

English, L 1999, 'Unsubtle differences' (editorial), *Australian Accounting Review*, vol. 9, no. 1, p. 2.

English, L 2003, 'Emasculating public accountability in the name of competition: transformation of state audit in Victoria', *Critical Perspectives on Accounting*, vol. 14, nos. 1–2, pp. 51–76.

Ferris, G, Mitchell, T, Caravan, P, Frink, D & Hooper, H 1995, 'Accountability in human resource systems', in G Ferris, S Rosen & D Barnum (eds), *Handbook of human resource management*, Blackwell Publishers, Oxford, pp. 175–190.

Guthrie, J 1998, 'Application of accrual accounting in the Australian public sector – rhetoric or reality?' *Financial Accountability and Management*, vol. 14, no. 1, pp. 1–19.

Hood, C 1991, 'A public management for all seasons?' *Public Administration*, vol. 69, no. 1, pp. 3–19.

International Monetary Fund 2001, *Government finance statistics manual 2001*, International Monetary Fund, Washington, DC.

Jubb, P & Kelso, R 1998, 'Ethics, pluralism and public service', *Accounting Forum*, vol. 21, no. 3–4, pp. 433–460.

Likierman, A 1992, 'Financial reporting in the public sector', in D Henley, C Holtham, A Likierman & J Perrin (eds), *Public sector accounting and financial control*, Chapman and Hall, London, pp. 10–42.

Ma, J & Hou, Y 2009, 'Budgeting for accountability: a comparative study of budget reforms in the United States during the progressive era and in contemporary China', *Public Administration Review*, vol. 69, no. 1, pp. 553–559.

Mulgan, R & Uhr, J 2000, 'Accountability and Governance', *Discussion Paper* No. 71, Australian National University Public Policy Program, Canberra.

Parker, L & Gould, G 1999, 'Changing public sector accountability: critiquing new directions', *Accounting Forum*, vol. 23, no. 2, pp. 109–135.

Ryan, C 1995, 'Australian public sector financial reporting 1976 to 1993: Reforming policy agendas', doctoral thesis, Griffith University, Queensland.

Ryan, C 1998, 'The introduction of accrual reporting policy in the Australian public sector: an agenda-setting explanation', *Accounting, Auditing and Accountability*, vol. 11, no. 5, pp. 518–539.

Sendt, R 2000, 'The taxpayers' right to know: keeping governments accountable', paper presented to the *IIR conference: Service Delivery in Government*, 11 May, The Institute for International Research, Canberra.

Stewart, R & Ward, I 1996, *Politics one*, 2nd edn, Macmillan Education Australia Pty Ltd, South Melbourne.

Taylor, D & Rosair, M 2000, 'The effects of participating parties, the public and size on government departments' accountability disclosures in annual reports', *Accounting Accountability and Performance*, vol. 6, no. 1, pp. 77–97.

Walker, R 1989, 'Should there be common standards for the public and private sectors', Government Accounting Research Lecture, ASCPA & ANU, ASCPA, Canberra, pp. 1–20.

Wanna, J, Kelly, J & Forster, J 2000, *Managing public expenditure in Australia*, Allen & Unwin, St Leonards, NSW.

Wanna, J, Ryan, C & Ng, C 2001, *From accounting to accountability: A centenary history of the Australian National Audit Office*, Allen & Unwin, Crows Nest, NSW.

Willoughby, W 1918, *The movement for budgetary reform in the States*, Institute for Government Research, New York.

Wines, G & Scarborough, H 2006, 'Behind the headlines: An analysis of Australian Commonwealth, State and Territory budget balance numbers', *Accounting Accountability and Performance*, vol. 12, no. 2, pp. 82–122.

Legislation

Audit Act 1901 (Cwlth)
Auditor-General Act 1997 (Cwlth)
Charter of Budget Honesty Act 1998 (Cwlth)
Commonwealth Authorities and Companies (CAC) Act 1997 (Cwlth)
Commonwealth of Australia Constitution Act 1900 (UK)
Financial Management and Accountability Act 1997 (Cwlth)
New South Wales Constitution Act 1855 (UK)

5 Westminster system, parliamentary sovereignty and responsible government

Executive accountability in New Zealand and Australia

David Gilchrist[1]

Introduction

James (1997) divided the British Empire's colonies into two groupings which I will paraphrase as 'exploitation colonies' and 'settler colonies'. Exploitation colonies are those colonies where British settlers saw an economic opportunity and sought to exploit it by spending a term 'in country' before returning home, having made their fortune.

These colonies were dangerous and mortality rates were high but so were the returns. Exploitation colonies, such as India, Burma and Ceylon, were not settled with a view to establishing a new, British country that would be a reflection of home. Often the settlers used local customs, took advantage of local political divisions and established administrations that were fit-for-purpose in the contexts of the existing society; the form of economic opportunity being pursued; and the military and political contexts within which the colony was being administered. The importation of British institutions was not as important as the peaceful, effective economic exploitation of the local resources. Though of a lesser class than the British colonialists, the original inhabitants were important as a source of labour, as a market for British products and for supporting the security of Imperial holdings by the manipulation of local political, religious and cultural differences (Ferguson 2008; Fox 2008 [1933]; James 1997; Young 1961).

This functional colonisation was very different from that undertaken in the settler colonies which were established as permanent, but imperfect, effigies of the Imperial centre (Belich 2009). Colonial pragmatism was a critical reality as survival (especially in the early period of establishment) and then economic development were central considerations of colonial elites. In the context of settlement, essentially, the British settlers displaced, and often ignored, the indigenes with a view to creating a new country in which they and their descendants would enjoy opportunities that were not available to them in Britain. Australia, New Zealand, Canada and South Africa are the prominent colonies of this type. They all had separate and unique histories but also enjoyed ties of kinship and commitment to each other and to England at the Imperial centre, including in relation to the political rhetoric and institutions transferred from Britain (for more details, see—amongst others—Belich 1998; Eddy 1969; Horner 2015; James 1997).

Most significantly, the settler colonies brought an inheritance from the Imperial centre in terms of culture, education, economic thinking, political thought, religion and literature (Gilchrist 2017). This inheritance framed much of the development and ultimately the independence of these colonies. It ensured that political ideas (such as liberalism and democracy) and methods of organisation impacted the institutions created to conduct government in each colony. However, the pragmatism needed to ensure physical and then economic survival meant these colonies were also comfortable in ignoring or opposing the Imperial government. This was aided in the earlier decades by distance and a European political context that often prevented Imperial resources and attention from being applied to far-flung colonies. In later years, it was as a result of the colonies developing their own political powers as they matured (Eddy 1969; Fox 2008 [1933]; Young 1961).

Growing maturity, combined with the Imperial inheritance, meant that settler colonies went their own way when pragmatically necessary: they worked together with other colonies (including against the Imperial government) when appropriate (Laidlaw 2005); they worked with the British government if political and/or economic dictates suggested they ought (Clarke 1977); sought to leverage the British government for political ends if thought useful (for instance, see Dowd 2014); and they competed with each other when it was in their interests. For instance, the economic opportunity in Imperial preference was pursued by many in the colonies who argued that access to significant British markets was necessary on the basis of Imperial ties of kinship and loyalty, thus reducing access to those same markets for non-British producers (Gollin 1965). Conversely, settler colonies also sought to avoid participation in Imperial defence, shifted expenses back to the Imperial government whenever they could, and experienced conflict between the local polity and the centre due to the vice-regal structures built into local political settlements (Gilchrist 2017; Wilson 1909; Young 1961).

This chapter considers a small but important section of this broad canvass. The political settlements in each of the settler colonies developed independently but, generally, concomitantly during the middle- to later-19th century. All settlements commenced their political trajectory as gubernatorial dictatorships and achieved responsible government before 1900. Significantly, each operationalised responsible government by implementing the Westminster system as a basis of Executive accountability. Institutional development in settler colonies was complex and focused on meeting the not-always mutually inclusive democratic expectations of a widening franchise and ensuring the capacity to govern. It also allowed the Imperial government to release the costs and inconvenience of local administration while still maintaining sufficient control over aspects such as international affairs (in order to defend and expand Imperial interests).

In all settler colony cases, local political and economic pragmatism affected the extent to which an apparent desire to see the implementation of Imperial institutions was realised in the actuality—impacting in turn the true accountability of the Executive. This is especially the case with regard to the Westminster system of government and the extent to which it was transplanted effectively into these colonies. Therefore, it is Executive accountability that is central to this chapter: does the rhetoric of the Westminster system support Executive accountability?

Chapter 5 begins by examining the realities of parliamentary sovereignty and responsible government—two important central tenets of the Westminster system. It does this by first considering the British case, being what might be termed the 'Mother Parliament', in order to explicate the system and to assess the extent to which the Westminster system is, in fact, deployed in that jurisdiction. The Westminster system—including responsible government and Executive review—is then considered in the context of the institutional framework used as a rhetorical device. The cases of New Zealand and Australia are used as prisms through which to examine the issues at hand. Ultimately, I will demonstrate that the accountability mechanisms used to hold the Executive to account are not as embedded in common historical roots or as central to controlling Executive government as they may be generally perceived.

The British case

The Westminster system is the appellation ascribed to the system of government and institutions that evolved in England over more than a millennium. It is a fundamental element of the unwritten constitution of the United Kingdom (UK) and, importantly for our purposes here, one distinguishing feature is the fact that the legislature and the Executive are not neatly separated in the way that they are, for example, in the presidential system underlying the constitution of the United States (Groves & Lee 2007). Under the Westminster system, the Executive is selected from the members of parliament holding the confidence of the popular house (usually because their party has a majority in that house but not necessarily so). This arrangement impacts the notion of parliamentary sovereignty as the Executive has the opportunity to significantly influence the legislature, as we will see.

Parliamentary sovereignty has been defined as parliament being the ultimate source, and exerciser, of power within a nation state (Goldsworthy 2010). In terms of what I call the machinery of review—the institutions, infrastructure and capacity of the parliament to exert its authority by overseeing the Executive—the Westminster system has also developed the idea of responsible government in which government ministers (the Executive) are individually and collectively responsible to the popular house. This arrangement establishes what Reilly et al. (2013, p. 18) called a 'chain of accountability'—the Executive is responsible to the legislature which is in turn responsible to the people.

Goldsworthy (2010) further suggested that there is a certain logic to considering the development and modern operation of the British Parliament in the context of parliamentary sovereignty and responsible government as these concepts have significant explanatory power. Archer (1980) demonstrated this explanatory power by identifying three definitions of responsible government, which have practical value in considering the extent to which the idea has real application beyond its use as a rhetorical device for those with a democratic turn of mind.

These three definitions are the responsiveness of the Executive to public opinion; providing prudent and consistent government by which unpopular but strong decisions are made by strong rulers; and ministers forming a government which is collectively accountable to an elected assembly—the primary definition used herein. In a modern democracy, should the Executive be more concerned with the wishes of the people or the wishes of the parliament? This question is especially problematic when it is considered that members of the parliament are likely to want an Executive place themselves.

When discussing the idea of Cabinet government in Australia (an extension of responsible government in which ministers are individually and jointly responsible to the parliament), Weller (2007, p. 6) wrote about these institutions as being 'part normative, part descriptive, part perception'. They have a role in communicating the ideas surrounding democratic government but do not necessarily facilitate the implementation of those ideas; they serve as vehicles for explanation rather than models for operation.

The extent to which the parliament is in fact sovereign and the Executive responsible to the popular house are important questions for this chapter. The Westminster system, sometimes inadvertently and sometimes intentionally (Monk 2010), creates opportunities in the accountability framework that allow the Executive to have undue influence on the effectiveness of the parliament to exercise its oversight role—even to the point of preventing any oversight at all. Aroney, Prasser and Nethercote (2008) considered this in relation to the UK, New Zealand and Australia when making the observation that the Executive controls parliament and not the other way around. As a result, there are two primary objections to the existence of parliamentary sovereignty beyond the rhetorical.

The first set of objections is what might be termed legalistic challenges to the very existence of parliamentary sovereignty and responsible government. These are philosophical rather than functional issues, and seem to support Goldsworthy's (2010) proposition that parliamentary sovereignty is on the wane (Rhodes 2005). Essentially, these challenges arise out of the logical reconciliation of parliamentary sovereignty and the reality of changing constitutional arrangements. For instance, in Archer's (1980, p. 24) view, parliamentary sovereignty would exist only where a responsible minister does not share their power with any 'outside body', including in terms of a federation, judicial review, bills of rights or even the rule of law.

Such legalistic challenges include that parliamentary power is restricted by the following five areas: (1) the fundamental expectation of the rule of law—for instance, parliament must consider ideas of fairness which is a particularly important issue in modern times when personal rights are considered inviolable; (2) the relative capacity of parliament to abdicate or transfer its powers and choose to be subject to those new power-holders—an example is the European Union and the agreement by the British Parliament to 'live by' the rules of that institution; (3) the place of common law and if that invalidates any measures the parliament may seek to implement—this is really a 'chicken and egg' argument where the Westminster system is said to arise from common law yet the parliament is said to have unfettered sovereignty—how can parliament be unfettered if its genesis is in common law?; (4) extending the issue of common law, British legislation is now subject to judicial review and, of course, the interpretation of the intent of statutes is carried out by the judiciary which may even strike down parliament's laws; and (5) the place of the people in a democracy serves to posit that ultimate sovereignty rests with electors rather than the parliament—for example, the recent 'Brexit' referendum which now requires the government to engineer a reversal of the European Union arrangements notwithstanding many politicians do not seem to agree with the decision.

The second set of objections to parliamentary sovereignty are practical realities, largely related to the political pragmatism of members of parliament and their desire to respond to their constituencies as the source of political reward (Degeling, Anderson & Guthrie 1996; Pilcher et al. 2013). While the legalistic challenges are of significance, probably these practical challenges present the most formidable difficulties in terms of holding the Executive to account.

For instance, because the Executive comes from the parliament and usually commands a majority, members of parliament who are also members of the party in government are not incentivised to attack the Executive—thus giving the Executive power over the parliament and negating the idea of parliamentary sovereignty (Bennet 1980). The majority can be used to both drive the acceptance of government policy and to hinder the committees and other parliamentary infrastructure used to check the Executive. The Executive will seek to guide the debate and to balance the constitutional limitations imposed on them with the political necessity to be seen to be strong and competent leaders by a less-than-well-informed public. The parliament itself can be let down by disinterested members from both government members and their opponents (who themselves desire to be the government one day and yet who are frequently inexperienced in the process of Executive oversight) (Benton & Russell 2012; Degeling, Anderson & Guthrie 1996).

The process is made more complicated by the multiple roles played by politicians, the need for and involvement of a public sector and the desire of politicians to respond directly (and, importantly, to be seen to respond) to the apparent wishes of the electorate. Theoretical prisms such as agency theory are difficult to apply (Pilcher et al. 2013) in this complex milieu. The infrastructure may well be in place but the behaviour of politicians—wittingly or unwittingly—prevents it being effectively deployed.

An example can be found in the institutions created by parliaments to support their sovereignty and to operationalise responsible government in relation to the raising and spending of public money—that is, public accounts committees, estimates committees and officers and inspectors of parliament including auditors-general (Balls 1963; Gilchrist & Coulson 2015; Woolmer 1998). Almost uniformly, these institutions are funded out of the government's appropriation (as is the parliament itself), giving the Executive financial leverage. The Executive can retain the institutions and be seen to be accountable, but may reduce their resources and render them ineffective (Gilchrist & Coulson 2015). This is equally so in New Zealand and Australia although some practical elements, such as having an opposition member of parliament chair the committee, are not followed in the Antipodes thus increasing the questionable value of these institutions as oversight mechanisms. It is not likely that a public accounts committee chaired by a government member will be encouraged to attack the Executive, regardless of the extent to which it may be deserved.

Finally, the Westminster system and the Imperial influence are still seen today in the supra-national infrastructure that has grown out of the Imperial structure. As the British Empire collapsed and was replaced by the British Commonwealth, concomitant institutions such as the Commonwealth Parliamentary Association and the Australasian Council of Public Accounts Committees formed to help ensure that new and not so new nation states that had been Imperial possessions (in the widest sense of the term) could retain their relationships. Such institutions do not, however, act as a catalyst for uniformity. Rather, they provide opportunities to discuss process and practice while reinforcing the recognition of sovereignty and difference by not developing policy positions regarding better practice or membership requirements other than in relation to such fundamentals as democratic institutions (Pilcher et al. 2013). Indeed, there is great diversity amongst these countries notwithstanding their common colonial histories and their recognition of the centrality of the Westminster system, whatever that has come to mean to them (Pelizzo 2011).

Nevertheless, the ideas of parliamentary sovereignty and responsible government are still of value as a means of explicating history as well as providing a normative description of what might be termed 'better-practice' governance in a Westminster-based parliamentary democracy (Rhodes 2005). They provide legitimacy to political systems built upon popular democratic institutions, as the rhetoric presents a vision of accountability and democracy regardless of the fact (Gilchrist & Coulson 2015). Practically, the description of these institutions and their intended operation provides a logical framework upon which the discourse of Executive accountability can be hung and judgements made about whether or not the structure of accountability is likely to be effective. This is particularly the case when considering the experience of New Zealand, discussed in the next section.

The New Zealand and Australian position

In this section I will review the extent to which the ideas of parliamentary sovereignty and responsible government were established in New Zealand and Australia: two nations that began as settler colonies which prized their connection to the parliamentary institutions of the Imperial government and rhetorically sought to demonstrate that they emulated those democratic principles (James 1997).

It can be thought that the Westminster system evolved in Britain and was then transplanted, fully matured, into the settler colonies. In fact, the model evolved in concert across the Empire (Bunn & Gilchrist 2013; Gilchrist & Coulson 2015). The British Parliament at Westminster certainly enjoyed a prominence and rhetorically was seen as the 'Mother of Parliaments'. However, the reality was that while the Westminster model was transplanted to these two settler colonies, as described by Rhodes and Weller (2005), this did not mean that the institutions remained static in response to local pragmatic imperatives and political environments. Colonies usually commenced government with the Westminster model but parliamentary systems and Executive governance were implemented in their own style and in response to the situation on the ground (Bunn & Gilchrist 2013). This experience supports Wehner's (2010) contention that consistency within parliaments is not there—the rhetorical devices and the nomenclature surrounding the infrastructure of accountability may exist but it operates differently within sovereign states.

To paraphrase Goldsworthy (2010), the assessment of New Zealand and Australia in the context of the Westminster system of government would seem to suggest that New Zealand would be an easier polity to consider, as it is a unitary state and has a unicameral parliament. This notion is reinforced when we consider the impression that these two countries made on 19th-century visitors with respect to the level of pragmatism practised and the lack of theoretical discussion or policy consistency extant in either country (for instance, see Metin 1977). In fact, political pragmatism and change have impacted the development of the Westminster system in both countries. These impacts manifested in differing ways, demonstrating the variation that constitutes the rule in terms of the development of parliamentary democracy in Westminster-based countries.

Both countries also share a conundrum that would fall into the category of legalistic concerns raised in the previous section. As the parliaments of each nation were 'enabled' by legislation emanating from the British Parliament, how can they be considered to have sovereign power? Such enabling legislation implies a condescension on the part of Britain. However, notwithstanding the provision of independence by the Imperial Parliament, it is also reasonable to query whether in reality Westminster had the power to deny such independence or was acting as a result of political realities. These colonies were actively lobbying for responsible government and may well have declared independence if it had not been offered (as had happened in the United States).

New Zealand achieved responsible government in 1852. Its political system has been described as 'more Westminster than Westminster' (Wanna 2005, p. 154) and as the 'purest form of the Westminster system' implemented (Levine 2004, p. 646). On the other hand, the idea of a New Zealand form of parliamentary sovereignty has also been attacked, with Lord Cooke (2007, p. 377) calling it a 'catchphrase' that could not survive in-depth analysis. New Zealand has also undergone radical change in terms of the way the parliament is elected, apparently, in turn, improving Executive accountability.

Historically, New Zealand adopted unicameralism (thus removing one element that reduces the relevance of parliamentary sovereignty in Australia—an upper house with almost identical powers to the lower or popular house) and an electoral system that resulted in the Executive wielding extraordinary power (Wanna 2005). This electoral system has been described as a 'winner-takes-all' process (Wanna 2005, p. 154), leaving the Executive in command of a majority in the House and the ability to use its voting capacity to dominate parliament.

The New Zealand Executive was able to dominate parliament for over 100 years with successive governments being subject only to an unwritten constitution and simple institutions (Levine 2004). While the government did not degenerate into authoritarianism, Wanna (2005, p. 154) described a descent into an 'agreeable "elected dictatorship"'. Wanna (2005) attributed this outcome to the Executive's willingness to behave as if it were a responsible government—that is, to maintain the rhetoric and appearance—and to the fact that New Zealand was such a small country that the ministry was personally accessible, making it directly account-able. Indeed, Wanna (2005) indicated that the political arrangements deliberately allowed the Westminster system to be adulterated, in order to insulate the govern-ment from parliament and the electorate.

By the 1980s, Levine (2004) described a growing dissatisfaction amongst vot-ers and the media regarding incompetent members of the Executive not being held to account by the parliamentary processes. As a result of this dissatisfaction and a royal commission, the New Zealand Parliament adopted what has been termed a mixed member proportional representation system where it is very difficult for any one party to obtain a working majority and certain seats are set aside for the local indigenes (Maoris) (Aroney, Prasser & Nethercote 2008). Wanna (2005) described this as a move away from the Westminster system on the basis that one-vote one-value is truer to it. However, in terms of parliamentary sovereignty, it is likely that the change has had a positive impact as it removed the original situation where the party holding the majority was effectively able to dominate parliament.

This apparent strengthening of parliamentary sovereignty must be balanced against other change processes underway in New Zealand. For instance, the unwritten constitution also allows for change to occur organically, as it does in the Westminster parliament itself. In this vein, Goldsworthy (2010) claimed that judges in New Zealand were actively dismantling the concept of parliamentary sovereignty and replacing it with a new framework that shared power between the parliament and the judiciary. Goldsworthy (2010, p. 2) called this 'bi-polar sovereignty' or 'dual sovereignty', to reflect that the courts are in no way seen to be subordinate to the parliament.

In the Australian context, the current states of the Commonwealth of Australia were once entirely separate British colonies which had all achieved responsible government from the Westminster parliament by 1890 (Galligan & Roberts 2007). Wentworth (1956) held that these parliaments developed within a unitary policy framework. However, that is not really the case. While each colony had 'received' the power to undertake responsible government from the Imperial Parliament, in fact the Imperial government retained control in important areas such as foreign policy, international trade and defence, and ensuring, amongst other things, that Australian soldiers fought in Imperial wars paid for by Australian governments right up until the effective (if not the actual) collapse of Empire during the Second World War (James 1997).

The logic of federation prevailed by 1900 and the Commonwealth of Australia was established in 1901 as a result, again, of the British Parliament passing an enabling act—an act which became the Commonwealth Constitution (Groves &

Lee 2007, Reilly et al. 2013). Therefore, the idea of Commonwealth parliamentary sovereignty suffers from the same legalistic 'chicken and egg' problem as the other Imperially-sanctioned parliaments. It is also true to say that the relatively late establishment of Australia meant that the Commonwealth Constitution was established with the benefit of 100 years of constitutional development experienced across the Empire (Gilchrist & Coulson 2015).

As a result of this development trajectory, there are a number of fundamental differences between Australia and New Zealand that impact the relative sovereignty of these parliaments and the ability of the Executive to be accountable to their parliament—even if they were of a mind to be so in fact and not just rhetorically. For instance, Australia has seven sovereign parliaments (one in each original state and the Commonwealth Parliament) and two parliamentary assemblies that have their origins in Commonwealth-enabling legislation and which are recognised as 'territories' rather than as states. Therefore, there is a complex policy environment and, by virtue of the Commonwealth Constitution, a division of powers between these erstwhile sovereign states. In consequence, it is hard to envisage any real sovereignty being retained by any one parliament. The powers and activities are intertwined such that no one parliament can operate without reference to the interests—political, financial or constitutional—of at least one other parliament, even if only to ensure it does have the power it thinks it has (Galligan & Roberts 2007). Simply put, ministers can also claim a lack of responsibility because another jurisdiction (usually the Commonwealth or vice versa) has prevented the preferred action or forced an unpopular action.

The bicameral nature of the Commonwealth Parliament and of all Australian state parliaments (save that of Queensland) also impacts parliamentary sovereignty. The Executive government is formed in the lower, popular house, usually elected via proportional representation. If the upper house is hostile to the Executive, the lower house will be thwarted even if the Executive holds its usual majority. Prosser and Denniss (2015) identified that parliamentary sovereignty may be enhanced in situations where the differences in party representation are small. However, there is a limit here. Recent Commonwealth parliaments have seen parliamentary sovereignty reduce markedly in hung parliaments, where individual members hold far greater power than they normally would and can effectively hold the Executive to ransom (Prosser & Denniss 2015).

A further constraint arises on these parliaments' powers because a federal political settlement requires the appointment of an umpire to rule in disputes between parliaments, to evaluate whether or not a particular law is valid under the constitutional settlement and to consider the impact of laws of one parliament on the interests of another (Goldsworthy 2010). This has also meant that, while the relationship between parliaments is justiciable in the context of the High Court (Australia's supreme national court), each state parliament is also subject to judicial review by their own supreme courts. Thus parliamentary sovereignty is reduced considerably, even within the accepted parameters of residual powers retained by states.

Concluding remarks

The Australian and New Zealand parliaments suffer from the same human weaknesses displayed by politicians in the UK. Where politicians can exploit the weaknesses inherent in the Westminster system (whether wittingly or unwittingly) in order to cultivate the rewards offered by electors, they have and will continue to do so. Practical difficulties associated with the idea of parliamentary sovereignty and responsible government are numerous and inherent in democratic political systems where the protection of citizens is as important as the constitutional capacity of the legislature.

There is also an argument here that the idea of parliamentary sovereignty can be destructive—a lack of understanding amongst electors (and often amongst members of parliament) means that the concept of parliamentary sovereignty and responsible government can be accepted without question while, as in the case of New Zealand prior to the reformation of the 1990s, the Executive is allowed to expand its power.

Laski (1948) argued that the theory of sovereignty provides that in every social order there has to be some single source of power, but that this is simply not true. He proposed that, in fact, the very idea of parliamentary sovereignty is of dubious value and equally dubious utility. Perhaps the time for considering unitary systems of Executive accountability has gone as the natural tensions between differing elements within the system are healthy in modern democracies and conceptions, such as the Westminster system with its components of parliamentary sovereignty and responsible government, are relics rather than useful modern tools.

I do not think so: there is still considerable value in maintaining the discourse surrounding this view even though its practical application is increasingly impossible as democratic ideas confine parliaments' capacity for action. For instance, the concept of parliamentary sovereignty provides a framework for this discourse. Rhodes and Weller (2005) described the elements of a sound political system (including an expert public service, an accountable administration, a pluralistic political system and an underlying respect for the law) as positioned within a conception of the Westminster system that often covers diverse contexts, histories and polities connected by family resemblance rather than a single, essential idea. Perhaps, then, a more useful frame for the broad changes occurring across Westminster-based polities would be that proposed by Goldsworthy (2010): an increased set of constitutional principles, rather than the establishment of a hard and fast conception of the idea of parliamentary sovereignty.

Note

1 University of Western Australia, Perth WA, Australia (david.gilchrist@uwa.edu.au).

References

Archer, JR 1980, 'The theory of responsible government in Britain and Australia', *Politics*, vol. 15, no. 2, pp. 23–31.

Aroney, N, Prasser, S & Nethercote, JR 2008, *Restraining elective dictatorship: the upper house solution?* University of Western Australia Press, Crawley.

Balls, HR 1963, 'The public accounts committee', *Canadian Public Administration*, vol. 6, no. 1, pp. 15–34.

Belich, J 1998, *The New Zealand wars and the Victorian interpretation of racial conflict*, Penguin Books, Auckland.

Belich, J 2009, *Replenishing the earth: the settler revolution and the rise of the Anglo-world, 1783–1939*, Oxford University Press, Oxford.

Bennet, WL 1980, 'The paradox of public discourse: a framework for the analysis of political accounts', *The Journal of Politics*, vol. 42, no. 3, pp. 792–817.

Benton, M & Russell, M 2012, 'Assessing the impact of parliamentary oversight committees: the select committees in the British House of Commons', *Parliamentary Affairs*, vol. 66, no. 4, pp. 772–797.

Bunn, M & Gilchrist, DJ 2013, ' "A few good men": public sector audit in the Swan River Colony, 1828–1835', *Accounting History*, vol. 18, no. 2, pp. 193–209.

Clarke, FG 1977, *The land of contrarities: British attitudes to the Australian colonies, 1828–1855*, Melbourne University Press, Carlton, VIC.

Degeling, P, Anderson, J & Guthrie, J 1996, 'Accounting for public accounts committees', *Accounting, Auditing and Accountability Journal*, vol. 9, no. 2, pp. 30–49.

Dowd, C 2014, *Faith, Ireland and empire: the life of Patrick Joseph Clune CSSR, 1864–1935 – Archbishop of Perth, Western Australia*, St Pauls Publications, Strathfield.

Eddy, JJ 1969, *Britain and the Australian colonies, 1818–1831: the technique of government*, Clarendon Press, Oxford.

Ferguson, N 2008, *Empire: how Britain made the modern world*, Penguin Group, Camberwell.

Fox, R 2008 [1933], *The colonial policy of British imperialism*, Oxford University Press, Oxford.

Galligan, B & Roberts, W (eds) 2007, 'Responsible government', in *The Oxford companion to Australian politics*, Oxford University Press, Oxford.

Gilchrist, DJ 2017, *Imperial theory and colonial pragmatism: Charles Harper, economic development and agricultural co-operation in Australia*, Palgrave Macmillan, Cham. Switzerland.

Gilchrist, DJ & Coulson, K 2015, 'Pragmatism, black letter law and Australian public accounts committees', in Z Hoque (ed), *Making governments accountable: the role of public accounts committees and national audit offices*, Routledge, London, pp. 141–157.

Goldsworthy, J 2010, *Parliamentary sovereignty: contemporary debates*, Cambridge University Press, Cambridge.

Gollin, A 1965, *Balfour's burden: Arthur Balfour and imperial preference*, Anthony Blond, London.

Groves, M & Lee, HP 2007, 'Australian administrative law: the constitutional and legal matrix', in M Groves & HP Lee (eds), *Australian administrative law: fundamentals, principles and doctrines*, Cambridge University Press, Cambridge.

Horner, D 2015, ' "Republicanism and responsible government: the shaping of democracy in Canada and Australia", by Benjamin Jones (review)', *Journal of Colonialism and Colonial History*, vol. 16, no. 3, doi:10.1353/cch.2015.0046

James, L 1997, *The rise and fall of the British empire*, Abacus, London.

Laidlaw, Z 2005, *Colonial connections, 1815–45: patronage, the information revolution and colonial government*, Manchester University Press, Manchester.

Laski, HJ 1948, *A grammar of politics*, George Allen and Unwin, London.

Levine, S 2004, 'Parliamentary democracy in New Zealand', *Parliamentary Affairs*, vol. 57, no. 3, pp. 646–665.

Lord Cooke of Thorndon 2007, 'The myth of sovereignty', *Otago Law Review*, vol. 11, no. 3, pp. 377–379.

Metin, A 1977, *Socialism without doctrine*, trans. R Ward, Alternative Publishing Co-operative Ltd, Chippendale, NSW.

Monk, D 2010, 'A framework for evaluating the performance of committees in Westminster parliaments', *The Journal of Legislative Studies*, vol. 16, no. 1, pp. 1–13.

Pelizzo, R 2011, 'Public accounts committees in the Commonwealth: oversight, effectiveness, and governance', *Commonwealth & Comparative Politics*, vol. 49, no. 4, pp. 528–546.

Pilcher, RA, Gilchrist, DJ, Singh, H & Singh, I 2013, 'The interface between internal and external audit in the Australian public sector', *Australian Accounting Review*, vol. 23, no. 67, pp. 330–340.

Prosser, B & Denniss, R 2015, *Minority policy: rethinking governance when parliament matters*, Melbourne University Press, Carlton, VIC.

Reilly, A, Appleby, G, Grenfell, L & Lacey, W 2013, *Australian public law*, Oxford University Press, Oxford.

Rhodes, RAW 2005, 'Australia: the Westminster model as tradition', in H Patapan, J Wanna & P Weller (eds), *Westminster legacies: democracy and responsible government in Asia and the Pacific*, University of New South Wales Press, Sydney, pp. 129–152.

Rhodes, RAW & Weller, P 2005, 'Westminster transplanted and Westminster implanted: exploring political change', in H Patapan, J Wanna & P Weller (eds), *Westminster legacies: democracy and responsible government in Asia and the Pacific*, University of New South Wales Press, Sydney, pp. 1–12.

Wanna, J 2005, 'New Zealand's Westminster trajectory: archetypal transplant to maverick outlier', in H Patapan, J Wanna & P Weller (eds), *Westminster legacies: democracy and responsible government in Asia and the Pacific*, University of New South Wales Press, Sydney, pp. 153–185.

Wehner, J 2010, 'Principles and patterns of financial scrutiny: public accounts committees in the Commonwealth', *Commonwealth & Comparative Politics*, vol. 41, no. 3, pp. 21–36.

Weller, P 2007, *Cabinet government in Australia, 1901–2006: practice, principles, performance*, University of New South Wales Press, Sydney.

Wentworth, WC 1956, 'Responsible government in Australia: State constitutions and federal power', *The Australian Quarterly*, vol. 28, no. 2, pp. 7–19.

Wilson, AJ 1909, *An empire in pawn: being lectures and essays on Indian, colonial, and domestic finance, 'preference', free trade etc.*, T. Fisher Unwin, London.

Woolmer, L 1998, 'Public accounts committee – checks and balances Queensland style', *Accountability & Performance*, vol. 4, no. 1, pp. 41–51.

Young, DM 1961, *The colonial office in the early nineteenth century*, The Royal Commonwealth Society, Longmans, London.

6 The relationship between pre-election reports in New Zealand local governments and voter turnout

Bikram Chatterjee,[1] *Ross Taplin, Nicholas Pawsey, Mary Low, and Grantley Taylor*

Introduction

Democracies depend on citizens' engagement in voting and politics (Knack 1992). Following the significance of voting, some democracies introduced compulsory voting while others opted for it to be voluntary. In New Zealand, *enrolment* [emphasis added] to vote is compulsory while *voting* [emphasis added] is not compulsory (Electoral Commission 2017). In a voluntary setting, the question of why individuals take the time and effort to vote has stimulated a significant amount of theoretical and empirical research (Geys 2006a). Voting behaviour is one of the most widely researched topics in political science (Denny & Doyle 2008). Given assertions that low voter turnouts 'conceivably cause democracy to break down' (Downs 1957, p. 268), it is envisaged that efforts are made to increase voter turnout.

Voter turnout in New Zealand local government elections has been historically low with numbers declining since 1989 and being about 30 percent lower compared to parliamentary elections (Reid 2016). The decline in participation reached a point whereby it attracted the attention of the then Minister for Local Government, Sandra Lee, who suggested that 'when it comes to local government, New Zealanders, as voters, are pretty switched off' (Morning Report 2001 cited in Reid 2016, p. 3) and considered the possibility of introducing mandatory voting (Reid 2016).

One of the ways to increase voter participation is to reduce their information acquisition costs before the election day (Geys 2006b). The introduction in July 2011 of a requirement for pre-election reports in the *Local Government Act 2002* (NZ) was expected to reduce the information acquisition costs of voters. This in turn was thought to contribute to higher voter turnout in the next election year, as the reports provide opportunities for local governments to convey to the community a summary of their past performance as well as their plans for the next three years (New Zealand Society of Local Government Managers 2012). The reports also meet the characteristics of popular reporting. Hence, using rational choice theory, the present chapter investigates the relationship between pre-election reports (seen by government as an additional accountability mechanism) and voter turnout.

The next section outlines previous literature on the factors affecting voter turn-out with section 3 outlining the theoretical framework. Section 4 provides the context of New Zealand local government elections and the pre-election report. Section 5 outlines the research method with the results appearing in the penulti-mate section. The chapter finishes with a section providing the discussion, conclu-sion and suggestions for future research.

Literature review

There has been a considerable amount of prior research exploring the incidence of voter turnout and voter behaviour. Caporale and Poitras (2014) investigated the factors affecting voter turnout in 34 US presidential elections from 1880 to 2012. They found that short-term macroeconomic conditions, particularly unemploy-ment, were related to voter turnout. Higher unemployment had a positive effect while price inflation had a negative effect on voter turnout. This finding can be attributed to the poor economic conditions, during which citizens participate in voting in order to contribute to addressing these issues.

Bednarczuk (2017) investigated the relationship between employment in the government sector and voter turnout in the United States spanning 16 elections from 1982 to 2012. No significant relationship was found. Bednarczuk (2017) attributed this finding to voter perception of work culture and advancement. If a government employee is concerned about budgetary issues and hence loss of employment due to the election of a specific party or individual, they are expected to vote. In contrast, if government employees believe that loss of employment or an adverse effect on that person's career is instead the result of poor individual performance, these employees will have no greater incentive to vote than those not employed in the government sector.

Geys (2006a) synthesised previous literature on the factors affecting voter turn-out, finding population size and election closeness were the two main influences. In a recent update to the Geys (2006a) study, Cancela and Geys (2016) conducted a meta-analysis of studies published between the years 2002 and 2015 to inves-tigate the factors affecting voter turnout. They reported that campaign expendi-tures, election closeness and registration requirements were the issues affecting national election voting, whereas population size and composition, concurrent elections and the electoral system played a more significant role in subnational election voting.

Smets and Van Ham (2013) reported that in their analysis of 90 articles, 170 independent variables were found to be associated with voter turnout. The authors reported that the factors consistently linked with voter turnout were age, educa-tion, residential mobility, region, media exposure, mobilisation (partisan and non-partisan), voting in a previous election, party identification, political interest and political knowledge.

As outlined earlier, multiple factors have been studied in analysing their effect on voter turnout, but none of the existing studies investigated the effect of report-ing on voter turnout.

Reporting reduces information asymmetry between voters and the government through the provision of information that allows voters to monitor the pre-election promises of elected officials (Chan & Rubin 1987; Laswad, Fisher & Oyelere 2005). In more practical terms, as described by Daniels and Daniels (1991), the accounting reports of government entities enable citizens to conduct comparisons against budget forecasts, assess the financial performance and position, review the extent of compliance with relevant rules and regulations, and support the evaluation of their efficiency and effectiveness (Laswad, Fisher & Oyelere 2005). At the very least, citizens are likely to be indirect users of accounting information through information intermediaries, and accounting information can complement other information that voters possess (Feroz & Wilson 1994). Standard setting agencies have long regarded the citizenry as a significant user group of governmental financial reports (Chan & Rubin 1987).

The significance of accounting information, and hence reporting, in the context of voting is evidenced in previous studies. Ingram and Copeland (1981) reported a significant association between accounting ratios and municipal election outcomes. In a more recent study, Feroz and Wilson (1994, p. 161) suggested that the role of accounting information is particularly significant in highly competitive elections:

> the greater the competition, the greater the amount of information generated by intermediaries. The greater the amount of information generated, the higher the probability that voters will impound this information in their voting decision.

In the context of Spanish local government election results, Brusca and Montesinos (2006) confirmed the significance of some accounting ratios in explaining the differences in the percentage of votes obtained by the political party which was in government. Brusca and Montesinos (2006) recommended provision of information, specifically financial information, in an easily accessible format.

Given the lack of studies investigating the relationship between reporting and voter turnout, and the introduction of pre-election reports in New Zealand local governments, the present study investigates the relationship between pre-election reports and voter turnout in New Zealand local governments.

Theoretical framework

A widely used framework to explain the reason for voting voluntarily is rational choice theory. This framework uses an economic approach to the study of voter behaviour and adopts underlying economic assumptions of rationality and utility maximisation (Chan & Rubin 1987). Based on the seminal work of Downs (1957), rational choice theory depicts the decision to vote as being based on an individual's assessment of the costs and benefits of voting and the determination of the expected utility of voting (Colomer 1991; Geys 2006b; Smets & Van Ham 2013).

From a rational choice perspective, the benefits of voting include the chance that an individual can affect the outcome of the election (Fowler 2013; Geys 2006b). As suggested by Geys (2006b), the costs of voting can be classified into two broad categories. The first is the information acquisition cost incurred before the election day, as the voters seek to become politically informed about the candidates and their policies. The second is that incurred on the election day, as individuals make their way to and from the polling station and incur opportunity costs from the time spent doing so and casting their vote. Given that the chance that an individual vote will influence an election is very unlikely (particularly in large electorates), rational choice theory posits that it will take very little for the costs of voting to exceed the benefits and many rational voters will be likely to abstain from voting (Colomer 1991; Geys 2006b; Knack 1992).

Despite rational choice predictions of large voter absenteeism, many voters still elect to voluntarily vote (Geys 2006b) and this has led to a wider consideration of the benefits of voting and other individual factors impacting voting behaviour. In this regard, rational choice theory has been extended to recognise how a sense of civic duty can motivate individuals to vote (Smets & Van Ham 2013). As discussed by Geys (2006b, pp. 18–19), 'some people may vote to see democracy continue . . . a voter turns out because he or she feels morally obliged to do so'.

Based on the aforementioned discussion, it is expected that voter turnout will increase if the information acquisition cost decreases. It has long been recognised that citizens demand 'easy-to-understand' financial information (see, for example, Daniels & Daniels 1991). Carcaba-Garcia, Lopez-Diaz and Pablos-Rodriguez (2002, p. 22) explained that:

> public accountability roots on the belief that citizens have the 'right to know,' in other words, the right to be provided with reliable data that makes possible the debate between citizens and elected representatives.

Against this backdrop, there has been an ongoing debate about the ability of existing forms of governmental financial reports to meet the needs of all citizens, given their diversity with regards to education, expertise and information requirements (Cohen & Karatzimas 2015). One trend which seeks to redress this issue is the development of 'popular reporting', which Cohen and Karatzimas (2015, p. 450) claimed:

> aims at informing citizens about the financial condition of the state/local government in a convenient and friendly manner. Popular reports are expected to be concise, short in length, and present in a simplified way public sector accounting information.

Such practices are said to be aligned with the interests of citizens as the demand for concise and easily understandable financial information is likely to stimulate the interest of these citizens (Cohen & Karatzimas 2015). If the intention of preparing popular reports is to provide information that citizens are really interested in, such as 'what are the results and outcomes of last year? what is new? and what is likely to happen in the future?' (Financial Management Capability Building Committee 2004, p. 2), then popular reporting is expected to increase voter turnout.

The audiences of local authority performance reporting are the local communities who need such information to hold elected representatives and entities to account and participate effectively in democratic decision-making (Controller & Auditor General 2008). Yusuf et al. (2013, p. 97) argued that popular financial reports 'contribute to the development of informed citizens who want to and are able to provide public input regarding current and emerging policy issues'. Individuals with more information can be more confident that they are selecting the right candidate and the value of changing the election outcome is higher (Geys 2006b).

The pre-election reports meet the characteristics of popular reports since they often include predictions for the future, are considerably less in volume than annual reports and include both financial and non-financial information. Hence, these reports are expected to reduce information acquisition costs and to result in an increase in voter turnout.

New Zealand local government elections and pre-election reports: the context

New Zealand local governments include 78 councils (also referred to as local governments) comprising 11 regional councils, 61 territorial authorities made up of 11 city councils, 50 district councils and 6 unitary councils (Local Government New Zealand 2017). Elected members are chosen by voters to represent them every three years. The activities of regional councils include environmental resource management, flood control, air and water quality, pest control, and in some cases public transport, regional parks and water supply. Territorial authorities engage in a wide range of services including roads, water reticulation, sewerage and refuse collection, libraries, parks, recreation services, local regulations, community and economic development, and town planning. Councils may differ in terms of activities undertaken following consultation with the local community. The main source of finance of local governments is property tax (rates). Local government is governed by the *Local Government Act 2002* (NZ) (Local Government New Zealand 2017). Under this legislation, local councils are required to prepare an annual report for the purpose of comparing actual activities and performance with intended activities and performance and to fulfil accountability to the community (s. 98). In addition, councils are required (by an amendment to the Act in 2011, s. 99A) to prepare a pre-election report to promote discussion about issues facing the local authority. This report must be completed and published no later than two weeks before the nomination day of elections.

Research method

Sample

As detailed above, the population of New Zealand local governments currently includes 78 councils (following the merging of some local governments). Out of the 78 local governments, voter turnout data for the 2010 election of five local governments could not be obtained since these organisations had merged with other organisations. This resulted in analysis of pre-election reports and voter turnout data for a final sample of 73 local governments.

Measurement and sources of variables

Table 6.1 outlines the measurement of seven variables. The independent variable is 'disclosure', referring to disclosure in the 2013 pre-election report in the area of environmental information and infrastructure information, including historical and prospective information. Electorates are expected to be interested in these disclosures when electing councillors and the mayor because infrastructure and the environment affect everyday life. Since these information items have been reported in pre-election reports, they are expected to affect voter turnout.

The five control variables used in this study are 'increase in debt to total assets', 'increase in revenue to expenditure', 'increase in per capita income' of residents, 'press visibility' and 'size'. These data (except 'press visibility' and 'per capita income' of residents) were collected from 2010 annual reports and 2013 pre-election/annual reports of each New Zealand local government. Data on 'press visibility' was obtained from the Index New Zealand website (National Library of New Zealand 2016). The 'per capita income' of residents in each local government area was obtained from Statistics New Zealand (2016) census data.

Table 6.1 Variable measurement

Variable	Measurement
Voter turnout (dependent)	Number of voters divided by number of residents (%)
Increase in debt to total assets (control)	Log(debt/total assets) for 2013 subtract Log(debt/total assets) for 2010
Increase in revenue to expenditure (control)	Log(revenue/total expenditure) for 2013 subtract Log(revenue/total expenditure) for 2010
Increase in per capita income (control)	Mean income per resident for 2013 subtract mean income per resident for 2010
Press visibility (control)	Log(number of news items 2008-2013)
Size (control)	Log(total assets in 2010)
Disclosure (independent)	Number of items disclosed (out of 57)

Financials of respective local government debt, assets, revenue and expenditure were included since this economic information is expected to affect voter turnout. A local government with higher debt and/or lower revenue is expected to attract higher public attention as these financial factors affect the funds available for provision of services. 'Press visibility' was included as local governments with high press visibility are expected to attract more voters in an election.

The dependent variable is 'voter turnout'. Information with regard to voter turnout was obtained from The Department of Internal Affairs, New Zealand (2016), website.

Statistical analysis

In addition to summary statistics of the variables, the change in voter turnout (voter turnout in the 2013 election minus the voter turnout in the 2010 election) was tested for a significant difference to zero using a paired *t*-test. Multiple regression was used to test for significant relationships between the change in voter turnout and the independent variables. Due to the reduced sample size for disclosures made by local councils, two multiple regressions are reported (Table 6.4): model 1 includes disclosure as an independent variable (and therefore has a smaller sample size), and model 2 excludes the disclosure variable and hence includes all the 73 councils. Statistical analysis was performed using SPSS software (version 22).

Results

Summary statistics for voter turnout in 2010 and 2013, and the change from 2010 to 2013, are provided in Table 6.2. The table shows that the number of voters varied between about one-third and two-thirds. The mean voter turnout decreased significantly ($p < 0.001$; paired *t*-test), by 3 percent. The correlation between voter turnout in the 2010 and 2013 elections is high ($r = 0.74$; $p < 0.001$).

Table 6.2 Summary statistics for voter turnout

Variable	Min	Max	Mean	St. dev
2010 election	34.0	66.0	50.2	7.7
2013 election	31.6	64.0	47.1	6.8
Increase	−17.8	14.6	−3.0[1]	5.4

[1] Decrease in voter turnout of 3 percent is statistically significant ($p < 0.001$).

Table 6.3 provides summary statistics for the independent variables. There is considerable variation in the changes in debt to total assets from 2010 to 2013. On average, there was an increase of 7 percent. Similarly, revenue to expenses increased on average by 2 percent, although many councils experienced a decrease between these two years. Disclosure levels were very low, with on average only 6.35 items disclosed out of the 58 disclosure items.

Table 6.3 Summary statistics for independent variables

Variable	Min	Max	Mean	St. dev
Increase in debt to total assets	−0.34	0.53	0.07	0.16
Increase in revenue to expenditure	−0.17	0.27	0.02	0.07
Increase in per capita income	0.01	0.15	0.08	0.02
Press visibility	0.00	3.84	1.67	0.74
Size	7.81	9.86	8.79	0.42
Disclosure[1]	3.00	15.00	6.35	2.53

[1] The sample size for disclosure is only 55, while for other variables it is 73.

Table 6.5 (Appendix) further outlines disclosures in pre-election reports. Disclosure data could only be obtained for 55 local governments. The highest number of disclosures was made with regard to 'infrastructure information': first, 'information with regard to whether infrastructure assets have increased during the current financial year', followed by 'information about the need for new infrastructure' and 'capital expenditure already committed with regard to infrastructure, such as contracts already entered upon'. Disclosure about infrastructure can be attributed to attracting voters. Comparatively, disclosure of environmental information was sparse, with the 'narrative environmental expenditure' recording the highest number of disclosures.

Regressions both including and excluding the disclosure variable are summarised in Table 6.4. Model 1 includes the disclosure variable but shows an insignificant relationship with the change in voter turnout ($p = 0.723$). Model 2, therefore, excludes this insignificant variable and therefore increases the sample size by including the councils where disclosure information was not available. Both models confirm a significant relationship between voter turnout and the increase in debt to total assets ($p = 0.001$) and press visibility ($p = 0.012$) and marginal evidence of a relationship with the size of the local council ($p = 0.079$). Although multicollinearity was not an issue (all variance inflation factors are less than 1.3), the correlation between size and press visibility was moderate ($r = 0.429$), providing evidence of the intuitive relationship that press visibility is higher for larger councils.

Table 6.4 Regressions predicting voter turnout

Variable	Model 1 (N = 55)[1]		Model 2 (N = 73)	
	Coeff	*P*	*Coeff*	*P*
Constant	−28.94	0.041	−20.94	0.117
Increase in debt to total assets	−12.33	0.003	−12.25	0.001
Increase in revenue to expenditure	−4.03	0.670	−5.42	0.527
Increase in per capita income	−21.71	0.406	−16.29	0.504
Press visibility	−2.29	0.026	−2.22	0.012
Size	3.57	0.031	2.71	0.079
Disclosure	0.09	0.726	0.00	–

[1] Model 1 includes the disclosure variable and therefore has a sample size of only 55 councils.

Discussion and conclusion

A requirement for a pre-election report was introduced in New Zealand from the 2013 local government elections to promote discussion about issues facing the local government authority. These reports meet the characteristics of popular reporting since they communicate the performance of local governments in a concise format, which is expected to increase the interest of voters. The pre-election report reduces the information acquisition cost for voters, reducing the costs of voting. Based on rational choice theory, the reduction of information acquisition cost is expected to increase voter turnout in local government elections following the introduction of these reports.

This study finds instead that disclosure of infrastructure- and environment-related information in these pre-election reports had no significant relationship to voter turnout. In addition, the voter turnout in the 2013 election actually decreased compared to the 2010 election. Contrary to our expectation, 'debt to total assets' and 'press visibility' were negatively related to voter turnout. The former finding may be attributed to voters not referring to the pre-election reports and/or annual reports of councils and hence being unaware of their level of debt. The latter finding needs further investigation with regard to the nature of information reported about councils in publications. If publications reported positive and/or neutral news, voters would probably not be concerned.

This chapter adds to literature in the area of voter turnout by analysing the relationship between voter turnout and an additional accountability mechanism, the pre-election report. The theoretical contribution of this chapter is the application of rational choice theory in analysing the effectiveness of pre-election reports on increasing voter turnout. Finally, the findings also contribute to practice in developing future accountability instruments for local governments. At the least, the required content of pre-election reports needs to be evaluated.

The study is limited to two election years. Since the requirement for a pre-election report was introduced before the election year 2013, it is possible that awareness of this report has increased over the years and voter turnout will further increase in future years. Future studies, including data from multiple election years, are suggested to further evaluate the effectiveness of these reports. Investigating voters' needs in pre-election reports will contribute towards further development of these reports. Finally, future studies are suggested to investigate the content of news reported in publications about local governments and the pattern of voting in individual local governments.

Appendix

Table 6.5 Disclosure items and number and percentage of the 55 local companies disclosing each item

Disclosure item	Number	Percentage
Provision for clean-up costs	3	5%
Contingent liability data	0	0%
Forecast of the impact of environmental expenditure on future results	0	0%
Prospective environmental expenditure	14	25%
Historical environmental expenditure	3	5%
Statement of progress on environmental performance against targets	0	0%
Others (please state)	0	0%
Statement of assurance from management of compliance with external standards	17	31%
Summary of results of environmental audits	0	0%
Local government environmental policy statement	5	9%
External verifier's report on the environmental audit	0	0%
Environmental impact assessments and site level reports	1	2%
Statement of intent with regards to environmental audits	0	0%
Specific accounting policies for environmental issues	1	2%
Narrative environmental disclosures	38	69%
Management's responsibilities for monitoring environmental performance	9	16%
Others (please state)	0	0%
Good news	0	0%
Bad news	4	7%
Valuation of infrastructure	1	2%
Depreciation on infrastructure	0	0%
Current year's actual maintenance expenditure	2	4%
Separate disclosure of actual routine and non-routine maintenance expenditure	2	4%
Infrastructure cash flows	1	2%
Five year infrastructure maintenance plan outlining the required maintenance each year	0	0%
Deferred maintenance expenditure	1	2%
Disclosure of required maintenance each year	3	5%
Cost of attaining target level of service if different from actual one	0	0%
Budget to actual spending on infrastructure	0	0%

Disclosure item	Number	Percentage
Capital expenditure already committed in regard to infrastructure, such as, contracts already entered upon	48	87%
Information about the need for new infrastructure	52	95%
Economic lives of infrastructure	5	9%
Asset management plan certified by an independent expert	1	2%
Physical description of infrastructure assets, such as, kilometres of road, pipes or cables	20	36%
Consumption of infrastructure	1	2%
Information in regard to whether infrastructure assets have increased during the current financial year	54	98%
Assessment of long term implications of current infrastructure management practices	2	4%
Replacement cycle	0	0%
Ageing schedule	0	0%
Report on service quality by an independent body	0	0%
Difference between target and actual level of service	0	0%
Comparative information of infrastructure consumed and replaced	0	0%
Infrastructure availability/disruption	1	2%
Complaint/satisfaction of infrastructure services	2	4%
Provision for clean-up costs	9	16%
Contingent liability data	0	0%
Prospective environmental expenditure	31	56%
Historical environmental expenditure	3	5%
Statement of progress on environmental performance against quantified targets	0	0%
Statement of assurance from management of compliance with external standards	5	9%
Summary of results of environmental audits	0	0%
Environmental Impact assessment and cite level reports	0	0%
Cost of securing infrastructure	3	5%
Elector satisfaction	0	0%
Projects to engage with the community	10	18%
Positive impact of projects on community	2	4%
Negative impact of projects on the community	0	0%
Future projects to engage with the community	3	5%

Note

1 University of Waikato, Hamilton New Zealand (bikramc@waikato.ac.nz)

References

Bednarczuk, M 2017, 'Voter turnout and bureaucrats across time: a further examination of the bureau voting model in the United States', *Public Administration Quarterly*, vol. 41, no. 2, pp. 386–421.

Brusca, I & Montesinos, V 2006, 'Are citizens significant users of government financial information?' *Public Money and Management*, vol. 26, no. 4, pp. 205–209.

Cancela, J & Geys, B 2016, 'Explaining voter turnout: a meta-analysis of national and subnational elections', *Electoral Studies*, vol. 42, June, pp. 264–275.

Caporale, T & Poitras, M 2014, 'Voter turnout in US presidential elections: does Carville's law explain the time series?' *Applied Economics*, vol. 46, no. 29, pp. 3630–3638.

Carcaba-Garcia, A, Lopez-Diaz, A & Pablos-Rodriguez, JL 2002, 'Improving the disclosure of financial information in local governments', *International Public Management Review*, vol. 3, no. 1, pp. 22–40.

Chan, JL & Rubin, MA 1987, 'The role of information in a democracy and in government operations: the public choice methodology', *Research in Governmental and Nonprofit Accounting*, vol. 3, pp. 3–27.

Cohen, S & Karatzimas, S 2015, 'Tracing the future of reporting in the public sector: introducing integrated popular reporting', *International Journal of Public Sector Management*, vol. 28, no. 6, pp. 449–460.

Colomer, JM 1991, 'Benefits and costs of voting', *Electoral Studies*, vol. 10, no. 4, pp. 313–325.

Controller & Auditor-General 2008, 'The Auditor-General's observations on the quality of performance reporting', *discussion paper*, June, Office of the Auditor-General, Wellington.

Daniels, JD & Daniels, CE 1991, 'Municipal financial reports: what users want', *Journal of Accounting and Public Policy*, vol. 10, no. 1, pp. 15–38.

Denny, K & Doyle, O 2008, 'Political interest, cognitive ability and personality: Determinants of voter turnout in Britain', *British Journal of Political Science*, vol. 38, no. 2, pp. 291–310.

The department of Internal Affairs 2016, 'Local Authority Election Statistics 2013', viewed 8 May 2016, www.dia.govt.nz/diawebsite.nsf/wpg_URL/Services-Local-Elections-Local-Authority-Election-Statistics-2013?OpenDocument#two

Downs, A 1957, *An economic theory of democracy*, Harper and Row, New York.

Electoral Commission 2017, 'New Zealand's system of government', viewed 9 August 2017, www.elections.org.nz/voting-system/new-zealands-system-government

Feroz, EH & Wilson, ER 1994, 'Financial accounting measures and mayoral elections', *Financial Accountability & Management*, vol. 10, no. 3, pp. 161–174.

Financial Management Capability Building Committee 2004, *FMCBC recommended practice: preparing popular reports*, CCAF-FCVI Inc., Canada.

Fowler, A 2013, 'Electoral and policy consequences of voter turnout: evidence from compulsory voting in Australia', *Quarterly Journal of Political Science*, vol. 8, no. 2, pp. 159–182.

Geys, B 2006a, 'Explaining voter turnout: a review of aggregate-level research', *Electoral Studies*, vol. 25, no. 4, pp. 637–663.

Geys, B 2006b, ' "Rational" theories of voter turnout: a review', *Political Studies Review*, vol. 4, no. 1, pp. 16–35.

Ingram, RW & Copeland, RM 1981, 'Municipal accounting information and voting behavior', *The Accounting Review*, vol. 56, no. 4, pp. 830–843.

Knack, S 1992, 'Civic norms, social sanctions, and voter turnout', *Rationality and Society*, vol. 4, no. 2, pp. 133–156.

Laswad, F, Fisher, R & Oyelere, P 2005, 'Determinants of voluntary internet financial reporting by local government authorities', *Journal of Accounting and Public Policy*, vol. 24, no. 2, pp. 101–121.

Local Government New Zealand 2017, 'Local government in New Zealand', viewed 22 August 2017, www.lgnz.co.nz/nzs-local-government/

National Library of New Zealand 2016, Index New Zealand, viewed 8 May 2016, http://natlib-primo.hosted.exlibrisgroup.com/primo_library/libweb/action/search. do?vid=NLNZ&tab=innz

New Zealand Society of Local Government Managers 2012, 'Pre-election reports: preparing a pre-election report under Section 99A of the Local Government Act', SOLGM, Wellington.

Reid, M 2016, 'Local authority turnout: what's the story?' *Policy Quarterly*, vol. 12, no. 4, pp. 3–9.

Smets, K & Van Ham, C 2013, 'The embarrassment of riches? A meta-analysis of individual-level research on voter turnout', *Electoral Studies*, vol. 32, no. 2, pp. 344–359.

Statistics NZ 2016, 'Census', viewed 8 May 2016, www.stats.govt.nz/topics/census

Yusuf, J, Jordan, MM, Neill, KA & Hackbart, M 2013, 'For the people: popular financial reporting practices of local governments', *Public Budgeting & Finance*, vol. 33, no. 1, pp. 95–113.

Legislation

'Local Government Act 2002' (NZ), viewed 22 August 2017, www.legislation.govt.nz/act/public/2002/0084/167.0/DLM170873.html

7 Watching the watchdogs

How auditing is contributing to governance

Peter Wilkins[1]

Introduction

External audit of the public sector is a basic and long-standing feature of Australian public administration. The fourth Act passed by the newly formed Commonwealth Parliament in 1901 created a public sector auditor (Australian National Audit Office 2017) and states had independent audit functions prior to (and after) the creation of the Federation (Bunn & Gilchrist 2013). The original role of these public sector audit institutions was financial auditing to provide assurance regarding transactions and the usefulness of the statements.

Contemporary public sector audit has diverse additional roles, including performance audits, assurance regarding statements of performance, audits of key performance indicators (KPIs), internal control assessments and information systems audits.

Like the rest of the public sector, it is important that the audit offices are accountable and that there is oversight of their performance. This chapter analyses four recent Australian statutory reviews of audit offices and presents insights into the reviews and the audit offices involved. The observations and conclusions are of interest to Parliaments and audit offices in Australia and elsewhere because this kind of review is not general practice outside Australia.

Literature review

There has been much written about performance audit (as detailed in the following chapter). However, given the focus of performance audit, it is surprising how little of this writing provides evidence-based analysis of what performance audit is achieving. A wide-ranging review of evidence for the impact of performance audit identified 14 relevant empirical studies assessing a range of factors that facilitate impact, including the report, the process used, diffusion and communication and the audit results (Loocke & Put 2011, p. 185). However, the authors concluded that there is still considerable uncertainty about the factors that contribute to the impact of performance audits (Loocke & Put 2011, p. 201).

Typically audit offices have a hierarchy of quality assurance systems that may include in-house 'cold' and 'hot' reviews, monitoring information such as surveys of parliamentarians and agencies, peer reviews and benchmarking with other audit offices (see, for instance, Victorian Auditor-General's Office (VAGO) 2016).[2] Sitting above these arrangements is the accountability framework imposed by the legislation and the role adopted by the Parliament. Parliamentary oversight committees often have a specific role in relation to the work of integrity agencies (Griffith 2006) and periodic statutory reviews can be an important component of this accountability framework. These reviews typically look at the performance of the audit office with the approach shaped by the specific provisions of the legislation and the terms of reference. Reviewers may also be required to consider the adequacy of the governing legislation in relation to issues such as protecting independence.

Statutory reviews were identified by Whitfield (2006, p. 89) as necessary and 'fundamental for Parliament to gain assurance that the Auditor-General is carrying out his role in an appropriate way'.

It is notable that the wide-ranging review on evidence for the impact of performance audit referred to earlier identified 14 empirical studies but did not include statutory reviews as a source (Loocke & Put 2011, p. 188). There has not been a previous analysis of a sample of statutory reviews to understand what is being learnt and what issues parliaments and reviewers might consider in future. Consequently, there is potential for drawing on statutory reviews as a further source of evidence about the impact of performance audit. This chapter is a first attempt to fill this gap. A complementary project is based on the legislative provisions and terms of reference. It assesses the role of reviews of watchdogs from a parliamentary perspective and has been reported separately (Wilkins 2017).

Research design

Four Australian jurisdictions had statutory review reports finalised in the 18-month period prior to the commencement of the project in April 2017.[3] These were three States and one Territory, each having its own parliament: the Australian Capital Territory (ACT), Queensland, Victoria and Western Australia (WA).

Framework for analysis of the reviews

The legislation and terms of reference set the scope and, to some extent, the approach adopted by each review. It would therefore be expected that reviews would differ between jurisdictions and between reviews within a jurisdiction.

A framework was developed to unpack key aspects of the reviews relevant to the focus of this chapter, based on five components:

- overall findings of the reviews
- improving public sector performance
- improving public sector accountability
- independence of the audit office
- transparency of the audit office.

The assessment of the reviews reported in this chapter focuses on performance audit functions as they most directly contribute to audit impact in terms of improving public sector performance and accountability and are commonly the predominant focus of parliamentary interest in the work of public sector audit. Additionally, in considering audit impact, emphasis is given to coverage of effectiveness over efficiency and economy, and also over issues of compliance.

Results

Overall findings

The overall findings of the four reviews were generally positive, having a tone of doing well in each case with some areas for improvement. For instance, the Queensland review found that audit office 'is fundamentally sound. . . . It is operating economically and efficiently, and in accordance with its legislation' (Smith & Carpenter 2017, p. 2).

The reviews made a wide variety of recommendations, ranging in number from 15 to 30 per review. While there were some common areas for improvement, they also identified different key issues in each jurisdiction.

Improving public sector performance

All four reviews provided information on how the audit offices contributed to public sector performance. For instance, the review of the Queensland Audit Office (QAO) explained its approach to assessing effectiveness by noting that it 'requires addressing the question of purpose and the outcomes that the QAO achieves' (Smith & Carpenter 2017, p. 6). The review used the QAO's articulation of its own objectives in its strategic plan and in its assessment of effectiveness, noting that one of the objectives is '[o]ur clients use the information we provide to improve accountability and performance' (Smith & Carpenter 2017, p. 6).

However, the reviews paid relatively little attention to coverage of factors that may contribute to ongoing high performance, such as aspects of public sector agency organisational culture like the capacity to deliver quality services with integrity and to innovate as the need arises. While not easy aspects for auditors to address on a firm evidence base, such factors can be important information providing insights relevant to the future performance trajectory.

Coverage of other key issues regarding public sector performance was addressed through a consideration of the topic selection processes used by each audit office, and through a consideration of the measures used to report performance. These two perspectives are assessed next.

Choosing relevant and high priority performance audit topics is a key ingredient of the information ultimately provided as a result of an audit programme.

The WA review found that the audit office's topic selection process was robust and incorporated better practices than those used in other jurisdictions. It noted that the process considered the essential elements of materiality, impact, previous audit and review coverage (including by other bodies), risk, auditability and context, and sought a balance across core audit themes. The Victorian review noted similarly that the audit office followed a comprehensive selection process for its performance audits and had the right balance of performance audits. However, it also found that the audit office was unable to provide any analysis to support its decisions regarding the total number and mix of the performance audits and recommended that this analysis be conducted. The ACT review also raised a significant concern, noting that 'a number of stakeholders expressed a desire for more reports to address outcomes and that they should focus on achieving improved operational efficiency and effectiveness' (Pearson 2016, p. 25). It also suggested that more analytical approaches and additional overt criteria should be adopted in selecting performance audit topics. Overall, it is not evident that the reviews sought to identify any 'blind spots' in topic selection such as performance audit coverage of central agencies.

It is therefore evident that there are limitations in how some audit offices undertake and explain their topic selection processes so that care needs to be taken in seeking to understand how they contribute to public sector performance. There is also very little review coverage of how the performance audit programme influences agencies other than those that are within the scope of the individual audits. However, other research has argued that there are lessons to be shared more widely because of systemic issues that exist across a wider range of agencies than those within scope (Loocke & Put 2011, p. 182).

This concern is given some consideration in relation to the issuing of better practice advice. The Victorian review addressed promoting improvements in public sector administration by taking a stronger role in identifying and promoting better practice. Suggestions included publishing better practice guidance and sharing checklists, assessment criteria and frameworks that have the potential of extending lessons learnt to a wider range of agencies (VAGO 2016).

It is evident from the four reviews that the Queensland audit office has in recent years gone further than the other three audit offices in seeking to measure how it is contributing to public sector performance, suggesting that there is scope for learning between audit offices using the observations of the individual reviews.

Improving public sector accountability

There is general coverage by the reviews of the role of audit offices in strengthening public sector accountability. It was addressed most directly by the review of the WA Office of the Auditor-General (OAG), which stated that '[t]here is evidence that OAG findings and recommendations have directly assisted Parliamentary scrutiny, influenced government decisions and improved public sector accountability and management practices' (Vista Advisory 2015, p. 71). Value for money in improving public accountability was considered, including a comparison with similar organisations, the OAG's KPI audits and communications with audited entities. The review also referred to the role of auditing agency KPIs which 'has provided visibility to Parliament, the public and successive governments of agencies' performance in key areas' as stakeholders can have greater confidence in reported performance information (Vista Advisory 2015, p. 71).

By contrast, the Queensland review considered the value of audit and indicated that the primary value of performance audits lies in the benefit to parliament and the public of public entities being held to account as the audits give assurance about the performance of public entities. However, while the review made findings and recommendations specific to improving public sector performance, it did not do so in relation to public sector accountability. Similarly, the Victorian review identified that the audit office's vision included being a catalyst for continuous improvement in the accountability (as well as performance) of the public service, but did not assess how this is being addressed by the audit office.

Independence

Independence of the auditor-general is an essential feature of the role and an underpinning of its effectiveness (Whitfield 2006, p. 88). Overall, it is evident that the reviewers gave considerable attention to issues of independence.

The Queensland report (Smith & Carpenter 2017, p. 7) addressed independence when discussing the concept of clients (auditees) and the extent to which an auditor can assist a client, noting that:

> [a]n auditor must be independent of the entity that it audits, so the auditor is not subject to the client's direction. The extent to which an auditor can assist and advise the client is limited, lest it results in the auditor auditing his or her own work.

This review also commented that there was a lack of independence in relation to the resourcing of the office and recommended that the auditor-general be recognised as an independent officer of Parliament and that Parliament's role be increased in matters such as appointment, setting the budget and monitoring performance. However, the report did not address specifically the implications for independence resulting from the executive government's control in appointing the reviewers and setting the terms of reference.

The ACT review observed that amendments to the Act in 2013 had established an unprecedented level of independence from executive government. Nevertheless, it identified the importance of determining a term of appointment for the auditor-general (Pearson 2016).

Transparency

Two of the reviews—the Queensland review and the WA review—addressed the transparency of the audit offices in relation to their own performance.

The Queensland review addressed performance monitoring and reporting by the audit office, finding that a balanced scorecard system was used to plan and monitor performance for internal reporting purposes, and that '[s]elected measures are reported externally in the QAO's Statement of Service Delivery and Performance Statement' (Smith & Carpenter 2017, p. 111). It commended the audit office for its reporting of performance audit recommendations implemented and benefits from performance audits. It also noted that the audit office adopted, in 2016, an integrated reporting approach and had commissioned an audit of its performance statement which it commended. Smith and Carpenter (2017, p. 111) observed that

> [p]ublication of performance information, both financial and non-financial, is an important part of a public entity's accountability. Audit gives the users of that information assurance that it can be relied on.

The WA review found that the audit office was leading other jurisdictions in its publication of a transparency report. It identified that transparency could be improved by reporting on the utilisation of contract audit firms and the auditor-general's methodology for providing opinions on ministerial notifications. It suggested that the Parliamentary Joint Committee could consider a requirement that the auditor-general develop and publish a forward audit work programme showing the audits in progress at the start of the financial year and planned and potential audits for future years (Vista Advisory 2015).

While the terms of reference for the Victorian review identified the transparency issues of the appropriateness of the performance indicators and the usefulness of measures to assess the impact of audit activities, they were not the subject of specific comment in the review report.

Although it is evident that some consideration has been given to the transparency of the audit offices, it seems a more detailed consideration of their annual reports, website material and KPIs could enrich the value of the reviews.

Discussion

The observation that the overall findings of the four reviews were broadly positive is in one sense reassuring, as it aligns with the generally high standing of the offices in the community and that the reviews accurately capture the balance between good performance and areas for improvement. On the other hand, it raises a note of caution as to whether the reviews are sufficiently probing in their analysis. For instance, could there be an element of 'capture' of the reviewers, who might be so close to auditing practices that they do not take a bigger picture view? There are critics who query the validity of the claims of the contribution of performance audit (see, for instance, Leeuw 2011), and a review of performance audit literature identifies seven critiques: 'anti-innovation', 'nit-picking', 'expectations gap', 'lapdog', 'headline hunting', 'unnecessary systems' and 'hollow ritual' (Kells 2011). Others highlight the potential for performance audit reports to remain silent on key issues (Morin 2016) and the role of the accounting profession in shaping audit practices, in particular in relation to performance audit (see, for instance, Saint-Martin 2004). These critiques are partially addressed by the reviews, but it is not evident that the risks involved are considered by the reviews in a systematic manner.

An intermediate view could be that the wording of the review reports matches a common feature of performance audit reports—using neutral language that tends to underplay the significance of the findings, leaving it to parliamentarians and the media to interpret and articulate the severity of the problems identified.

As these differing perspectives are not addressed directly in the reviews, the discussion in this section considers the key issues raised in relation to improving public sector performance and accountability, and the independence and transparency of audit offices.

Improving public sector performance and accountability

The concerns expressed about the topic selection process for performance audit indicate that notwithstanding quite detailed processes to inform decisions, there is an inherently subjective element to these decisions. This, in turn, leaves the work open to challenge. By way of example, the Deputy Chair of the Queensland Finance and Administration Committee, Mr R. A. Stevens MP, queried, during hearings following completion of the review report, the value of some performance audits as their scope was too broad and they appeared to highlight problems that were already well known (Queensland Finance and Administration Committee 2017a, p. 3). Furthermore, the tensions between improving public sector performance and accountability, characterised as conflicting roles of 'consultant' and 'watchdog' (Sharma 2007, p. 292), were touched on in the reviews but were not explored in depth.

In relation to the *wider impact of performance audits*, little is understood about how the performance audit programme influences agencies other than those that are within the scope of the individual audits. Internationally, some audit offices do seek to incorporate a consideration of the potential factors underlying observed public sector performance issues. For instance, the Belgian Court of Audit undertakes a risk analysis when selecting topics that seeks to characterise the reasons for poor performance, these being identified as poorly designed policy, poor implementation or the effect of external circumstances, also termed 'bad luck' (Put & Turksema 2011, p. 61). Using an analysis framework of this kind and including factors such as agency organisational culture could assist in identifying the causes underlying the level of performance and accountability.

Some audit offices actively promoted better practice by issuing general guidance material and the reviews encouraged this approach. However, it also raised concerns for some authors about the effect on independence. Saint-Martin (2004, p. 137) observed that once an audit office gave a focus to the usefulness of its work to agencies audited, 'it can conflict with its original mission of fearlessly reporting waste, inefficiency and ineffectiveness'.

There is also a need to better understand how audit offices affect public sector legitimacy and trust, these being aspects of public value that are 'difficult to quantify but of immense importance' (Talbot & Wiggan 2010, p. 64).

The contribution of audit offices to *improving accountability* is identified in general terms in the reviews, and the WA review identified more directly that audit findings and recommendations had directly assisted parliamentary scrutiny, influenced executive government decisions and improved public sector accountability.

It is evident that the issues of wider impacts and improving accountability would benefit from more detailed consideration in future reviews or through other research.

Independence and transparency of the audit office

The reviews demonstrated a clear recognition of the importance of audit independence, raising issues specific to the jurisdiction. These included issues related to the governing legislation as well as practices such as the resourcing of the audit office.

For instance, the WA review recommended that the Parliamentary Joint Committee consider strengthening the auditor-general's information gathering powers and independence by giving Parliament, or one of its committees, an approval or veto right before the appointment of a nominee for the role of auditor-general.

The Queensland review identified barriers to effectiveness that included under-resourcing of both financial and performance auditing and the legislation preventing the audit office from employing all the staff that it needs because it could not offer adequate remuneration. The parliamentary committee considered the reviewers' report and recommended that the audit office prepare a detailed analysis of any additional funding required, but it did not support removing the requirement that the Treasurer approve audit fees (Queensland Finance and Administration Committee 2017b).

One review considered the implications of strengthening independence in relation to administrative support for the ACT Speaker as a result of legislative amendments that involved the Speaker in issues such as the budget and administrative arrangements for the auditor-general (Pearson 2016). However, none of the reviews commented directly on the important consideration identified by Whitfield (2006, p. 88), that parliamentary oversight should not encroach on the independence of the auditor-general.

In relation to *transparency*, only the Victorian and WA reviews explored some aspects of the significance of measures of coverage. It was presented by some audit offices as a component of the decision-making process and subject to targets ahead of the decision about whether to audit specific topics. For instance, a criterion established by the Victorian review was that 'VAGO has logical criteria for selection including materiality, risk, extent of coverage, value-add, public interest and data available from other jurisdiction' (Deloitte 2016, p. 38) and the WA review posed the specific question '[d]oes the OAG's audit coverage provide a reasonable level of scrutiny into the efficient and effective expenditure of public money?' (Vista Advisory 2015, p. 61). However, none discussed the tension between choosing the best individual topics one-by-one, compared with prioritising broad coverage over the choice of the best individual topics. In the former case, coverage is an interesting measure that describes what has arisen from a number of separate decisions but it would not be a measure of effectiveness with related targets (as is the case with the WA OAG).

All the audit offices reviewed covered some of the common *audit office performance measures* identified by Loocke and Put (2011, p. 196). The reviews identified by implication that the information disclosed can be interpreted in different ways. For instance, whether:

- a high proportion of recommendations accepted indicates that the audit office did a good job in explaining the need for the changes involved, or if it means that the recommendations avoided changes that were not likely to be accepted;
- a high proportion of recommendations implemented indicates that the audit office did a good job developing implementable recommendations, or if it avoided changes that were not likely to be implemented;
- partial capturing of costs and benefits can meaningfully establish the merits of a performance audit programme.

More generally, there is a potential that agencies accept and implement recommendations by the auditor-general because of the associated public pressure rather than strictly on their merits, further clouding the significance of measures based on rates of acceptance and implementation.

The progress in reporting on how audit offices contribute to public sector performance is limited by the absence of any absolute measures of, or changes in, that performance. Even if such measures could be created, it would be difficult to understand the extent to which any changes can be attributed to the general or specific components of the work of the audit office. Many factors can influence the impact of performance audits, including direct dialogue with agencies as well as how they perceive the performance audit (Reichborn-Kjennerud 2013; 2014). In the absence of a general theory, it was not evident that reviews were adequately taking into account the factors relevant in the local context. Further, it was unclear if factors underlying performance problems were being identified and addressed or if it is the case that they were, in essence, only addressing symptoms.

The advances by the Queensland audit office in better reporting of the contribution of performance audit raises questions about the lack of similar initiatives being identified by the reviews for the other three jurisdictions. Even with more comprehensive reporting, the considerable uncertainty about the factors that contribute to the impact of performance audits (identified by Loocke & Put 2011, p. 201) indicates that this needs to be a continuing focus for audit offices and parliaments.

More generally, it is not possible to conclude whether the broadly positive overall findings of the four reviews provide full assurance about the audit offices, or whether the review limitations leave key issues inadequately addressed. In particular there is potential for future reviews to focus on the extent to which audit offices are addressing the factors underlying performance problems, how they assess and report their performance and how they contribute to learning and improvement across the wider public sector.

Conclusion

The analysis of the four statutory reviews indicates that there were both similar and different issues identified across the audit offices, intimating that the reviews can contribute to improving their performance both through direct feedback and learning from the reviews of other audit offices. While the reviews were, in the main, positive about audit office performance, they also found areas for improvement that included limitations in the prioritisation of their performance audit work and possible changes to legislation and practices to strengthen their independence.

It also indicates that parliaments can consider the potential for future reviews to focus on the extent to which audit offices are addressing the factors underlying performance problems, how they assess and report their performance and how they contribute to learning and improvement across the wider public sector. However, in considering what to include and exclude from an individual review, care is needed to ensure that the scope of a review is manageable and provides for depth as well as breadth of coverage (Wilkins 2017), and whether there are other means to better gather the information and analysis being sought.

Parliaments can also learn from statutory reviews of audit offices in other jurisdictions. For instance, the WA review raised the concept of a Whole-of-Government Audit Committee to follow-up implementation of unassigned and cross-agency recommendations, and other parliaments could consider this innovative proposal without waiting for the possibility it is raised in their next review. It potentially provides a cost-effective approach to ensuring that value is achieved from the work of the audit offices, both for the agencies audited and across the public sector more generally. Periodic statutory reviews of audit offices are not general practice outside the Australian context, and as a consequence the observations in this chapter are of interest internationally.

While the four reviews make many useful observations both about the public sectors involved and the audit offices, there are a number of areas where further research could strengthen understanding. These include the contribution of the reviews to the accountability and performance of the audit offices, and ultimately to the accountability and performance of the public sectors involved. In particular, research could usefully compare the work of statutory reviews against other findings on relevant features of the public sector to provide a stronger foundation for future statutory reviews. This could help guide consideration of whether periodic reviews are the most effective and efficient way to hold watchdogs to account and help improve their performance.

Notes

1 Curtin University, Perth WA, Australia (p.wilkins@curtin.edu.au)
2 The term 'auditor-general' is hyphenated and generally lower case in this book, although individual jurisdictions may use variants of this.
3 The WA report is dated 27 November 2015; it was released publicly in August 2016.

References

Australian National Audit Office (ANAO) 2017, 'The history of the Auditor-General and the Australian National Audit Office', viewed 26 May 2017, www.anao.gov.au/about/history

Bunn, M & Gilchrist, DJ 2013, 'A few good men: public sector audit in the Swan River Colony, 1828–1835', *Accounting History*, vol. 18, no. 2, pp. 193–209.

Deloitte 2016, 'Performance audit of the Victorian Auditor-General and the Victorian Auditor-General's Office', viewed 5 April 2017, www.parliament.vic.gov.au/file_uploads/Performance_Audit_of_the_Victorian_Auditor-General_s_Office_00txBCvf.pdf

Griffith, G 2006, 'Parliament and accountability: the role of parliamentary oversight committees', *Australasian Parliamentary Review*, vol. 21, no. 1, pp. 7–46.

Kells, S 2011, 'The seven deadly sins of performance auditing: implications for monitoring public audit institutions', *Australian Accounting Review*, vol. 21, no. 4, pp. 383–396.

Leeuw, FL 2011, 'On the effects, lack of effects and perverse effects of performance audit', in J Lonsdale, P Wilkins & T Ling (eds), *Performance auditing: contributing to accountability in democratic government*, Edward Elgar, Cheltenham, pp. 231–247.

Loocke, EV & Put, V 2011, 'The impact of performance audits: a review of the existing evidence', in J Lonsdale, P Wilkins & T Ling (eds), *Performance auditing: contributing to accountability in democratic government*, Edward Elgar, Cheltenham, pp. 175–208.

Morin, D 2016, 'Democratic accountability during performance audits under pressure: a recipe for institutional hypocrisy?' *Financial Accountability & Management*, vol. 32, no. 1, pp. 104–124.

Pearson, D 2016, 'Strategic review of the ACT Auditor-General', viewed 6 April 2017, www.audit.act.gov.au/auditreports/Independent%20review%20of%20the%20office/2016%20Strategic%20Review%20of%20the%20ACT%20Auditor-General.pdf

Put, V & Turksema, R 2011, 'Selection of topics', in J Lonsdale, P Wilkins & T Ling (eds), *Performance auditing: contributing to accountability in democratic government*, Edward Elgar, Cheltenham, pp. 51–74.

Queensland Finance and Administration Committee 2017a, 'Public briefing – strategic review of the Queensland audit office', *Transcript of proceedings Wednesday 19 April 2017 Brisbane*, viewed 7 May 2017, www.parliament.qld.gov.au/documents/committees/FAC/2017/QAOStrategicReview/trns-pb-19Apr2017.pdf

Queensland Finance and Administration Committee 2017b, 'Consideration of the recommendations of the strategic review of the Queensland Audit Office', viewed 13 October 2017, www.parliament.qld.gov.au/documents/tableOffice/TabledPapers/2017/5517T2042.pdf

Reichborn-Kjennerud, K 2013, 'Political accountability and performance audit: the case of the Auditor General in Norway', *Public Administration*, vol. 91, no. 3, pp. 680–695.

Reichborn-Kjennerud, K 2014, 'Performance audit and the importance of the public debate', *Evaluation*, vol. 20, no. 3, pp. 368–385.

Saint-Martin, D 2004, 'Managerialist advocate or "control freak"? The Janus-faced Office of the Auditor General', *Canadian Public Administration*, vol. 47, no. 2, pp. 121–140.

Sharma, N 2007, 'Interactions and interrogations: negotiating and performing value for money reports', *Financial Accountability and Management*, vol. 23, no. 3, pp. 289–311.

Smith, P & Carpenter, G 2017, 'Strategic review of the Queensland Audit Office (2016)', viewed 5 April 2017, www.parliament.qld.gov.au/Documents/TableOffice/TabledPapers/2017/5517T493.pdf

Talbot, C & Wiggan, J 2010, 'The public value of the National Audit Office', *International Journal of Public Sector Management*, vol. 23, no. 1, pp. 54–70.

Victorian Auditor-General's Office (VAGO) 2016, 'Assuring VAGO's quality', viewed 6 June 2017, www.audit.vic.gov.au/about_us/assuring_vagos_quality.aspx

Vista Advisory 2015, 'Statutory review of the performance of the Auditor General for Western Australia (the OAG review)', in Joint Standing Committee on Audit, Legislative Council of Western Australia 2016, *Report 7: Review of the operation and effectiveness of the Auditor General Act 2006*, viewed 5 April 2017, www.parliament.wa.gov.au/ Parliament/commit.nsf/(Report+Lookup+by+Com+ID)/990219A1B6E07E0B4825801 A000DD7AB/$file/ac.rev.160825.rpf.007.xx.pdf

Whitfield, T 2006, 'Parliamentary oversight an auditor-general's perspective', *Australasian Parliamentary Review*, vol. 21, no. 1, Autumn, pp. 88–93.

Wilkins, P 2017, 'Parliaments and their watchdogs: the role of statutory reviews', paper presented at the Australasian Study of Parliament Group 2017 Annual Conference, Hobart.

8 Same, same but different

A comparison between performance audit and operational audit

Elnaz Vafaei, David Gilchrist, Glennda Scully, and Harjinder Singh[1]

Introduction

Globally, both performance audits (PAs) and operational audits (OAs) have a long history in the public and private sectors. However, these terms have been applied interchangeably both in theory and practice. Ambiguities exist around their similarities and differences which, in turn, potentially impact the quality of their performance and, therefore, of the outcomes associated with these important assurance activities (Vafaei 2016). Such impacts may include: that practice can become very organisationally specific, reducing transferability of skills and an increase in self-review risk; inhibiting the development of improvements, tools and processes; quality assurance can be less impactful in terms of enhancing practice due to a lack of established perceptions of quality and practice as well as an agreed set of professional expectations; and training and professional development can be less effective as a result.

Fundamentally, OAs and PAs may seem to be essentially the same—just named differently due to the environments in which they are practised—the one being predominantly practised in the private sector, the other chiefly in the public sector. Nonetheless, we consider that there are, in fact, major and important differences between the two. These differences are largely germane to purpose and environment rather than necessarily connected to the application of standards or the fundamentals of practice. Importantly, we see OA as an internal form of assurance practised by internal auditors in private corporations while PA describes the external form of assurance practised by auditors-general.[2]

This chapter seeks to contribute to the reduction of the concerns noted above by comparing the two types of audit as practised in the developed world, after examining briefly the broad development of the idea of PA and OA internationally. We focus on the Australian context in order to contain the length of the required discussion and because the two concepts are well developed in this federated jurisdiction. We have used a focused literature review process, examining both academic and industry literature, in order to confirm the existence of the problem so that subsequent research and analysis can consider appropriate responses.

In concluding, we suggest that the findings do support the dichotomisation between the two practices and that this dichotomisation is not a sound basis for the creation of better training, tools and practice specific to the needs of each practitioner area. Without an adequate understanding of the similarities and differences between these two assurance practices, it is difficult to see how standards, training processes and efficient audit practice itself can all be achieved.

We report on our review by dividing the chapter into five sections. In section 2, we provide a brief overview of the modern development of PA and OA. In sections 3 and 4, the development of OA and PA in the context of corporate governance law and New Public Management (NPM) reforms is discussed. A comparison between OA and PA in the Australian context is presented in the fifth section as a case study, with concluding remarks presented in the sixth and final section.

An overview of performance and operational audits' development in the western world

In western democracies during the second half of the 20th century, PA increasingly became an important tool of auditors-general, who typically report directly to the legislature regarding the executive's efficiency and effectiveness (Kells & Hodge 2009; Pollitt et al. 1999). However, performance auditing is not new. Indeed, ideas relating to this form of assurance have been traced back to antiquity. For instance, it is believed that a primitive form of PA was conducted in China around 1000 BC and evidence of PA has also been found in Egypt, Rome, Greece and Persia between 3000 BC and 500 BC (Adams 1986; Kells & Hodge 2009). Nevertheless, the provenance of the emergence of the modern form of practice remains opaque.

According to Lonsdale (2000), modern PA emerged after the Second World War and practitioners in Sweden, Germany, Japan, Britain, Canada and the United States (US) all claim to be the pioneers of modern practice (Kells & Hodge 2009; Lonsdale 2000). Reviewing the discourse also shows that, in different parts of the world, modern PA initially emerged in different sectors (Kells & Hodge 2009). For instance, in the US, Canada and Sweden, OA appears to have first developed within internal audit departments of the private sector before spreading to the public sector (Flesher & Zarzeski 2002; Kells & Hodge 2009). In contrast, it appears that PA was first conducted in the public sector in Australia and New Zealand (Flesher & Zarzeski 2002).

This is also a confused story. For instance, in 1972, the General Accounting Office of the US expanded the government auditors' roles to non-financial areas (Flesher & Zarzeski 2002). Further, some evidence suggests that, during the early 1970s in Australia, PA emerged in the public sector in the guise of value for money reviews (Flesher & Zarzeski 2002; Hossain 2010). Efficiency-based PA was identified in the 1976 *Report of the Royal Commission on Australian Government Administration* (Coombs 1976), demonstrating an evolution of thinking over the previous decade beyond the limited format of PA (McPhee 2012). Since then, PA has developed gradually to a point where every Australian jurisdiction's auditor-general routinely carries out some form of PA.

Additionally, it has been argued that Australian PA objectives were limited to reviewing efficiency and economy (Adams 1986; Guthrie & Parker 1999; Hossain 2010). However, in 1983, the Victorian Parliament's Economic and Budget Review Committee extended the scope of PA to include effectiveness (Hossain 2010). It does appear that modern PA in Australia has a relatively short history and that it has been mostly practised in the public sector focusing on the efficiency, effectiveness and economy of government programmes (the three Es).[3]

In contrast, there is evidence that the practice of OA commenced much earlier. It was practised around 150 years ago in the US (Spraakman 2001) and a primitive form of OA was performed by internal auditors in the early 19th century (Flesher & Zarzeski 2002; Spraakman 2001). Different terms have been used to describe this form of non-financial audit, although it appears that modern OA was officially added to the internal audit toolbox in the early 1940s in the US and the nomenclature 'operational audit' was added to the audit lexicon for the first time in 1948 (Flesher & Zarzeski 2002; Vafaei 2016). This was a turning point for the internal audit function, which had been traditionally limited to financial and compliance audits. OA expanded the internal audit function and assisted internal auditors in developing a value-adding role by helping management improve organisation performance (Flesher & Zarzeski 2002; Spraakman 2001). Consequently, OA practice in internal audit departments appears to have increased as a result of the global financial crisis and the subsequent large corporate collapses of the 2000s (Stuebs & Sun 2010; Talebnia & Dehkordi 2012).

In the Australian context, OA has been said to be focused increasingly on the three Es (as noted previously). This concept has significant audit relevance as it drives much auditor practice. Nevertheless, recent research shows that the three Es, while featuring prominently in the discourse regarding audit quality and purpose, do not, in fact, inform OA practice—predominantly because the three Es are unclear in practice (Vafaei 2016). Therefore, practitioners are more focused on 'risk', rather than the three Es in OA projects (Vafaei 2016).

The modern forms of OA and PA have been developed further in the last two decades by the emergence of corporate governance law (primarily affecting the private sector) and NPM reforms affecting the public sector. The impact of these reforms on OA and PA, and their backgrounds, are discussed in the following sections.

The emergence of corporate governance and operational audits

The emergence of corporate governance goes back to the mid-1970s when it was a vague concept and considered as one of the subsets of corporation law. An early draft of corporate governance principles was published by the American Law Institute in 1982. Corporate governance was a controversial topic at the time and different committees and councils were simultaneously working to define corporate governance principles. Hence, these principles were not officially confirmed until 1992 (Veasey 1993).

In the early 21st century, large corporate collapses—including those of Enron, World-Com, HIH and One.Tel—led to reformative actions around the world. Legislative reforms, such as the *Sarbanes-Oxley Act 2002* in the US and the *Corporate Law Economic Reform Program (Audit Reform and Corporate Disclosure) Act 2004* in Australia, were enacted to improve corporate governance in public companies. These acts have increased management responsibility for effectively managing resources (Agrawal & Chadha 2005; Rezaee 2009).

A controlling mechanism of corporate governance is internal audit (Goodwin 2004; Rezaee 2009). In the early stages of internal audit development, it was believed that the function had been substantially different in public and private sector organisations (Carhill & Kincaid 1989; Coupland 1993). Public sector internal auditors seem to have started the OA practice earlier than their counterparts in the private sector (Carhill & Kincaid 1989; Coupland 1993). Coupland (1993) noted that public sector internal auditors are more focused on value for money audits, due to the necessity of controlling public resources and decreasing waste. However, it is believed these differences have been diminished due to the public sector reforms (Goodwin 2004; Pilcher et al. 2013). Goodwin (2004) found that internal auditors of public and private sectors spend similar time on different activities including OA.

Conducting OAs is now one of the main activities of internal audit departments for three reasons (Swinkel 2012; Vafaei 2016). First, stakeholders have become more interested in non-financial information and the operational consequences of management decisions (Tooley, Hooks & Basnan 2010). Second, the organisation's success depends on managing operational risks and increasing the efficiency and effectiveness of organisational operations (Paape, Scheffe & Snoep 2003; Soh & Martinov-Bennie 2011). Third, practising OA in internal audit departments enhances governance within the organisation (Daujotait & Mačerinskiene 2008; Skærbæk 2009).

The emergence of New Public Management and performance audits

NPM reforms have continued in many developed countries since the 1970s and have had a considerable impact on modern public administration (English 2003; English & Guthrie 2000; Johnston 2000). NPM was a response to the increasingly perceived need for delivering services effectively and managing resources efficiently—in its essentials, it posits that the introduction of management processes used in commercial enterprises is likely to improve efficiency and effectiveness in the public sector (Funnell 2015). NPM has increased the accountability of public sector organisations and enhanced the importance of the three Es in the context of PA (English & Guthrie 2000; Everett 2003; Funnell 2015; Hood 1995; Kells & Hodge 2010). Funnell (2015) noted that the PA role has been evolved from a quasi-judicial one of monitoring managers' actions to that of reviewing highly politicised topics such as auditing Treasury's management of the Special Purpose Vehicle in 2009.

As such, NPM reforms have had a significant impact on the PA process (Power 2003). According to Funnell and Cooper (1998), PA has gone through three different eras since the commencement of NPM reforms. Initially, PA had followed what was termed a 'traditional administrative model', which reviewed management performance and expenditures to ensure that they were undertaken in accordance with an approved parliamentary programme. In the 1980s, PA moved to what was described as a 'corporatist model', having more financial and operational independence from managers. Finally, in the 1990s, a more complicated model was identified, called the 'contestable model'. In this model, various providers were considered for conducting PA, including internal and external auditors (English & Guthrie 2000; Funnell & Cooper 1998). It has been posited that the second and third evolutionary changes in PA have occurred in Australia (English & Guthrie 2000; Houghton & Jubb 1998; Taylor 1998).

PA has a critical role in maintaining public accountability (English 2003; Johnsen et al. 2001; March & Olsen 1995). PA assists in reviewing organisational processes and outcomes and in controlling management performance (Everett 2003). It clarifies the decision-making processes in public organisations and improves the connection between the public and authorities (Kells & Hodge 2010). Furthermore, practising PA in public organisations has several benefits for management and stakeholders (Skærbæk 2009). Operationally, PA is seen to improve organisational systems, identify repetitive tasks and evaluate property risk management (Lapsley & Pong 2000; Skærbæk 2009). Strategically, PA reduces the maintenance and administration costs and improves tax collection (Lapsley & Pong 2000). Also, recent research shows that PA has considerable positive impacts on auditees' motivation and performance (Morin 2008). Therefore, PA improves the performance of the organisation (Funnell 2015) and it has a significant impact on public management (Guthrie & Parker 1999; Lapsley & Pong 2000; Pollitt 2003; Radcliffe 1998).

Comparison of operational audits and performance audits in the Australian context

In arriving at a more nuanced perspective of these two closely related assurance activities, it is useful to examine the similarities and differences suggested by the evidence when considering the related auditing standards, organisational status and mandates. These three elements are discussed in detail in the following subsections and summarised in Table 8.1.

Auditing standards and PA/OA

While various standards are available for practising PA, such as the Yellow Book (US) and ASAE 3500 (Australia), OA is guided, generally, by the *International Professional Practices Framework* (IPPF) (The Institute of Internal Auditors

2017). However, there are no comprehensive, specific standards aplicable to this area of audit. Instead, internal auditors commonly use a risk-based approach (Chambers & Rand 2010).

In October 2008 (updated 2017), the Australian Government Auditing and Assurance Standards Board (AUASB) issued ASAE 3500 for conducting PAs in assurance engagements (AUASB 2017). This standard provided relatively specific advice for performing the differing parts of PA, while also setting certain minimum elements such as the requirement for the PA report to include a conclusion (Vafaei 2016). Importantly, and reinforcing the external nature of PA as compared to OA, ASAE 3500 also connected the PA process to the full suite of auditing concepts established by the AUASB and the ethical standards established by the Australian Professional Ethical Standards. This brought the practice of PA into the orbit of the full auditing framework—entirely appropriate for a function performed by practitioners external to the subject organisation.

While auditors generally undertake a risk-based approach when selecting topics for their PA programme, OA practitioners take a risk-based approach in their audit practice itself using the three phases of audit as their template: planning, performing and reporting (Chambers & Rand 2010). Audit objectives are generally based on the organisation's goals so that scope is informed by where the organisation is going. Having identified the audit scope, internal auditors then assess the inherent risk that audit resources are appropriately allocated and conduct the audit with a focus on the three Es. The report then highlights organisational weaknesses (Chambers & Rand 2010).

To summarise, the available models and standards for OA and PA resemble more general guidelines rather than a detailed, step by step approach. In fact, considering the malleable nature of OA and PA, it is difficult to put them into a detailed standard box (Parker & Guthrie 1993; Vafaei 2016). Hence, although different standards or guidelines have been used for conducting OAs and PAs, the nature of available standards are similar and they are more like general guidelines, especially when contrasted with the standards relating to financial statement audits. In the case of Australia, the relevant standards connect the PA process to the full suite of ethics and practice standards, while, for OA, no such connectivity exists.

Organisational status and independence

Another aspect worthy of examination relates to the practitioners' relationship with the auditee organisation and independence. In a PA, auditors-general are independent and they report directly to parliament. In the internal form of OA, practitioners should arguably functionally report to the audit committee. Yet, administratively they report to the chief executive officer (The Institute of Internal Auditors 2015). As such, internal auditors' independence has been routinely questioned by researchers (Roussy 2013, 2014).

Auditors-general have a strong and independent position. According to section 8(4) of the *Auditor-General Act 1997* (Cwlth), the Federal Australian

Auditor-General is an independent external auditor who has absolute discretion in performing PA and is a parliamentary officer. In other words, the Australian Auditor-General is not subject to oversight when determining the audit topic, methodology and priority. Furthermore, the auditor-general is nominated by public executives, appointed by the governor-general and approved by parliament (English & Guthrie 2000).

In contrast, internal auditors have a much less powerful position in the organisation. The internal audit plan needs to be approved by the audit committee and the board (Australian Stock Exchange 2014; The Institute of Internal Auditors 2015). Also, the audit committee has the responsibility of appointing and removing the chief audit executive and of approving the scope of internal work (Australian Stock Exchange 2014). Therefore, the scope and priority of internal audit projects, including OA, needs to be approved by the audit committee.

Although auditors-general seem to have a relatively more powerful position than internal auditors, the independence of both is still questioned. The independence of auditors-general has been a controversial issue. Some researchers have raised concerns about auditor-general independence due to political pressures (Radcliffe 2008; Skærbæk 2009; Tillema & Bogt 2010). Houghton and Jubb (1998) noted that although auditors-general report to parliament, governments are still involved in their employment process. However, recent research shows that auditors-general still act with integrity and independence in the context of PA projects despite serious political disputes (Funnell 2015).

Internal auditors' independence has also been questioned by researchers (Ahmad & Taylor 2009; Roussy 2013, 2014). Internal auditors are supposed to act with independence in mind and appearance, yet it is difficult for internal auditors to act independently due to their inherent role conflicts and confusion (Ahmad & Taylor 2009; Roussy 2013). In this respect, Roussy (2013) introduced the concept of 'grey independence' whereby internal auditors experience role conflicts in practice, so they lose their absolute independence and prioritise management interests higher than audit committee interests (Roussy 2013, 2014). Hence, Roussy (2013) concluded that considering internal auditors as independent corporate governance watchdogs is not appropriate.

While this discussion may seem to suggest that the independence of both auditors-general and internal auditors practising PA and OA respectively are similarly compromised, in fact this is not the case. The independence question faced by an auditor-general is very different from that faced by an internal auditor. Auditors-general are subject to pressure—both political and financial—applied by the government of the day. However, fundamentally, the auditor-general's position is never threatened in the way that an internal auditor's can be.

For instance, that role reports to the legislature, is supported by specific purpose legislation—which includes powers allowing the auditor-general to compel cooperation and also increasingly to audit beyond the public sector to related private sector organisations, may be included as a mandatory office under constitutions, has avenues for airing difficulties via committees of the legislature, has the capacity to speak directly to the public media and, in Australian jurisdictions, requires approval from a significant majority of the legislature before removal from office. Perhaps most importantly, the auditor-general's reports are made public and so the avenues for the auditor-general to respond to inappropriate pressure from government are substantial.

In contrast, internal auditors practising OAs are subject to considerable pressure as, notwithstanding that they often report to the board or a committee of the board, they are direct employees of the company, are directly controlled and overseen by the internal governance structure of the organisation and have no external reporting mechanism allowing for protection or the airing of concerns. Indeed, often the only avenue available for internal auditors to voice concerns is to resign. Therefore, the independence issues facing auditors-general are much less effective in preventing the auditor-general from conducting the audit and reporting.

Mandates

OA and PA mandates are different. While conducting PA is compulsory in the public sector, there is no legal obligation for an OA to be conducted in internal audit departments. In Australia, the *Auditor-General Act 1997* obligates monitoring the operational and financial performance of public executives and a 'separate appropriation of funds' is considered by parliament for the Australian National Audit Office. Also, under this act, auditors-general are authorised with 'complete discretion' to perform any types of audit, including PAs, to review federal government activities (English & Guthrie 2000). Hence, PA practice is highly supported by the government even though it might be subject to inadequate funding during difficult times (Kells & Hodge 2009).

In contrast, conducting OA is not compulsory in internal audit departments. The authorities of internal audit departments are described in the charter of internal audit departments (The Institute of Internal Auditors 2015). The internal audit budget is also approved by the audit committee and the board (The Institute of Internal Auditors 2015). Ideally, internal auditors should have unlimited access to 'all relevant, functions, records, property, and personnel within the law' and 'have full access to the Audit & Risk Committee' (The Institute of Internal Auditors 2015, p. 55). However, it has been observed that management can easily limit the internal audit access if they disagree with the OA process (Vafaei 2016). Furthermore, internal audit departments are usually faced with limited resources which negatively affect the OA practice (Al-Twaijry, Brierley & Gwilliam 2003; Vafaei 2016).

Therefore, PA has a stronger mandate in comparison with OA. Auditors-general are entitled to perform PA, and their budget is approved by parliament. In contrast, there is no legal obligation for performing OA in internal audit departments, and the required budget is approved inside the organisation. Hence, internal audit is in a weaker position regarding legal mandate to perform OA than are auditors-general.

This comparison of OA and PA is summarised in Table 8.1.

Table 8.1 The comparison of OA and PA

Criteria	OA	PA
Auditing Standards[1]	IPPF/general guideline	Yellow book, ASAE3500 / General guideline
Organisational Status	Report to the audit committee or board	Report to parliament
Independence	Partially independent/subject to intra-organisational pressures	Highly independent/subject to political pressures
Mandate	No legal obligation	Compulsory

[1] Although the mentioned audit standards are classified in the same group, they are not equivalent and their structures and applications are different.

Conclusion

This discussion on OA and PA indicates that they are different in context. We did state at the outset that we believed one major difference to be the extent to which practitioners of PA and OA are integrated into the auditee organisation. This is a fundamental issue, as the practice of external and internal audit generally raises a number of concerns regarding independence, resourcing and impact of findings, to name a few. While it may have appeared that there are concerns regarding independence on both sides of the dichotomy, we found, in fact, that these concerns are substantially dissimilar and that the context is also different.

Findings also revealed that the central mandate of each assurance process is different and that this also impacts practice. The mandate for PA in the public sector context is essential to the maintenance of constitutional arrangements, while OA is very much an internally focused and practised form of assurance. The lack of compulsion with respect to even practising OA in a private enterprise, let alone the absence of obligation to comply with any standards, reveals serious differences between the practice of OA and the practice of PA.

The want of a clear definition is also a difficult issue to mitigate because, in fact, PA and OA have many similarities in terms of their objectives—especially in relation to the three Es—and they can be very wide in their application, objectives and fundamental purpose. Similarly, they both are risk-focused processes and generally seek to contribute to all aspects of an auditee organisation. However, this lack of clarity in definitions is an important weakness that needs to be addressed by future research.

Without clear delineations between the two processes, and in the context of the audiences for the audit reports generated, it will be difficult to achieve the development of effective training materials, standards and clarity of professional expectations beyond general concepts. Additionally, in the context of NPM reforms, public sector managers may also seek to emulate the practice of OA practitioners in the private sector in order to better understand their own organisations, drive improvement and to provide a risk mitigation strategy.

Finally, a strong separation between the two practices can also enhance the capacity of practitioners themselves to be able to learn from the practice of the other area. That is, PA practitioners can always learn from OA practioners and vice-versa. At the very least, there is a clear need for the professions, academics and the practitioners themselves to have a robust understanding of this practice in order to ensure that, if nothing else, the discourse in this area is universally understood and effective in raising the bar on OA and PA practice.

Notes

1 David Gilchrist, University of Western Australia, Perth, Australia (david.gilchrist@uwa. edu.au).
2 The public sector auditor is referred to as the auditor-general or auditor-general in most developed western countries. The inclusion or exclusion of the hyphen in this title can be contentious for many readers. In this book, we have adopted the hyphenated format.
3 There is some discrepancy between the Australian Government Auditing and Assurance Standards Board (AUASB) initial definitions of economy, efficiency and effectiveness (AUASB 2008) and their 2017 definitions (AUASB 2017). Initial definitions (AUASB 2008, p. 15):

> *Economy* means the acquisition of the appropriate quality and quantity of resources at the appropriate times and the lowest cost; *Efficiency* means the use of resources such that output is optimised for any given set of resource inputs, or input is minimised for any given quantity and quality of output; and *Effectiveness* means the achievement of the objectives or other intended effects of activities at a programme or entity level.

Later definitions were somewhat different (AUASB 2017, p. 7):

> *Economy* means the minimisation of the costs of resources, within the operational requirements of timeliness and availability of required quantity or quality; *Efficiency* means 'the minimisation of inputs employed to deliver the intended outputs in terms of quality, quantity and timing;' and *Effectiveness* means the extent to which the intended objectives at a program or entity level are achieved.

References

Adams, N 1986, 'Efficiency auditing in the Australian audit office', *Australian Journal of Public Administration*, vol. 45, no. 3, pp. 189–200.

Agrawal, A & Chadha, S 2005, 'Corporate governance and accounting scandals', *Journal of Law and Economics*, vol. 48, no. 2, pp. 371–406.

Ahmad, Z & Taylor, D 2009, 'Commitment to independence by internal auditors: the effects of role ambiguity and role conflict', *Managerial Auditing Journal*, vol. 24, no. 9, pp. 899–925.

Al-Twaijry, AAM, Brierley, JA & Gwilliam, DR 2003, 'The development of internal audit in Saudi Arabia: an institutional theory perspective', *Critical Perspectives on Accounting*, vol. 14, no. 5, pp. 507–531.

American Law Institute 1982, *Principles of corporate governance and structure: Restatement and recommendations*, Tentative draft no. 1, The American Law Institute, Philadelphia.

Auditing and Assurance Standards Board (AUASB) 2008, *Standard on assurance engagements ASAE 3500 performance engagements*, Auditing and Assurance Standards Board, Melbourne, Australia.

Auditing and Assurance Standards Board (AUASB) 2017, *Standard on assurance engagements ASAE 3500 performance engagements*, Auditing and Assurance Standards Board, Melbourne, Australia.

Australian Stock Exchange 2014, *Corporate governance principles and recommendations*, ASX Corporate Governance Council, Sydney, NSW, Australia.

Carhill, KM & Kincaid, JK 1989, 'Applying the standards in governmental internal auditing', *The Internal Auditor*, vol. 46, no. 5, pp. 50–55.

Chambers, A & Rand, G 2010, *The operational auditing handbook: auditing business and IT processes*, John Wiley and Sons (Ltd.), Hoboken, NJ.

Coombs, HC 1976, *Royal Commission on Australian government administration: report*, Australian Government Publishing Service, Canberra.

Coupland, D 1993, 'The internal auditor's role in public service orientation', *Managerial Auditing Journal*, vol. 8, no. 1, pp. 3–13.

Daujotait, D & Mačerinskiene, I 2008, 'Development of performance audit in public sector', in A Pabedinskaitė (ed), *Business and management 2008: selected papers of the 5th international scientific conference*, 16–17 May, Vilnius Gediminas Technical University Publishing House, Vilnius, Lithuania, pp. 177–185.

English, L 2003, 'Emasculating public accountability in the name of competition: transformation of state audit in Victoria', *Critical Perspectives on Accounting*, vol. 14, nos. 1–2, pp. 51–76.

English, L & Guthrie, J 2000, 'Mandate, independence and funding: resolution of a protracted struggle between parliament and the executive over the powers of the Australian Auditor-G-eneral', *Australian Journal of Public Administration*, vol. 59, no. 1, pp. 98–114.

Everett, J 2003, 'The politics of comprehensive auditing in fields of high outcome and cause uncertainty', *Critical Perspectives on Accounting*, vol. 14, nos. 1–2, pp. 77–104.

Flesher, DL & Zarzeski, MT 2002, 'The roots of operational (value for money) auditing in English speaking nations', *Accounting and Business Research*, vol. 32, no. 2, pp. 93–104.

Funnell, W 2015, 'Performance auditing and adjudicating political disputes', *Financial Accountability and Management*, vol. 31, no. 1, pp. 92–110.

Funnell, W & Cooper, C 1998, *Public sector accounting and accountability in Australia*, University of New South Wales Press, Sydney, Australia.

Goodwin, J 2004, 'A comparison of internal audit in the private and public sectors', *Managerial Auditing Journal*, vol. 19, no. 5, pp. 640–650.

Guthrie, JE & Parker, LD 1999, 'A quarter of a century of performance auditing in the Australian federal public sector: a malleable masque', *ABACUS*, vol. 35, no. 3, pp. 302–332.

Hood, C 1995, 'Contemporary public management: a new global paradigm?' *Public Policy and Administration*, vol. 10, no. 2, pp. 104–117.

Hossain, S 2010, 'From project audit to performance audit: evolution of performance auditing in Australia', *Journal of Accounting Research & Audit Practices*, vol. 9, no. 3, pp. 20–46.

Houghton, K & Jubb, C 1998, 'The function of the auditor-general: independence, competence and outsourcing – the policy implications', *Australian Accounting Review*, vol. 8, no. 1, pp. 30–35.

The Institute of Internal Auditors 2015, 'Internal audit charter', The Institute of Internal Auditors, Sydney, Australia.

The Institute of Internal Auditors 2017, 'International professional practices framework (IPPF)', The Institute of Internal Auditors, Altamonte Springs, Florida.

Johnsen, Å, Meklin, P, Oulasvirta, L & Vakkuri, J 2001, 'Performance auditing in local government: an exploratory study of perceived efficiency of municipal value for money auditing in Finland and Norway', *European Accounting Review*, vol. 10, no. 3, pp. 583–599.

Johnston, J 2000, 'The new public management in Australia', *Administrative Theory & Praxis*, vol. 22, no. 2, pp. 345–368.

Kells, S & Hodge, G 2009, 'Performance auditing in the public sector: reconceptualising the task', *The Journal of Contemporary Issues in Business and Government*, vol. 15, no. 2, pp. 36–60.

Kells, S & Hodge, G 2010, 'Redefining the performance auditing space', *Asia Pacific Journal of Public Administration*, vol. 32, no. 1, pp. 63–88.

Lapsley, I & Pong, CKM 2000, 'Modernization versus problematization: value-for-money audit in public services', *European Accounting Review*, vol. 9, no. 4, pp. 541–567.

Lonsdale, J 2000, 'Developments in value-for-money audit methods: impacts and implications', *International Review of Administrative Sciences*, vol. 66, no. 1, pp. 73–89.

March, JG & Olsen, JP 1995, *Democratic governance*, Free Press, New York.

McPhee, I 2012, 'The evolving role and mandate of the Australian National Audit Office since federation', *Papers on Parliament*, no.57, pp. 59–87.

Morin, D 2008, 'Auditors general's universe revisited: an exploratory study of the influence they exert on public administration through their value for money audits', *Managerial Auditing Journal*, vol. 23, no. 7, pp. 697–720.

Paape, L, Scheffe, J & Snoep, P 2003, 'The relationship between the internal audit function and corporate governance in the EU – a survey', *International Journal of Auditing*, vol. 7, no. 3, pp. 247–262.

Parker, LD & Guthrie, J 1993, 'The Australian public sector in the 1990s: new accountability regimes in motion', *Journal of International Accounting, Auditing and Taxation*, vol. 2, no. 1, pp. 59–81.

Pilcher, R, Gilchrist, D, Singh, H & Singh, I 2013, 'The interface between internal and external audit in the Australian public sector', *Australian Accounting Review*, vol. 23, no. 4, pp. 330–340.

Pollitt, C 2003, 'Performance audit in Western Europe: trends and choices', *Critical Perspectives on Accounting*, vol. 14, nos. 1–2, pp. 157–170.

Pollitt, C, Girre, X, Lonsdale, J, Mul, R, Summa, H & Waerness, M 1999, *Performance or compliance? Performance audit and public management in five countries*, Oxford University Press, Oxford.

Power, MK 2003, 'Auditing and the production of legitimacy', *Accounting, Organizations and Society*, vol. 28, no. 4, pp. 379–394.

Radcliffe, VS 1998, 'Efficiency audit: an assembly of rationalities and programmes', *Accounting, Organizations and Society*, vol. 23, no. 4, pp. 377–410.

Radcliffe, VS 2008, 'Public secrecy in auditing: what government auditors cannot know', *Critical Perspectives on Accounting*, vol. 19, no. 1, pp. 99–126.

Rezaee, Z 2009, *Corporate governance and ethics*, John Wiley and Sons (Ltd.), Hoboken, NJ.

Roussy, M 2013, 'Internal auditors' roles: from watchdogs to helpers and protectors of the top manager', *Critical Perspectives on Accounting*, vol. 24, no. 7–8, pp. 550–571.

Roussy, M 2014, 'Welcome to the day-to-day of internal auditors: how do they cope with conflicts?' *AUDITING: A Journal of Practice & Theory*, vol. 34, no. 2, pp. 237–264.

Skærbæk, P 2009, 'Public sector auditor identities in making efficiency auditable: the national audit office of Denmark as independent auditor and modernizer', *Accounting, Organizations and Society*, vol. 34, no. 8, pp. 971–987.

Soh, DS & Martinov-Bennie, N 2011, 'The internal audit function: perception of internal audit roles, effectiveness, and evaluation', *Managerial Auditing Journal*, vol. 26, no. 7, pp. 605–622.

Spraakman, G 2001, 'Internal audit at the historical Hudson's Bay company: a challenge to accepted history', *The Accounting Historians Journal*, vol. 28, no. 1, pp. 19–41.

Stuebs, M & Sun, L 2010, 'Business reputation and labor efficiency, productivity, and cost', *Journal of Business Ethics*, vol. 96, no. 2, pp. 265–283.

Swinkel, WHK 2012, 'Exploration of a theory of internal audit: a study on the theoretical foundations of internal audit in relation to the nature and the control systems of Dutch public listed firms', doctoral thesis, Universiteit van Amsterdam, Amsterdam, The Netherlands.

Talebnia, G & Dehkordi, BB 2012, 'Study of relation between effectiveness audit and management audit', *GSTF Business Review (GBR)*, vol. 2, no. 1, pp. 92–97.

Taylor, JC 1998, 'Public sector audit in Victoria: leading where?' *Australian Accounting Review*, vol. 8, no. 1, pp. 36–39.

Tillema, S & Bogt, HJ 2010, 'Performance auditing: improving the quality of political and democratic processes?' *Critical Perspectives on Accounting*, vol. 21, no. 8, pp. 754–769.

Tooley, S, Hooks, J & Basnan, N 2010, 'Performance reporting by Malaysian local authorities: identifying stakeholder needs', *Financial Accountability & Management*, vol. 26, no. 2, pp. 103–133.

Vafaei, E 2016, 'Operational auditing within Australian internal audit departments: developing a framework', doctoral thesis, Curtin University, Perth, Australia.

Veasey, EN 1993, 'The emergence of corporate governance as a new legal discipline', *The Business Lawyer*, vol. 48, no. 4, pp. 1267–1270.

Legislation

Auditor-General Act 1997 (Cwlth)

Corporate Law Economic Reform Program (Audit Reform and Corporate Disclosure) Act 2004 (Cwlth)

Sarbanes-Oxley Act of 2002 (PL 107–204, 116 Stat. 745) (USC)

9   Just do it? A cautionary tale on implementing performance management regimes

Joseph Drew[1] and Sasindu Gamage

Introduction

There is a vast scholarly literature on performance management in the context of the public sector (see, for instance, Bevan & Hood 2006; de Bruijn 2007; Pollitt 2013). The literature is mostly pessimistic with respect to the efficacy of performance management and has a large focus on the performance paradox (the discord between performance on paper and actual performance (de Bruijn 2007)), gaming (the exploiting of grey areas to present a more favourable impression of performance than might otherwise be warranted (Bevan & Hood 2006)), and motivation (with particular reference to the dominant dichotomy of knights and knaves (Le Grand 2003)). However, two rather curious features stand out in relation to the extant literature. First, the leading scholars in the field are drawn from the ranks of political science and management and, second (perhaps as a consequence), there is only a nascent literature on the use of audited financial data for compiling performance indicators. Yet, as we will demonstrate below, there are specific challenges posed as a result of employing audited financial data. To explicate, we review the use of audited financial accrual data in the recent forced amalgamations of New South Wales (NSW) councils—dubbed *Fit for the Future* (FFTF).

FFTF is a particularly useful case study in order to explain the challenges faced in employing audited financial data in high stakes public performance management. This is because, as part of FFTF, different incentives were offered at discrete periods of time, appealing to both sides of the public sector motivation dichotomy. As a result we have a valuable natural experiment regarding the response of executives to increasing levels of incentives over time. FFTF was initially conceived as a sector-led reform within the constraints of a firm state government policy of no forced amalgamation (Drew & Grant 2017a). However, in January 2014 the Independent Local Government Review Panel (ILGRP)—charged by the state government to investigate evidenced based reforms to enhance the sustainability of local government in NSW—surprised the sector by releasing a report which called for 'amalgamations [as] another essential component of reform, notably in metropolitan Sydney' (Drew 2018; ILGRP 2013, p. 15). The major empirical evidence relied upon by the ILGRP was a sustainability assessment, based on ten financial ratios, conducted by the NSW Treasury Corporation (TCorp 2013).

Therefore, well before the end of the 2013–2014 financial year, local governments were alerted to the fact that amalgamations were proposed and that financial data were being used to justify these. This was followed by the state government launch of a self-assessment programme in September 2014, whereby councils were directed to demonstrate financial fitness with reference to just seven financial performance indicators and to propose 'voluntary' amalgamations (by 30 June 2015) in the event that they did not satisfy certain benchmarks. Thus, the stakes were raised from 'mooted amalgamation' to an 'amalgamation directive' by the end of the 2014–2015 financial year.

The aim of this chapter is to demonstrate that employing audited accounting data as the basis of a performance management regime in no way guarantees that the regime will be free of material distortion (and hence does not necessarily represent a sound basis for important public policy decision-making).

The balance of the chapter is organised as follows. First, the extant literature on performance management, with a particular emphasis on the unique challenges posed when audited financial data form the foundation of performance indicators, is reviewed. We then set out the two fundamental assumptions which must be met in order for valid comparisons to be made with respect to financial performance indicators. There is then an outline of the research design employed. This is followed by a discussion of our results which suggest that neither of the necessary assumptions were satisfied in the case of the Greater Sydney councils with respect to FFTF, therefore casting doubt on the empirical legitimacy of the entire programme. The chapter concludes with an enumeration of the important lessons for public policy architects intending to employ financial data for high stakes performance management.

Lessons from the literature

The performance paradox is a discord between performance on paper and actual performance and is well attested in the corpus of scholarly literature on performance management (see, for example, Bevan & Hood 2006). There are three causes of the performance paradox (see Figure 9.1): unintended distortions (measurement error and the like), synecdochical gap (the disparity between the whole entity—comprised of measurable and unmeasurable elements of performance—and the parts which are measured) and intended distortions (which might be either cheating (outright fabrication) or gaming (exploiting the grey areas)).

Unintended distortion

Unintended distortion is undoubtedly the most neglected cause of the performance paradox. However, it has particular importance for performance management based on audited financial data (Drew & Grant 2017b). Frequent users of financial report data are aware that misstatements do occur and that these occurrences persist despite the presence of internal and external auditing. A salient example of this is the recent revelation of 'an $8.68 million depreciation "system

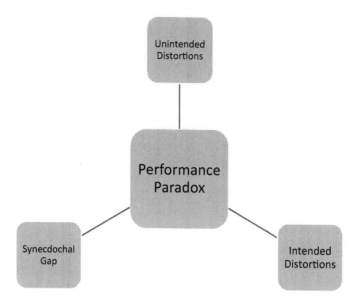

Figure 9.1 The three causes of performance paradox.

error"' at Newcastle City Council (McCarthy 2014, p. n.p.). No doubt misstatements also occur in non-audited financial data—the important difference is that in the case of accounting data there is widespread confusion regarding the meaning of internal and external auditing of financial data. Many end users are under the erroneous impression that auditing is an absolute assurance that the data are free of error, when in fact auditing is only intended as reasonable assurance that the data are free of material misstatement (Drew & Dollery 2015). Moreover, what is considered material in a financial statement sense is very different from what might be considered material in a performance management sense—particularly if dichotomous benchmarks are detailed in advance (as was the case in FFTF). That is, if pass/fail benchmarks are detailed in advance and strictly observed, then materiality comes down to the adjustment that is necessary in order to correct what might otherwise be a performance deficit for the entity.

Synecdochical gap

When we come to the question of synecdochical gap, we find a much more thorough treatment in the literature (see, for instance, Bevan & Hood 2006; Pollitt 2013). Synecdoche is an Aristotelian rhetorical trope in which a part is taken to represent a whole (*pars pro toto*) or the whole is taken for the part (*totum pro parte*) (Hamilton 2003). When it comes to performance management, focus has rested on the disparity between the whole (which is comprised of things both measurable and unmeasurable) and the part which is actually measured. Synecdochical gap is problematic because naïve interpretation by end users can result in some seriously misleading conclusions (Walker, Boyne & Brewer 2010). This presents particular problems when financial data are used because lifting just a few pieces of information out of financial statements, which often run to a hundred or more pages, is not only an extreme example of synecdoche but also denudes the numbers used of the sense that they are, in fact, comprised of countless transactions and professional judgements. In so doing, performance indicators based on financial data may give an unwarranted impression of ontological truth (at the expense of a prudent cognisance of the role of professional accounting judgement). Moreover, the received wisdom is that the degree of synecdochical gap is proportional to the amount of gaming and strategic behaviour opportunities.

Intended distortions

Gaming has attracted the bulk of the attention of scholars—not least because of the 'thrill of the chase' felt when uncovering discrepancies that invalidate the claim of politicians seeking to employ performance management data for political purposes (Bevan & Hood 2006; Drew 2018; Drew & Dollery 2015; Drew & Grant 2017b). Before examining the types of gaming, it is important to establish the difference between gaming and cheating. Gaming exploits grey areas to put the best gloss possible on performance, whereas cheating involves outright fabrication. In an accounting sense, gaming may be manipulation of discretionary accruals data to achieve a particular purpose such as income smoothing (Copeland 1968; Marquardt & Wiedman 2004), whilst cheating is fraud pure and simple (Rezaee 2005). In the former case, one can rely on professional judgement to get out of jail; in the latter there is no defence. Gaming has three main effects: threshold effects, ratchet effects and strategic behaviour. Threshold effects occur when performance benchmarks are communicated in advance—creating an incentive to perform to the benchmark level, but no incentive to perform at an entity's utmost capacity. Ratchet effects, on the other hand, occur when executives rightly or wrongly perceive that performance in the present period will be used to set benchmarks for performance in later periods. If this belief is held, then executives are actively dis-incentivised to perform above the bare minimum. The parallels between ratchet effects and the near zero balance public accounts literature (whereby it is hypothesised that executives manipulate discretionary accruals—particularly depreciation accruals—to achieve 'Goldilocks' results) are striking (see, for instance, Pilcher & Van der Zahn 2010; Stalebrink 2007). By way of contrast, strategic behaviour occurs when executives of entities emphasise only the areas of performance which are measured or pursue short-term goals at the expense of long-term performance. When solely financial data is used, strategic behaviour may take the form of reducing service levels in order to enhance operating results (Drew & Dollery 2015) or extending the useful life of assets (knowing that there will be a cost when assets are ultimately sold or scrapped (Marquardt & Wiedman 2004)).

The extent of intended distortions within a performance monitoring regime is largely dependent on the conjunction between dominant public sector motivations and the specific incentives posed to executives. In a well-known dichotomous framework, Julian Le Grand (2010, p. 56) portrayed public servants as being either knights (motivated by 'a spirit of altruism and the desire to perform a public service' regardless of personal cost) or 'knaves' (motivated 'completely by self-interest'). Bevan and Hood (2006) noted that all performance management regimes must assume that the ranks are dominated by the former rather than the latter and, moreover, that the balance of knights and knaves does not shift as a result of incentives posed by the regime. In most instances, gaming and other subversive practices are attributed to knaves. However, Drew (2018) provided a convincing argument that there are situations in which knights may also participate in subversive activities. To understand this claim it is useful to think about the framework for accounting fraud incentive[2] outlined by Rezaee (2005). Rezaee (2005, p. 283) proposed just three incentives which explain most fraud: egocentric incentives (which clearly map nicely onto knavish motivations and the extant literature on gaming of public performance management regimes), economic pressure (which is not so relevant to public servants in the absence of performance bonuses and share prices) and ideological apologetics (which allow 'individuals to think their behaviour or cause is morally superior'). Drew and Grant (2017b) contended that ideological apologetics can, in quite specific circumstances, result in knights also engaging in subversive activity. For instance, the Woollahra Council Mayor argued that local government amalgamations 'have a huge impact on our community both in cost and in the loss of our community's interest' (Glanville 2016, p. n.p.). If affected council executives were to believe claims of impending doom for their local communities, then this might indeed result in a conjunction between knightly motivations and ideological apologetic incentives. Moreover, were this to be the case—that incentives were posed for both sides of the public service motivation dichotomy—then we might expect to see evidence of widespread gaming.

Specific challenges associated with using accounting data

Thus, we can see that the use of accounting data as the basis for high stakes performance management regimes in no way escapes the well-documented pitfalls detailed in the literature. In fact, using accounting data also poses additional problems which have largely escaped the attention of the scholarly community—notable exceptions include Drew (2018) and Drew and Grant (2017b). First, there is an additional clear mechanism for gaming, which provides perpetrators with a ready excuse of 'professional judgement' (in the case of distortion of depreciation accruals). In FFTF, three of the seven ratios could easily be manipulated by distorting depreciation accrual data—the operating ratio (operating surplus divided by operating revenue), the buildings and infrastructure renewal ratio (asset renewals divided by depreciation on infrastructure assets) and the 'efficiency' ratio (operating expenditure divided by resident population)—and our (subsequent) analysis focuses on this accrual item. Second, the NSW state government fell into the trap of eschewing performance management data audits presumably on the basis that most of the data inputs came from audited financial data. Yet, as noted earlier, the purpose (and materiality concerns) of financial statement audits are quite different to the purpose and materiality concerns of performance management audits—particularly where the bench-marks are nominated in advance. The final additional problem posed by use of accounting data in performance management is that the performance indicators thus generated tend to obscure the accounting judgements which lie behind the numbers. For instance, it would not have been evident to most end users that the nominal dollars per capita cited for the 'efficiency' ratios were dependent on depreciation accrual estimates (which represent around one-fifth of NSW local government expenditure (Grant & Drew 2016)).

We now outline two crucial implicit assumptions which must be true for FFTF process to have been empirically legitimate.

Research design

In order to make valid decisions (and implicit comparisons) on council financial performance indicators it is necessary to accept two important assumptions:

(i) that financial inputs (to performance indicators) are the result of consistent practice across the cohort;
(ii) that egocentric and ideological apologetic incentives do not result in a material change to practice.

Our focus is on the depreciation accruals which are an obvious vehicle for material gaming as per our discussion (although clearly the assumptions apply to all inputs). Marquardt and Wiedman (2004), Mulford and Comiskey (2002), Pilcher and Van der Zahn (2010) and others have measured the quantum of unexpected depreciation according to the following algorithm:

$$\text{UDEP}_{j,t} = \left[\text{DEP}_{j,t} - \left(\text{DEP}_{j,t-1} * \text{Gross IPPE}_{j,t} / \text{Gross IPPE}_{j,t-1} \right) \right]$$

(where UDEP is unexpected depreciation, DEP is depreciation, and IPPE is infra-structure, property, plant and equipment).

In simple terms, the methodology asserts that the rate of depreciation should remain consistent in consecutive financial years and can thus form the basis for calculating expected depreciation (and hence unexpected depreciation) with reference to current carrying values. We also employ this method. Initially we adapt the general premise of comparing rates of depreciation in order to assess whether the first assumption was valid, before applying the method more directly to assess the second assumption.

In both cases we have elected to make a few changes to the methodology in order to enhance its accuracy. First, it seems important to ensure non-depreciable IPPE assets are excluded from gross IPPE in view of the fact that around

37 percent of IPPE in NSW local government accounts is non-depreciable (Drew & Grant 2017b). Failure to remove these items (a prominent example is land—as found in the IPPE notes (Note 9a) of all NSW local government audited financial statements) confounds the analysis, particularly in view of the fact that individual items are often subject to contrariwise (upwards) revaluations. Therefore, UDEP and DEP in our analysis refer to the depreciable portion of IPPE only. Second, we believe that the unexpected depreciation should be calculated separately for each class of assets given that discordant useful lives (of, say, buildings, with lives of 80 years or more compared with books, with lives of three years or so) would otherwise result in conflated expected depreciation quantum (this is particularly important when new long-lived assets are acquired by a local government during the period of study). In other words, calculating the depreciation rate by employing a single depreciation expense figure derived from the Income Statement effectively imputes a weighted average useful life to all depreciable assets (which is best mitigated by calculating the expected depreciation by each asset class). We therefore made 18 separate calculations (one for each distinct class of depreciable IPPE asset) and summed these, in lieu of the one calculation employed in the extant literature. Notably, acceptance of the need for this second innovation to the methodology necessarily dictates that the first innovation is also observed. We also expressed the unexpected depreciation as the percentage variance from expected depreciation, in order to facilitate valid comparisons across the cohort.[3]

To test the first assumption, we calculated the average rate of depreciation for each of the 18 distinct depreciable asset classes in 2013 over the cohort of 38 councils in the Greater Sydney region and used this average rate in place of '$DEP_{j,t-1}$/Gross $IPPE_{j,t-1}$' in the previous algorithm. We then expressed the sum of quantum of unexpected depreciation for each asset class as a percentage of expected depreciation for each council. The results were summarised (Table 9.1) with particular attention to measures of spread as a basis of assessing the validity of the reasonableness assumption.

To test the second assumption, we used the rate of depreciation for each asset class in the 2012–2013 financial year as the basis of calculating the quantum of expected depreciation in 2014 *and* 2015 respectively with reference to the relevant carrying value for each asset class. It should be noted that the rate of depreciation used was the specific rate employed by each individual council in the 2012–2013 financial year (not the average rate). We used the 2013 asset class rate of depreciation for both years because at the time that the 2012–2013 financial year accounts were being finalised, there was no suggestion that council amalgamations might occur. The 2013 rates of depreciation therefore were largely free of amalgamation inspired incentives for gaming which occurred in 2014 (when amalgamations were officially mooted) and 2015 (when councils were directed to pursue amalgamations). The results of these analyses are detailed in Table 9.2 below.

Finally, to test the composite effect of both assumptions being violated, we calculated the consistency of depreciation practice (as per the method employed for testing the first assumption) and present the results in Table 9.3.

Results

For valid comparisons to be made on the financial performance indicators, it is clearly necessary to assume that practice is more or less consistent (certainly that the degree of inconsistency is immaterial with respect to achievement or non-achievement of the pre-determined performance benchmarks). This was always a rather heroic assumption given existing scholarly evidence to the contrary (see, for example, Pilcher 2006) and the reservations expressed by the Audit Office of NSW (2012). Moreover, as the measure of spread (inter-quartile range) in Table 9.1 shows, this assumption was violated by a rather alarming margin. Clearly, if practice was not consistent before the advent of FFTF, there is little reason to expect that fair comparisons could be made for the three performance indicator benchmarks which used depreciation data. We acknowledge that there might be some legitimate variation owing to, for instance, different classification of assets within the 18 different IPPE classes; however, the scale of the variation suggests that there is something more at work here.

Moreover, as Table 9.2 demonstrates, the incentives posed by FFTF resulted in rather startling changes to practice in both the 2013–2014 and 2014–2015 financial years. Specifically, the typical council appears to have adjusted depreciation practice downwards (median of -2.83 percent in 2013–2014 and -6.54 percent in 2014–2015) in an apparent effort to convey a more favourable impression of performance against the FFTF criteria. In addition, the downward shift seems to have become more pronounced as the incentives became greater (that is, as we moved from mooted amalgamation in 2013–2014 to an amalgamation directive in 2014–2015). In addition, the shifts in behaviour seem to have been widespread—thus suggesting that the particular incentives posed by FFTF found a response in a large proportion

Table 9.1 Inconsistent depreciation, Greater Sydney councils 2013 (percent)—testing the first assumption

Financial Year	Smallest	Largest	Q1	Median	Q3	IQR
Inconsistent Depreciation 2012–2013	−39.21	45.27	−19.44	−4.09	25.3	44.74

Table 9.2 Unexpected depreciation, Greater Sydney councils 2014–2015 (percent)

Financial Year	Smallest	Largest	Q1	Median	Q3	IQR
Unexpected Depreciation 2013–2014—mooted amalgamation	−38.42	10.26	−11.67	−2.83	1.24	12.91
Unexpected Depreciation 2014–2015—amalgamation directive	−46.07	16.46	−20.19	−6.54	0.86	21.05

of the local government executive ranks. This observation is, in turn, consistent with our conjecture that there are circumstances (such as local government amalgamation) which might give rise to a conjunction of knightly *and* knavish motivations. This stands in contrast to the scholarly consensus that only knaves are responsible for subversive activity in performance management regimes (see, for example, Bevan & Hood 2006). All of this evidence is consistent with the media reports that that 'some councils. . . "played games" with their books by extending the useful life of their public assets to an "unrealistic" age' (Bell 2015, p. n.p.).

However, the question remains as to the overall consequence of inconsistent practice *combined* with subsequent changes to practice that may be elicited from egocentric and ideological apologetic incentives. There are two ways of thinking about this composite effect. The first is to replicate the methodology employed to test the first assumption (but using 2014–2015 data instead of 2012–2013 data). This approach tells us how much variation in practice existed with the cohort of local governments at the end of the FFTF process and is presented in the first row of Table 9.3. Curiously, the spread of results (as measured by the inter-quartile range) narrowed from 2012–2013 levels, suggesting that there was some convergence in practice by the end of 2015, although practice was still far too discordant for anyone to believe that valid judgements could be made regarding FFTF on the basis of the data. Moreover, whilst convergence in practice might have occurred, we have no way of thinking about how the practice for the whole cohort had also changed in response to incentives posed by FFTF. Therefore, in the second row we calculate the inconsistent depreciation practice across the cohort by employing the depreciation rates as at 2012–2013 (before incentives for distortion became apparent). Once again, the results suggest a convergence in behaviour. Yet, the results also clearly show a large shift downwards in the depreciation practice of the entire cohort (which might be expected given the results detailed in Table 9.2). What this means is that there is strong empirical evidence that FFTF did significantly reduce depreciation accruals, notwithstanding the fact that there was some convergence amongst peers.

Table 9.3 Inconsistent depreciation, Greater Sydney councils 2015 (percent)—testing the composite effect of violating both assumptions

Financial Year	Smallest	Largest	Q1	Median	Q3	IQR
Inconsistent Depreciation 2014–2015 (using 2014–2015 depreciation rates	−43.48	67.19	−24.22	−7.33	14.25	38.47
Inconsistent Depreciation 2014–2015 (using 2012–2013 depreciation rates)	−46.59	57.42	−26.67	−11.54	8.22	34.89

In sum, our analyses of Greater Sydney councils suggest that audited financial data is not, in and of itself, a sufficiently firm foundation for high stakes performance management regimes. Moreover, we note that the 'pass' or 'fail' assessments for each of the three performance indicators (operating ratio, buildings and infrastructure renewal ratio and efficiency ratio) provided absolutely no indication that one of the key financial inputs to the said ratios (depreciation) was typically distorted by around 11.54 percent. This 'obscurement' of the accounting judgements which underlie financial performance indicators is a key area of concern moving forward.

Discussion

The foregoing analysis of Greater Sydney councils has demonstrated that public performance management regimes based on financial data are not only subject to the large number of problems identified in the scholarly work on performance management, but also to additional problems specific to the nature of accounting data. These additional problems include new opportunities for gaming based on professional (accounting) judgement, the temptation to eschew performance auditing and rely instead on financial statement auditing, and the likelihood that end users might remain oblivious to the fact that performance indicators are strongly reliant on accounting judgement. Specifically, we note that significant levels of manipulation of depreciation accrual data for the Greater Sydney councils undermined the essential assumptions of the FFTF performance management and that these distortions occurred despite the fact that the financial statements had been audited. We also note that the FFTF pass/fail dichotomy—in the absence of analysis such as this—gives no indication of the performance indicator's reliance on heavily distorted depreciation data. This fact highlights the danger that accounting judgements are obscured when performance indicators are collated (especially in the absence of sensitivity analysis and concomitant indicators for margin of error).

It is clear that high stakes public performance management regimes require higher audit effort and that reliance cannot be made of financial audit alone. This is particularly the case where performance benchmarks have been communicated in advance (as was the case for FFTF) as 'complete specification of targets and how performance will be measured almost invites reactive gaming by managers' (Bevan & Hood 2006, p. 533). Our evidence indicates that reliance on financial auditing does little to change this assessment. Moreover, the failure to take measures to combat gaming and other subversive actions is likely, in time, to provide testament to the assertion of Bird et al. (2005, p. 10) that:

> to buy cheap methodology is to buy dear in the longer term if subsequent audit or independent critique [such as our analysis above] discovers problems with performance data which have been influential in public policy debate.

Conclusion

Lest this chapter be interpreted as a gloomy assessment of public policy performance management regimes, we now detail some of the measures which might have been taken to prevent the decision to spend 'up to a billion dollars' on local government reform in NSW being made on clearly unreliable empirical data (Drew & Dollery 2015, p. 80).

First and foremost, a system of thorough performance management audit must form the foundation of any competent performance management regime (with emphasis placed on materiality with respect to performance benchmarks). Analysis, of the type conducted above, would have allowed regulators to understand the reliability of the performance indicators used in public policymaking. Moreover, sensitivity analysis might have been conducted with a view to constructing confidence intervals for performance indicators. Second, indicators might have been constructed with the purpose of discouraging manipulation of obvious targets for gaming—for instance, a depreciation rate presented as a proportion of depreciable assets would have put potential gamers on notice that their efforts would attract attention (Drew & Dollery 2015). In addition, the responsible regulator might have made executives aware that attention would be paid to unexpected movements in accrual items and that consequences would be imposed on individuals caught distorting data—a 'hang the admirals' approach as discussed by Bevan and Hood (2006). Fourth, efforts might have been made to increase the unpredictability of the performance management product. Process, on the other hand, should be clearly outlined in order to promote trust in the regime. Undoubtedly there are some constraints imposed when using financial data, although the financial year is fixed, unpredictability can be introduced in other ways. For instance, a larger set of performance indicators might have been specified, but attention focused on the smaller subset (although not so small as to elicit conclusions of extreme synecdoche). Another effective way of increasing the cost of gaming is to commit to continuing use of the performance indicators—in so doing, gamers are presented with a smaller subset of suitable gaming devices (changes which commit the organisation to future actions are no longer appealing) and are also more likely to incur the costs of gaming (for example, the cost of extending the useful life of assets will continue into a future time). In similar vein, mandating independent audit committees, requiring audit committees to sign off on the performance management inputs and committing to a future review of FFTF outcomes would have increased the likelihood of gamers being detected.[4]

In short, the emphasis should be on increasing the cost of gaming and ensuring end users are aware of the potential error imputed into individual performance indicators.

In view of both the unreliability of the performance indicators employed to guide the billion dollar reform to NSW local government and the fact that the embarrassing flaws might have been avoided, it is clear that the accounting profession needs to engage more fully in the development and scholarly evaluation of performance management regimes. Political and management scientists have made very important advances in many fields—but when it comes to performance management on the basis of financial data, there is a clear role for the expertise which only an accounting professional can provide.

Notes

1 University of Technology, Sydney NSW, Australia (Joseph.Drew@uts.edu.au)
2 Although, as noted earlier, the focus of our chapter is on gaming rather than cheating, the framework of incentives is still useful for understanding how and why the dichotomy of public sector motivations might respond to particular incentives.
3 We concede that the methodological innovations (along with extant methodology) would fail to detect some manipulations, such as incorrectly classifying assets as non-depreciable items or keeping items as 'work in progress' beyond commissioning date.
4 Only around half of NSW councils had audit committees at the commencement of FFTF. Moreover, most audit committees are not truly independent.

References

Audit Office of New South Wales 2012, *New South Wales Auditor-General's report performance audit – monitoring local government*, Audit Office of NSW, Sydney.
Bell, A 2015, 'Blacktown Mayor Stephen Bali rejects IPART Fit for the Future findings', *Daily Telegraph*, 20 October 2015, viewed 23 December 2016 2015, www.dailytelegraph.com.au/ newslocal/news/blacktown-mayor-stephen-bali-rejects-ipart-fit-for-the-future-findings/ news-story/af9a5472ebb39fbcdb43ebc11d0de58c
Bevan, G & Hood, C 2006, 'What's measured is what matters: targets and gaming in the English public health care system', *Public Administration*, vol. 84, no. 3, pp. 517–538.
Bird, S, Cox, D, Farewell, V, Goldstein, H, Holt, T & Smith, P 2005, 'Performance indicators: good, bad, and ugly', *Journal of the Royal Statistical Academy*, vol. 168, no. 1, pp. 1–27.
Copeland, R 1968, 'Income smoothing', *Journal of Accounting Research*, vol. 6, no. 1, pp. 101–116.
de Bruijn, H 2007, *Managing performance in the public sector*, Routledge, Taylor and Francis Group, London.
Drew, J 2018, 'Playing for keeps: local government distortion of depreciation accruals in response to high stakes public policy-making', *Public Money & Management*, vol. 38, no. 1, pp. 57–64.
Drew, J & Dollery, B 2015, 'Less haste more speed: the fit for future reform program in New South Wales local government', *Australian Journal of Public Administration*, vol. 75, no. 1, pp. 78–88.
Drew, J & Grant, B 2017a, 'Multiple agents, blame games and public policy-making: the case of local government reform in New South Wales', *Australian Journal of Political Science*, vol. 52, no. 1, pp. 37–52.
Drew, J & Grant, B 2017b, 'Means, motive and opportunity: distortion of public policy making performance management data', *Australian Journal of Public Administration*, vol. 76, no. 2, pp. 237–250.
Glanville, B 2016, 'Woollahra Council loses legal challenge against NSW government over forced amalgamation', *Australian Broadcasting Commission*, 20 July, viewed 22 December 2016, www.abc.net.au/news/2016-07-20/woollahra-council-loses-legal-challenge-over-forced-amalgamation/7643776

Grant, B & Drew, J 2016, *Local government in Australia: history, theory and public policy*, Springer, Palgrave Macmillan, Singapore.

Hamilton, P 2003, 'The saliency of synecdoche: the part and the whole of employment relations', *Journal of Management Studies*, vol. 40, no. 7, pp. 1569–1585.

Independent Local Government Review Panel (ILGRP) 2013, *Revitalising local government: final report of the NSW Independent Local Government Review Panel*, ILGRP, Sydney.

Le Grand, J 2003, *Motivation, agency, and public policy: of knights & knaves, pawns & queens*, Oxford University Press, Oxford.

Le Grand, J 2010, 'Knights and knaves return: public service motivation and the delivery of public services', *International Public Management Journal*, vol. 13, no. 1, pp. 56–71.

Marquardt, C & Wiedman, C 2004, 'How are earnings managed? An examination of specific accruals', *Contemporary Accounting Research*, vol. 21, no. 2, pp. 461–491.

McCarthy, J 2014, 'Silence greets call to double check audits', *The Newcastle Herald*, 23 July, viewed 24 December 2014, http://newsstore.smh.com.au/apps/viewDocument.ac? page=1&sy=afr&kw=Silence+greets+call+to+double+check+audits&pb=nch&dt=sele ctRange&dr=5years&so=relevance&sf=text&sf=headline&rc=10&rm=200&sp=nrm& clsPage=1&docID=NCH140723A46R235R4A4

Mulford, C & Comiskey, E 2002, *The financial numbers game: detecting creative accounting practices*, John Wiley and Sons, New York.

Pilcher, R 2006, 'The smoothing potential of depreciation for local authorities', *Journal of Contemporary Issues in Business and Government*, vol. 12, no. 2, pp. 67–80.

Pilcher, R & Van der Zahn, M 2010, 'Local governments, unexpected depreciation and financial performance adjustment', *Financial Accountability & Management*, vol. 26, no. 3, pp. 299–323.

Pollitt, C 2013, 'The logics of performance management', *Evaluation*, vol. 19, no. 4, pp. 346–363.

Rezaee, Z 2005, 'Causes, consequences, and deterrence of financial statement fraud', *Critical Perspectives on Accounting*, vol. 16, no. 1, pp. 227–298.

Stalebrink, O 2007, 'An investigation of discretionary accruals and surplus-deficit management: evidence from Swedish municipalities', *Financial Accountability & Management*, vol. 23, no. 4, pp. 441–458.

TCorp 2013, *Financial sustainability of the New South Wales local government sector*, TCorp, Sydney.

Walker, R, Boyne, G & Brewer, G (eds) 2010, *Public management and performance: research directions*, Cambridge University Press, Cambridge.

10 The intention and the reality

A commentary on the not-for-profit reform Agenda in Australia

David Gilchrist[1] and Robyn Pilcher

Introduction

The Australian not-for-profit (NFP) sector is the third component of the national economy (the other two being the public and private sectors) and represents a fundamental part of the national social infrastructure. Its importance and centrality to social cohesion and community development was early identified in that country when various sub-national governments established legislation designed to enable the incorporation of associations.[2] This Australian legislation has now been in place for over 100 years, initially passed in South Australia with the Parliament of Western Australia (WA) legislating a few years later in 1895 (Huntly 1999a). The early legislation was world-leading. Indeed, antipodean parliaments were often decades ahead of the remainder of the Anglophone world regarding many aspects of social legislation (Gilchrist 2009, 2017; Metin 1977).

By modern standards, however, this legislation was relatively unsophisticated, essentially enabling the incorporation of non-trading, socially focused entities including clubs, sporting teams and hospitals. Nevertheless, it did have the effect of establishing a corporate vehicle for social activities of all types, including charitable activities. It ensured that, when the Australian federation was established in 1901, the states (and subsequently the territories) retained the power to create associations. Importantly, the legislation also focused these corporation styles on non-trading or mission-focused activities.

The place of mission, purpose and/or objects of these organisations subsequently created the separating factor between them and commercial concerns, becoming the foundation for eligibility decisions regarding the provision of favourable tax arrangements for NFP organisations of which charities are a subset. While there are now many methods available for the incorporation of NFP organisations, we are concerned only with associations in this chapter. The purpose, mission and/or objects of an association have become central to debates regarding governance, sustainability, efficiency and arrangements associated with government procurement—particularly of human services—from NFP organisations (Frumkin 2005; Wilkins & Gilchrist 2016).

Over the succeeding century, the various sub-national legislative arrangements for NFP organisations were reformed and amended to increase: the supervisory and regulatory capacities of government; the responsibility of those charged with the governance of these corporations; the options available for incorporation styles; and the relative diversity relating to this area of law across the Commonwealth. The Commonwealth also impacted these reform processes by stipulating taxation arrangements, ultimately adding a regulatory framework at a national level—and concomitant with the sub-national jurisdictions' arrangements—for the charities subset of the NFP sector when the *Australian Charities and Not-for-profits Commission Act 2012* (Cwlth) and the *Charities Act 2013* (Cwlth) added both a taxation definition of charities and a regulatory body to the Australian NFP landscape.[3] Further, with the powers to regulate companies transferred from the states to the Commonwealth parliaments by the last three decades of the 20th century, enabling legislation was also established at the Commonwealth level supporting the incorporation of NFP organisations. As such, companies limited by guarantee became able to be incorporated under the *Corporations Act 2001* (Cwlth).

NFP organisations incorporated under the various sub-national legislations now play an important part in virtually all social and community building activities and enjoy a reputation for commitment to all manner of social development (for example, Gilchrist & Knight 2017a). Setting aside that substantial social contribution, the NFP sector in Australia is also an extremely important element in the national economy. This was identified by the Australian Government Productivity Commission (AGPC 2010), which reported that NFP organisations contribute in excess of $43 billion in national Gross Domestic Product (GDP), employ 8 percent of the national workforce and that there are currently around 59,000 economically significant NFP organisations out of an estimated 600,000 NFP organisations nation-wide. The AGPC also estimated that the 4.6 million volunteers deployed by NFP organisations contributed a wage equivalent value of $15 billion (AGPC 2010). Since then, several studies have been undertaken at the national and sub-national level confirming the importance of the sector in terms of employment, contribution to GDP and the work it does on behalf of governments and others (for example, see Cortis et al. 2016; Gilchrist 2011; Gilchrist & Knight 2017b, 2017c).

Of equal importance—and although not strictly relevant to regulation or supervision—there is a growing nexus between governments and the Australian NFP sector. In general, the connection is created out of an accelerating predilection for governments to purchase services from these mission-based organisations rather than provide services directly (Wilkins & Gilchrist 2016). This nexus also acts as a regulatory framework in the sense that the arrangements established for procurement, reporting and acquittal impact the way NFP organisations do business, organise themselves and their survivability (Alford & O'Flynn 2012). These arrangements also affect the relative mission-centricity of these organisations as economic survival is often a challenge and sources of funding usually come with some strings attached.

The purpose of this chapter is to review the experience and the complexity associated with the reform of WA associations by examining charities' regulation reform at a national level (which impacts a subset of these organisations) and associations' regulation at a sub-national level—that is, by reviewing the reform process in WA. This review constitutes two essential elements: first, an examination of the establishment of the Australian Charities and Not-for-profits Commission (ACNC) at the national level and, second, an examination of the *Associations Incorporation Act 2015* (WA) and procurement reform at the sub-national level in WA. This is done by initially considering the purpose of associations and the nature of such corporations. The impact of regulatory reform is then reviewed in the context of the chapter's purpose: that mission, rather than commercial concern, is the principal consideration for a NFP organisation.

The chapter is divided into five sections. In the next section there is a review of the nature of associations in the context of their purpose, whilst in the third and fourth sections the Commonwealth and WA reform processes are examined. The final section contains concluding remarks and future research.

Associations' definition and primary purpose

Prior to examining the reform processes themselves, it is necessary to understand the nature of associations in WA as this better frames the discussion pertaining to the impact of regulatory arrangements.[4] In WA the current enabling legislation, the *Associations Incorporation Act*, has its head of power based in the Australian and WA Constitutions, wherein the power to make laws in relation to corporations are residual to the states within the federation.[5] *Inter alia*, this legislation provides for the purpose and regulation of associations incorporated in WA.

As identified in the introduction, the current legislation has its origins in the *Associations Incorporation Act 1895* (WA). Importantly, Huntly (1999a) drew a very significant division between the incorporation of NFP organisations and the incorporation of trading entities, and considered that the establishment of separate legislation for each class of corporation was deliberate. Huntly (1999a) emphasised that this separate legislation confirmed that incorporated associations are *sui generis*, or unique to their own purpose. However, it might also be argued that while the original intention was to separate the various forms of incorporation for particular purposes, government policy since those early times has changed considerably while the legislative precedent does not necessarily reflect these changes. With the increase in complexity and size of the sector as well as the increasing importance of the government/NFP nexus (Butcher & Gilchrist 2016), the original *sui generis* nature of incorporated associations has been eclipsed, making them less mission-focused and more market orientated.

While Schwabenland (2006) considered that commentators and others are obsessed with definition, it is important to note that many of the reforms implemented over the past decade were created out of a commercial perspective that is expected to have a negative impact on the sector (Barraket 2008; Butcher & Gilchrist 2016). Such an effect is likely to come from inappropriate or confused reform undertaken independently at the Commonwealth and sub-national level (discussed later), and also from the confusion resulting from commercial emphasis on directorial priorities and governance processes.

Consequently, a definition is important to: the application of law concerning the objectives of NFP organisations (mission and/or commercial); the development of policy by government; and the identification of the responsibilities of directors and members of NFP organisations themselves. For example, Anheier (2005) identified several starting points when considering the definition of a NFP organisation. Commencing with a legal definition, Anheier (2005) also introduced an economic definition, a functional definition and a structural-operational definition.

From a legal perspective, Fletcher (1986), in his review of the various Australian and New Zealand NFP legislation, described the primary purpose of such legislation as not to regulate NFP corporations, but rather to provide them legal status. Fletcher (1986) considered that, in the absence of specific legislated regulatory arrangements, one must revert to the commercial corporation regulatory model. This lack of real regulation, supported by an appropriate legislative framework, has led advisers, committee members and others to assume that the legal framework for commercial corporations can apply readily to the associations they work in and for. This acceptance at the individual director and advisor level has made the government reform agenda, within a commercial and market economy framework, much more readily agreeable. These reforms are seen to simply build on a perception of NFP organisations already accepted by many within the sector, working with the sector and providing services to it.

The commonality between commercial corporations and incorporated associations has tended to be emphasised in the context of committee members' responsibilities, accounting and financial reporting and contract law. Fletcher (1986) emphasised this similarity by stating that the committee member and the director are in the same position. Fletcher (1986, p. 289) went on to mitigate this initial comment by reflecting that such a position is not established in case law, but that it is *probable* (author's italics) that 'committee members owe, in the same measure, the common law and equitable duties which law and equity impose on company directors'. Huntly (1999b) discussed this idea by reference to what he saw as the common characteristics of companies, including: perpetual succession; ability to sue and be sued; and the ability to hold and dispose of property. However, here Huntly (1999b) drew the line on commonality and emphasised the differences between the two forms of corporation.

Huntly (1999a, p. 5), also taking a legal perspective, described essential characteristics of an incorporated association as including the fact that such corporations are made corporations *sui generis* (as noted earlier), and do not 'fit into the framework, structure or operations of companies or the law of companies'. He went on to ascribe further attributes to such entities, including: associations are usually incorporated to pursue a dominantly socially beneficial purpose(s); they often manage their affairs on a 'domestic' basis;[6] government funding is often extended;[7] and the majority of such organisations operate on a modest scale (as detailed above, less than 10 percent of NFPs are economically significant). These differences, Huntly (1999a) argued, meant the analogy between corporations and associations is questionable. As such, reform programmes need to consider these attributes in terms of the nature of reforms being attempted and the capacity of those reforms to be absorbed by the NFP organisations themselves. This consideration is occurring in Australia where, for instance, the Australian Accounting Standards Board (AASB) is reviewing the current financial reporting framework to test its continued suitability (AASB 2017).

Setting aside the legal nuances, there are also a number of functional differences that are important to consider here. These differences relate to the central purpose of a trading concern compared to that of a NFP organisation. Clearly, a trading corporation has as a central purpose the creation of sustainable wealth for the benefit of shareholders. Shareholders then participate, to the extent of their proportional ownership, in the wealth created, either by selling their shares or enjoying dividends directly paid by the company. On the other hand, a cardinal marker in the identification of a NFP organisation is the prohibition on the distribution of the association's wealth to members as dividends. In other words, NFP organisations have an alternate purpose—their mission. However, it is the accounting, taxation and corporate definitional elements that seem to be emphasised in the reform debates, the primacy of which resulted in the *Inquiry into the Definition of Charities and Related Organisations* (Treasury Department 2001).

As a further example, Kilcullen, Hancock and Izan (2008) explored the definition of a NFP organisation for accounting purposes. In essence, their paper sought evidence as to what those in the public sector, the NFP sector and the commercial sector considered to be essential criteria for the identification of a NFP organisation. The top scoring useful criterion for the identification of a public sector agency was 'an entity whose principle objective was not the generation of profit' (Kilcullen, Hancock & Izan 2008, p. 21). A second criterion identified was 'may not distribute surpluses', while 'operating purpose other than profit' was the third essential criterion for identifying NFP organisations (Kilcullen, Hancock & Izan 2008, p. 23). Other key elements included the enjoyment of tax privileges and volunteer contributions. It is probable that a study with an accounting focus would tend to highlight accounting or business criteria in defining a NFP organisation.

Lyons (2001), offered a more nuanced definition, claiming NFP organisations should: be private organisations; act voluntarily; have members who do not seek personal profit; aim to provide benefits to themselves and/or others; be democratically controlled; and are such that any material benefit gained by a member is proportionate to that member's use of the organisation. This definition is still deficient in that, while it does invoke the non-profit element, it does not consider the issue of mission as central to the purpose of the organisation. In other words, the definition here predates Kilcullen, Hancock and Izan's (2008) definitional elements which focus on material resource allocations and benefits rather than on mission. Frumkin (2005) argued that there are only three essential elements required to identify a NFP organisation: a lack of coercion in terms of participation; a lack of capacity to distribute profits to stakeholders; and a lack of clear lines of ownership and accountability. The first two elements here are consonant with those already discussed, while the third emphasises the somewhat confusing nature of

NFP accountability—stakeholders of a NFP organisation are often numerous and can vary considerably. However, again, Frumkin (2005) does not consider mission to be a necessary element in defining a NFP organisation.

The definitions above have one thing in common. They recognise attributes of NFP organisations rather than provide a working definition. The difficulty commentators, academics and others experience in arriving at a suitable definition of NFP organisations is confirmation that incorporated associations are *sui generis* and that the legal and operational bases of definitions created out of commercial and public sector ideas are not able to be usefully applied to NFP organisations. Such organisations do not fit the general definitions of commercial or government organisations because they do not have the same purpose and profile as such organisations. Therefore, by extension, the regulation of such organisations can only be successful if regulators first recognise the purpose of NFP organisations and their central mission.

Regulatory reform at the commonwealth level

As indicated in the previous section, there have been a number of reports prepared by agencies of the Commonwealth Government as a result of a long-term discourse. These reports include the Senate Standing Committee on Economics' report on the disclosure regimes of NFP organisations (2008), the AGPC's report into the contribution of the sector (2010), and the Henry Tax Review (2010)—all of which recognised the common desire for a national regulator to be established and for the introduction of uniform legislation and simplification of regulation to the benefit of NFP organisations.

Prima facie, the call for a national regulator, the creation of a one-stop-shop for NFP regulation and supervision, and the introduction of uniform legislation across the sector at a national level are logical. The culminating step in the Commonwealth's regulatory reform evaluation agenda was its final report in April 2011 (Treasury Department 2011a) which informed the Commonwealth budget initiatives discussed later (Treasury Department 2011c). In essence, this final report brought together several recommendations and ideas that had been developed in other reports over an extended period (for instance, in relation to taxation and NFP organisations, Treasury Department 2011b) and effectively set the scene for the Federal budget and development of the ACNC over the coming three years.

Additionally, and very importantly, the report also considered the work of several other bodies at the national level and constitutes what might pass for the only national reform agenda and description of all reforms being attempted. The report, somewhat predictably, provided recommendations pertaining to: the establishment of a national regulatory and supervisory regime; the establishment of a single NFP form of incorporation (over time); the establishment of a national definition of the term 'charity'; the development of a single information portal; the development of guidance and educative material at a national level; and the development of specific financial reporting arrangements (Treasury Department 2011a).

Significantly, the report recommended the ongoing establishment of effective communication between the national regulator and the AASB. It also recognised the importance of the Council of Australian Government's process in the context of the negotiations to come with the states and territories. The report served to bring together ideas and prospective improvements as well as identifying the various bodies through which the reforms may be developed.

A formal structure for the establishment of a reform agenda was implemented when the Not-For-Profit Sector Reform Council was established in December 2010. The Council included a number of high-profile leaders from the sector and Linda Lavarch (a former politician and respected academic) was appointed chair. Amongst other things, the Reform Council was charged with: examining the scope of a national one-stop-shop regulator, including its role, feasibility and structure; streamlining Commonwealth government (not state/territory government) tendering and contracting processes for government-funded NFP organisations (including developing a common form contract); and the harmonisation of fund raising and other Commonwealth, state and territory laws.

These are all useful and appropriate considerations for such a council, and the body went about its work providing policy advice to the government that resulted in, amongst other things, several provisions addressing these issues in the 2011 Federal Budget. Included in the announcement in the 2011 Federal Budget was the establishment of the ACNC, the implementation of new taxation arrangements for those NFP organisations undertaking trading activities and the forecasting of the introduction of several further reforms over the 2012 and 2013 calendar years (Treasury Department 2011c).

The establishment of a national regulator and the aspiration to create a one-stop-shop to which all NFP organisations in the country report represented an opportunity for substantial, long-term and real reform. As part of the Budget, the ACNC would establish a 'report-once-use-often' general reporting framework for charities. Finally, that Budget also provided for the enhancement of the taxation regime with the intention that it focus on increasing compliance activity in the area of income unrelated to the charitable purpose of an organisation.

Western Australian reform

In regard to associations, the current WA legislation is the *Associations Incorporation Act 2015* (WA). This Act was passed in that state's Parliament after a ten-year review of the previous legislation (the *Associations Incorporation Act 1987* (WA)). Over the course of the ten years between commencing the review of the 1987 legislation, in part via the *Associations Incorporation Bill 2006* (WA) (tabled as a Green Bill for the purposes of public comment), and the passing of the new legislation in 2015, the ACNC was established, the *Charities Act* passed, and the National Standards Chart of Accounts was established and adopted by the WA Government. All these factors increased pressure on the WA Government to respond by enacting the new legislation.

The 2015 legislation followed many attributes that are present in the national charities regulatory legislation. For instance, this legislation provides for differing reporting requirements for associations depending upon the tier they fall into (of which there are three, based on size by turnover)—these tiers equate to those described in the national legislation. Further, the state legislation also provides for accounting and auditing requirements, based on tiers but invoking the Australian Accounting Standards (requiring the preparation of accounts that are accepted as 'true and fair'), and allows for the pursuit of commercial activities by associations on the proviso that such activities support their purpose. Additionally, the state legislation requires committee members to act in the best interests of the association and for a proper purpose. Unfortunately, that purpose does not include prioritising mission above any other activities.

The path toward reforming the associations' legislation in WA was also impacted by the work of the Economic Audit Committee (EAC). The EAC had a remit to, amongst other things, make recommendations regarding the effectiveness of government agencies in service delivery, the increased delivery of services by the NFP sector and the increased use of competition to deliver government outcomes (Government of WA EAC 2009). The committee was given a very wide mandate to review every aspect of government service delivery and it devoted a considerable portion of its time and, ultimately, of its final report to the nexus between the WA NFP organisations and the government. Recommendations (of which there were 43) included: building an enhanced government/NFP sector relationship; a more mature procurement process; reducing the 'administrative burden'; establishing a grants programme to promote social innovation; replacing current procurement arrangements with a new 'collaboration for Community' policy effectively aimed at contractual arrangements; and introducing an option for low-interest loans for community organisations (Government of WA, EAC 2009, pp. iii–xiii).

Overall, the EAC's report looked to re-establish the public sector as a service facilitator, where NFP and commercial organisations compete for funds to act as direct providers. In the report the EAC claimed that '[a]n increasing number of WA's community sector organisations will have the opportunity to develop as social enterprises, run along business lines and become financially sustainable' (Government of WA, EAC 2009, p. i), suggesting that NFP organisations will be more like businesses and will, in essence, implement the government's agenda.

Clearly, the issue of the *sui generis* nature of incorporated associations was denied here. Additionally, the proposal to establish a centralised procurement capacity, with the main purpose of monitoring policy and efficiency gains, was suggestive of a view that procurement of services is uniform across service delivery (Government of WA, EAC 2009). Rainnie et al. (2012) examined the implications for the NFP sector and the community resulting from the EAC recommendations. Amongst other issues, they identified that the EAC report made several assumptions regarding the capacity and efficiency of both the WA public sector and the NFP sector. Rainnie et al. (2012) claimed that the EAC's conclusions lacked evidential support and that a number of negative outcomes would emanate from the recommendations. These outcomes included, in the context of this chapter's discussion, a predisposition within the report for emphasising financial outcomes over human outcomes and a reference to international experience where mission drift, amongst other things, resulted from the kinds of changes being sought by EAC (Rainnie et al. 2012).

The idea of mission drift, consonant with the idea of the uniqueness of associations and the ongoing theme of this chapter, was not considered by the EAC report. As well, the 'commercialisation' of the NFP sector targeted by the EAC could be seen as an attempt to progress the sector further along the NFP/commercial spectrum—not necessarily an intended attempt or knowing attempt, but an attempt all the same—by requiring business operations and economic considerations to become central to the concern of NFP directors.

The extent to which the reforms were rolled out were also examined annually for three years and it was discovered that a lack of capital and training in both government procurement offices and NFP organisations, as well as the complexity of measuring outcomes, held back the effective implementation of the scheme (Knight & Gilchrist 2015). Clearly, with reform also being undertaken at the federal level, there is an opportunity to slow down the reform itself and take more time over the reform's design and implementation.

Concluding remarks

The role of NFP organisations in the Australian economy and in the building of civil society is both axiomatic and critical. These organisations constitute infrastructure that is leveraged by government for services delivery, to achieve policy outcomes and to facilitate feedback and advocacy. Members of the community also leverage this infrastructure to gain support, enable participation and to enhance their community opportunities.

The place and role of associations is thus very varied and complex. They are different in size, purpose and in terms of their resourcing, formality of their governance and mission. Adding to this complexity is the impact of the government/NFP nexus where government policy and funding impacts the way these associations operate. Further, the sub-national and national governments regulate and supervise associations based largely on their activities in the context of their taxation arrangements.

Overall, this complexity informs the regulatory and supervisory arrangements and appears to drive the focus on commercial and financial governance and reporting frameworks rather than on what should be the mission of the organisation. This complexity is exaggerated by the federal nature of the Australian polity and the fact that there is considerable work to go before one single jurisdiction has responsibility for this area. It is suggested that this simplification is necessary before any regulatory and supervisory regime can extend to focus on mission rather than the commercial and/or financial position and performance of an organisation.

It is acknowledged here that measuring and regulating mission is a fraught process. However, there does not appear to be even the slightest level of regulatory infrastructure aimed at preserving the mission of these organisations.

While this is an important finding in itself, the purpose of these organisations and the development of a regulatory environment that supports their purpose are critical. We know that the regulatory, supervisory and funding environments all impact the way an organisation operates, and we also know that the mission of an association is central to its definition—that is, its *raison d'etre*. Without a focus on mission as a critical regulatory frame, we suggest that the difference between corporations incorporated under legislation such as the *Associations Incorporation Act 2015* (WA) will drift increasingly toward commercial corporate governance arrangements, impacting negatively on Australia's social fabric.

Notes

1 University of Western Australia, Perth WA, Australia (David.gilchrist@uwa.edu.au)
2 Australia is a federal constitutional monarchy and was established in 1901 as the Commonwealth of Australia. Further details on the origin of the Australian states as sovereign entities can be found in Chapter 5 as well as Mendes (2007); Reilly et al. (2014); Ville and Withers (2015).
3 This definition was relevant to all Commonwealth purposes, but the overriding impact relates to the taxation issue.
4 Companies limited by guarantee are incorporated under the federal corporations' law and are not considered in this chapter – as they are impacted by the Commonwealth legislation.
5 The current state of the federal corporations' law is based on an agreement between the states and the Commonwealth wherein the states relinquished their rights to make laws with respect to corporations law (in the context of commercial corporations) in return for which the federal government committed to paying compensation to the states for loss of revenue on an indexed basis.
6 That is, governance finance and corporate style management is often not implemented in many small associations incorporated with volunteer officers and a minimum of staff.
7 Arguably, in the case of federal government funding particularly, this distinction may be becoming less useful as commercial corporations are also attracting considerable government funding under the purchaser provider arrangements currently in play.

References

Alford, J & O'Flynn, J 2012, *Rethinking public service delivery: managing with external providers*, Palgrave Macmillan, Basingstoke.

Anheier, H 2005, *Nonprofit organizations: theory, management, policy*, Routledge, Milton Park.

Australian Accounting Standards Board (AASB) 2017, 'Improving financial reporting for Australian charities', *Discussion Paper*, November, Australian Government, Canberra.

Australian Government Productivity Commission 2010, 'Contribution of the not-for-profit sector', Research Report, Commonwealth of Australia, Canberra.

Barraket, J (ed) 2008, *Strategic issues for the not-for-profit sector*, University of New South Wales Press, Sydney.

Butcher, J & Gilchrist, D (eds) 2016, *The three sector solution: delivering public policy in collaboration with not-for-profits and business*, Australian University Press, Canberra.

Cortis, N, Young, A, Powell, A, Reeve, R, Simnett, R, Ho, K & Ramia, I 2016, 'Australian charities report 2015', Centre for Social Impact and Social Policy Research Centre, UNSW, Australia.

Fletcher, K 1986, *The law relating to non-profit associations in Australia and New Zealand*, Law Book Company Limited, London.

Frumkin, P 2005, *On being nonprofit: a conceptual and policy primer*, Harvard University Press, Cambridge.

Gilchrist, D 2009, *'Le Socialisme sans doctrines* – Charles Harper and the foundation of co-operative agriculture in Western Australia', paper presented at the *History of Economic Thought Society of Australia Conference 2009*, Fremantle, 14–17 July, viewed 10 November 2017, www.hetsa.org.au/hetsa2009/abstracts_index.html

Gilchrist, D 2011, 'Devil's in the detail', *Public Accountant*, 1 August 2011, viewed 10 November 2017, www.pubacct.org.au/features/devils-in-the-detail-2

Gilchrist, D 2017, *Imperial theory and colonial pragmatism: Charles Harper, economic development and agricultural co-operation in Australia*, Palgrave Studies in the History of Economic Thought series, Palgrave MacMillan, London.

Gilchrist, D & Knight, P 2017a, 'WA's not-for-profit sector 2017: the first report on charities and other not-for-profits in WA', A Report for the Western Australian Council for Social Service, Perth, Australia.

Gilchrist, D & Knight, P 2017b, 'Australia's disability services sector 2017: report 2 – financial performance – summary of key findings (national benchmarking project)', A Report for National Disability Services, Canberra.

Gilchrist, D & Knight, P 2017c, 'Value of the not-for-profit sector 2017: an examination of the economic contribution of the not-for-profit human services sector in the Northern Territory', A Report for the Northern Territory Council of Social Service, Darwin, Australia.

Government of Western Australia (WA), Economic Audit Committee 2009, 'Putting the public first: partnering with the community and business to deliver outcomes: final report', Department of Premier and Cabinet, Perth.

Henry, K 2010, *Australia's future tax system: report to the Treasurer*, Commonwealth of Australia The Treasury, Canberra.

Huntly, C 1999a, 'The origin & function of the Associations Incorporation Act 1987 (WA) in three scenes', *Working paper series 99.03*, Curtin University of Technology, School of Business Law, Perth Western Australia.

Huntly, C 1999b, 'The Associations Incorporation Act 1987 (WA) & corporate law reform: challenges for the accounting profession', *Working paper series 99.04*, Curtin University of Technology, School of Business Law, Perth Western Australia.

Kilcullen, L, Hancock, P & Izan, I 2008, 'Defining a not-for-profit entity in Australia – one size may not fit all', Paper Presented to the University of Notre Dame Australia School of Business Not-for-profit Seminar Series, Fremantle.

Knight, P & Gilchrist, D 2015, *2014 Evaluation of the sustainable funding and contracting with the not-for-profit sector initiatives and associated procurement reforms*, Government of Western Australia, Perth.

Lyons, M 2001, *Third sector: the contribution of nonprofit and cooperative enterprises in Australia*, Allen & Unwin, Crows Nest.

Mendes, P 2007, *Australia's welfare wars revisited: the players, the politics and the ideologies*, University of New South Wales Press, Sydney.

Metin, A 1977, *Socialism without doctrine*, trans. R Ward, Alternative Publishing Co-operative Ltd, Chippendale, NSW.

Rainnie, A, Fitzgerald, S, Gilchrist, D & Morris, L 2012, 'Putting the public first? Restructuring the West Australian human services sector', *International Journal of Employment Studies*, vol. 20, no. 1, pp. 104–125.

Reilly, A, Appleby, G, Grenfell, L & Lacey, W 2014, *Australian public law*, 2nd edn, Oxford University Press, South Melbourne, VIC.

Schwabenland, C 2006, *Stories, visions and values in voluntary organisations*, Corporate Social Responsibility Series, Ashgate Publishing Limited, Aldershot.

Senate Standing Committee on Economics 2008, *Disclosure regimes for charities and not-for-profit organisations*, Australian Parliament, Canberra.

Treasury Department 2001, *Report of the inquiry into the definition of charities and related organisations*, Australian Government Publishing Service, Canberra.

Treasury Department 2011a, *Final report: Scoping study for a national not-for-profit regulator*, Commonwealth of Australia, Canberra.

Treasury Department 2011b, *Better targeting of not-for-profit tax concessions: consultation paper*, Commonwealth of Australia, Canberra.

Treasury Department 2011c, *Budget Paper No. 3 2011–12*, Commonwealth of Australia, Canberra.

Ville, S & Withers, G (eds) 2015, *The Cambridge economic history of Australia*, Cambridge University Press, Port Melbourne.

Wilkins, P & Gilchrist, D 2016, 'Accountability for the public policy contribution of not-for-profit organisations: who is accountable to whom and for what?' in R Pablo Guerrero & P Wilkins (eds), *Doing public good? Private actors, evaluation and public value*, Comparative Policy Evaluation, vol. 23, pp. 49–56, Routledge, New York.

Legislation

Associations Incorporation Act 1895 (WA)
Associations Incorporation Act 1987 (WA)
Associations Incorporation Act 2015 (WA)
Australian Charities and Not-for-profits Commission Act 2012 (Cwlth)
Charities Act 2013 (Cwlth)
Corporations Act 2001 (Cwlth)
Parliament of Western Australia 2006, *Associations Incorporation Bill*

11 Utopia

Joined-up government in Australia and New Zealand

David Gilchrist[1] and Karen Knight

Introduction

The term 'joined-up government' (JUG) first gained prominence after the then-British Prime Minister, Tony Blair, invoked it in 1997 on the launch of the Social Exclusion Unit in Britain (Bogdanor 2005). It became an umbrella term encapsulating a wider narrative about government reform in western countries that commenced at the close of the 20th century and centred on horizontal intra-government coordination and integration. In contrast to the New Public Management (NPM) reforms of the 1980s and early 1990s, which emphasised increased vertical and horizontal specialisation, JUG approaches have developed from a strong central core of government employing both top-down and bottom-up approaches, and developing supportive architectures to promote horizontal coordination and access to local mechanisms (Ling 2002; Matheson 2000; Stewart 2002).

Although coordination within government has been an age-old challenge, the expansion of government functions in the 20th century in countries including Australia, Britain and New Zealand (NZ) has brought the relative ineffectiveness of government agencies working in silos into stark relief—particularly in the context of the growth of the welfare state and increased government responsibility for human service delivery.

The modern discourse has particularly focused on how government coordination can be improved to address 'wicked' problems—problems that tend to be resistant to policy resolution. Such problems have tended to be complex social issues rooted in cultural contexts such as those related to social exclusion, homelessness, domestic violence, alcohol and drug abuse and crime prevention (Briggs 2012; Six 2004).[2] Since the late 1990s, governments in both Australia and NZ—at the national and sub-national levels—have introduced different JUG reforms for the delivery of services in these policy areas. Both countries have also taken advantage of the digital transformation and the internet to create more accessible and personalised public services. While the two nations' JUG experiences have differed in form, implementation and levels of success, there are also similarities with a shared history of hierarchy, 'top-down' approaches and the impact of the British Imperial inheritance that affected both constitutional practice and government organisation (Six 2004).

The form of JUG in Australia and NZ continues to evolve. JUG has extended beyond a simple narrative and catchcry as researchers, politicians and public servants develop clearer conceptual and institutional frameworks and taxonomies to describe, assess and look for ways to improve JUG practice. Importantly, the idea of JUG has been extended to incorporate non-government organisations external to the public sector.

This chapter provides some historical context of government coordination and integration generally, outlining, initially, more clearly various definitions and meanings that have become associated with the catch-all phrase, 'joined-up government'. The Australian and NZ experiences of JUG are examined in Sections 3 and 4 respectively, ending with a conclusion and suggestions for future research.

Background

Coordination is an old administrative doctrine and improving it horizontally has been a perennial challenge for governments across the ages (Peters 1996). In terms of the modern policy frameworks that are of interest here, Hood (2005) provided an historical perspective of JUG as it manifested in Britain via the New Labour Party reforms of the 1990s and early 2000s. He (2005, p. 19) viewed JUG as a new term for an old practice and showed examples in the history of public administration to highlight various governments' preoccupations with how otherwise separate government agencies could 'interconnect, complement one another, and pool related information'.

Hood (2005) also emphasised exceptions to the broader observation that JUG is really just a new term for an old concept by framing two general questions. First, how does the current expression differ in scope from earlier doctrines; and, second, have different means and mechanisms been developed in order to implement public administration coordination? In answer to the first question, Hood (2005) points to a move from a preoccupation of coordination at the margin, or in response to extraordinary events (such as war or plague), to a call for coordination as a general condition and the impacts of digital transformation. In answer to the second, historical perspective is given to the choice of methods of coordination set against distinct political and bureaucratic settings. Hood (2005) identified four broad types of coordination mechanisms: authority; architecture (physical or virtual); group interaction; and market-type entrepreneurship. Historically, however, hybrids of these broad approaches have tended to emerge.

The preceding historical perspective underlines that public administration coordination (or JUG) is an evolving concept and JUG practice continues to adapt to social conditions and political frameworks (Davies 2009; Hill & Hupe 2009; Meyrer & Dillon 1999; Richards 2001; Sandfort 1999). So, whereas Six (2004) provided a useful Neo-Durkheimian account of cross-national differences in JUG, identifying Australia and NZ as falling within hierarchical and 'top-down' styles of coordination, more recent research suggests this is changing. The literature indicates that there is growing emphasis being placed on horizontal, matrix and 'bottom-up' approaches to government coordination and collaboration with other local-level agents (Carey, McLoughlin & Crammond 2015; Keast 2011; O'Flynn et al. 2011; Ross et al. 2011). For example, the growing role and contribution of not-for-profit organisations to modern western economies presents significant potential to both the scope and mechanisms of JUG. Christensen and Laegreid (2007, p. 1067) described that potential as being 'to a great extent, about lower-level politics and getting people on the ground in municipalities, regions [and] local government organisation[s]' to work together.

Terminology related to JUG since its invocation late last century has also become diverse. This chapter uses the term 'joined-up government' (or JUG) in a broad sense. It has been used to refer to public administration as an approach, a form of coordination and an implemented action. Other descriptors that fall within the notions of JUG as outlined earlier include 'whole-of-government' (Halligan, Buick & O'Flynn 2011; Vincent 1999), 'integrated services' (McDermott et al. 2010; Vincent 1999), 'horizontal governance', 'boundary-spanning' and 'cross-boundary initiatives' (Carey, McLoughlin & Crammond 2015).

There is no broadly accepted definition of JUG in the literature, though Pollitt (2003, p. 35) offered the following:

> "Joined-up government" is a phrase which denotes the aspiration to achieve horizontally and vertically co-ordinated thinking and action. Through this co-ordination it is hoped that a number of benefits can be achieved. First, situations in which different policies undermine each other can be eliminated. Second, better use can be made of scarce resources. Third, synergies may be created through the bringing together of different key stakeholders in a particular policy field or network. Fourth, it becomes possible to offer citizens seamless rather than fragmented access to a set of related services.

Here Pollitt (2003) referred to JUG as an aspiration or approach. However, elsewhere in the literature distinctions have been made between JUG as narrative and praxis (Carey, Crammond & Riley 2014; Six 2004). There have also been efforts to develop broad frameworks outlining JUG in more detailed ways, extending consideration to best practices, identifying barriers and enablers to successful implementation, and considering the strengths and weaknesses of its use in different policy settings (Keast 2011; O'Flynn et al. 2011; State Services Authority 2007). It is in the Australian and NZ context that we explore some of these ideas further.

The Australian experience

Australia operates as a federation with six sovereign parliaments at state level, two territory parliaments and the Commonwealth parliament at the national level. At the national level, the Commonwealth government made early forays into the exploration of horizontal coordination of, and collaboration between, government agencies before the narrative of JUG became internationally popularised in the late 1990s.

The first clear emergence of government coordination as a deliberate policy priority was associated with the Labour party and the strong social policy programme of the then-prime minister, Gough Whitlam, during the early to mid-1970s (Hunt 2005). This focus must have struck both an administrative and a populist chord, as it extended beyond the life of one government. The report of the Royal Commission on Australian Government Administration (RCAGA), held after the fall of the Whitlam government, for example, identified a number of different agencies and levels of government where functions could be joined-up and investigated ways that local level mechanisms could achieve this (RCAGA 1976). These early forays were not without critique. Wilkins (2002), amongst others, subsequently noted that the RCAGA had provided limited guidance on accountability within such frameworks. Since this time, Australia's focus on JUG has emerged in national, state and regional settings and has included policy reforms aimed at addressing a diverse range of wicked issues and the application of digital transformation.

In relation to the Australian federation, in which differing governments have differing responsibilities for differing policy areas, complex inter-governmental coordination has been maintained formally via the Council of Australian Governments (COAG). COAG was established by the Labour government (under Bob Hawke, Prime Minister 1983–1991), and, subsequently, strengthened by the Liberal government (under John Howard, Prime Minister 1996–2007) which placed early emphasis on coordination and integration mechanisms at the local level (Hunt 2005). After announcing a range of whole-of-government priorities in 2002, the Commonwealth government formed the Management Advisory Committee (MAC), a forum for secretaries and heads of agencies within the Australian government. The MAC developed broad guidelines supporting JUG approaches in Australia. These guidelines made reference to overarching structures and processes, culture and capability, information management and infrastructure, budget and accountability frameworks and guidelines for making connections outside of the Australian public service.

The Commonwealth government continued to place greater emphasis on JUG as an approach that agencies could adopt when it offered clear advantages. Notably, this need was identified in MAC's *Connecting Government* report released in 2004. This report offered a checklist of issues related to JUG approaches that 'should be adopted as routine practice' (MAC 2004, p. 1). It also identified areas of potential for increased collaborative efforts in federal government, identified challenges to be faced in the century ahead and recommended frameworks that could support JUG.

It is interesting to note, however, that these documents do not define collaboration nor do they raise the idea of JUG. Rather, Halligan, Buick and O'Flynn (2011, p. 86) observed that these 'collaboration-rich' documents underpinned major experiments which became collectively known as 'whole-of-government', formally referring to the undertaking of action across portfolios but, more practically, working across agencies in order to support inter-organisational collaboration.

The increased focus on JUG approaches in Australia has been notable in policy reforms relating to regional and remote areas, predominantly in the context of service delivery within indigenous communities. Indeed, an experiment under the auspices of COAG—the 'COAG trials'—was launched in 2002. These trials introduced opportunities for government to partner with indigenous communities via Shared Responsibility Agreements. The creation of Indigenous Coordination Centres emerged from these trials in 2004, amongst other things, providing the opportunity for researchers to examine the architecture of JUG implementation more closely (O'Flynn et al. 2011).

Other national JUG initiatives directed at wicked issues also arose. For instance, in 2005 the National Homeless Strategy was launched (Commonwealth Department of Family and Community Services 2005). This heralded a more ambitious programme targeting social exclusion, which was to emerge two years later in the form of the Social Inclusion Agenda (SIA), launched by the Australian government as a wide-ranging initiative designed to broadly address social disadvantage in the country. Additionally, reform was introduced in the education, employment and health sectors and extended to infrastructure including law, financial and economic services. Running until 2013, the SIA was notable for its breadth of coverage and the unprecedented singling out of non-government organisations as a source of partnering for delivery at local levels (Carey, Crammond & Riley 2014).

The effectiveness of the SIA's JUG approach has since provided the opportunity for researchers to evaluate the effectiveness of JUG as it was applied to wicked policy issues and implemented on a wider scale. Carey, Crammond and Riley (2014) were critical of how JUG was implemented in the SIA. They argued that the agenda was weakly implemented by a reliance on top-down approaches and that this impeded the successful engagement of non-government organisations. Carey, Crammond and Riley (2014) highlighted the unique context and relationships existing between the non-government and government sectors in Australia and two broad conclusions were drawn from this research. First, referencing the work of O'Flynn et al. (2011), it was argued that stronger supportive architecture for JUG should take a matrix form, emphasising both vertical and horizontal integration and utilising bottom-up approaches. Second, referencing the work of Keast (2011, p. 227), the need for 'fit-for-purpose' strategies was emphasised (see also Carey & Dickinson 2017; Carey, McLoughlin & Crammond 2015).

By 2010, JUG was fully articulated within the Australian government as an approach that could improve social delivery via partnerships, networks and collaboration. JUG is now well established both in terms of the broader narrative and policy development in the Commonwealth policy space. However, how best to implement JUG and to ensure its integration continues to evolve.

Notwithstanding the challenges, individual states also focused upon JUG in order to effect change. The development of JUG at state and local government level in Australia has followed the federal trajectory, although the arrangements have naturally varied between jurisdictions. Initiatives have appeared in both the economic and social policy arenas and in the development of whole-of-government approaches, including in relation to service delivery.

Directional statements with strong emphasis on JUG have emerged from state governments across Australia. For example, the then-Labour government in Queensland developed a strong JUG narrative in the early 2000s that encouraged multi-sector partnerships and community engagement, reflected in the following comment by the then-Premier, Peter Beattie (Queensland Government 2001, p. 10):

> There is . . . an emerging service delivery model involving governments working in partnership with communities to determine need, devising strategies for meeting these needs, implementing activities consistent with these strategies and ultimately monitoring results. The emphasis is on community empowerment and not on traditional functional program delivery.

Between 1998 and 2003, the Queensland government developed JUG-related approaches that included both economic and social policy initiatives. Some of these included: the Wide Bay 2020 Regional Growth Management Framework strategies for population growth, fostering partnerships and agency coordination; the Breaking the Unemployment Cycle Initiative that drew on public, private and community partnerships to create employment and labour market programmes; and the Cape York Partnerships that integrated both social and economic policy initiatives to form cross-sector partnerships aimed at addressing disadvantage (Smyth, Reddel & Jones 2004).

Social policy units have also emerged in the states, underscoring the requirement for partnership approaches to address social issues. For example, the Social Policy Unit in Western Australia and the Social Inclusion Unit in South Australia that subsequently became subsumed in state departments. JUG has also been articulated as specific state policy. Examples include the *Western Australian Whole of Government Interoperability Policy* (Office of the Government Chief Information Officer 2017a) and the South Australian Government's *Working Together: A Joined-up Policy Guide* (Senior Management Council 2016). Other states have applied JUG approaches for specific strategies such as the *Whole of Government Ageing Strategy* (New South Wales Government 2011) and the *Tasmania Together 2020* long-term plan (Tasmania Together Progress Board 2006). The Victorian government has undertaken a wide range of JUG initiatives through cross-cutting policy issues, place-based initiatives, targeting populations, and across levels of government (State Services Authority 2007).

JUG has also been facilitated at the regional level through local council collaborations. These emerged in Tasmania as early as 1922, when the first Voluntary Regional Organisation of Councils was formed. Regional Organisations of Councils have formed four types of partnerships: bilateral; regional; state-wide; and sector or issue specific. At the federal level, the COAG trials and Sustainable Regions programme are examples of the national government partnering with local councils (Department of Infrastructure Regional Development and Cities 2003).

JUG has also been driven by changes in technology. In 1997, the formation of Centrelink created a service delivery network of 25 government agencies in Australia, but 'one-stop-shops' supported by digital transformations have emerged in most states and territories. Compatibility of supportive architecture has been a strong driver between federal and state/territory agencies. For example, the *Western Australian Enterprise Architecture Framework (WEAF) 1.0*, released in December 2017 (Office of the Government Chief Information Officer 2017b), identified collaboration as a key driver in providing an enterprise architecture framework that will facilitate the state's continuing compatibility with the Australian Government Architecture and Federal Enterprise Architecture Framework. Other projects have highlighted the potential of joined-up data to support joined-up policy solutions. The Western Australian Developmental Pathways Project, for example, involved connecting a large number of de-identified administrative databases in order to inform thinking related to wicked problems impacting children and young adults (Data Linkage Western Australia 2018; Stanley et al. 2011).

Clearly, JUG will continue to represent both an opportunity and a challenge in a country like Australia where political settlement is complex and where both the allocation of responsibility and control of resources makes clarity of authority and capacity very difficult. It does appear, though, that JUG remains a fixed element in the armoury of public service organisation at the national and sub-national levels. It is evident that such JUG (or 'collaboration', or 'whole-of-government') approaches will continue to be used in attempts to achieve better outcomes for service delivery.

The New Zealand experience

The unitary state of NZ, leading up to the 1980s, was highly centralised and bureaucratic in contrast to Australia's early forays into collaborative governance approaches at around the same time. In the late 1980s the country was faced with a significant fiscal crisis. During this time the World Bank threatened loss of access to loan funds unless radical action was taken. The result was a later and more radical response to the NPM reforms based on market-based management practices that had emerged earlier in other western countries.

Reforms in NZ were pervasive and notable for a greater disaggregation of government than that experienced in Australia. Central government was weakened by changes to the *State Sector Amendment Act (No. 2) 1989* and the *Public Finance Amendment Act 1992* via the formation of multiple agencies led by chief executives (Scott & Boyd 2017). As Gregory (2003, p. 43) observed, 'the reformist pendulum of the 1980s and 90s swung sharply away from "rule-drive administration" to "results-orientated management"'.

The changes to NZ's public sector during the 1980s and early 1990s led to a focus on agency performance and accountability, and increased the emphasis placed on efficiency and output delivery. Under this regime, the country recovered spectacularly from the earlier fiscal crisis. The success of the NZ reform subsequently gained international recognition and interest (Boston et al. 1996). The flip side of the 'efficiency/output' coin was the emergence of new problems in the form of constrained internal governance coordination. The challenge inherent in addressing wicked problems, which in NZ were particularly difficult in the areas of family violence and gang violence, was exacerbated by the fragmentation of service delivery across multiple agencies. Although innovation had thrived internally amongst agencies under the new governance model, the emphasis on achieving efficient output had come at the cost of limited matrix capacity for government across levels to join-up (Eppel et al. 2008). Central mechanisms that could coordinate joining-up, such as cabinet committees, had also been significantly weakened.

In 2001 in response these challenges, the NZ government made several recommendations based on a commissioned report entitled *Review of the Centre* (Ministerial Advisory Group 2001). As Halligan, Buick and O'Flynn (2011, p. 87) observed, a rebalancing and renewing of public management outcomes in NZ became crucial and several reform themes became dominant including 'capability, outcomes, integration and central agency roles within a philosophy supportive of the public sector'. The report also notably placed greater focus on cross-agency cooperation and the role of community and citizen involvement in the policy creation process (Pollitt & Bouckaert 2004, pp. 277–281; Wintringham 2002).

One of the measures advocated in the *Review of the Centre* was the establishment of 'super networks' to counter agency fragmentation (Gregory 2003). A further early response to the report was the development of 'Managing for Outcomes', a programme that required agencies to collaborate to articulate a joint description of their collective impact. Essentially this consisted of the development of value statements that widened the previously narrow output focus for benchmarking effectiveness. The programme ran from 2002 to 2004 but faded as interest waned. This early foray in JUG was largely viewed as ineffectual in three ways. First, there were no clear links between group actions and desired outcomes or opportunities for reflective practice and response. Second, reporting mechanisms to parliament led managers to be both conservative and defensive in their ambitions. Third, there had been debate whether reporting lines should point to the executive (cabinet and ministers) or the legislative branch (parliament) (Scott & Boyd 2017). Although the Managing for Outcomes programme was never officially cancelled, agencies gradually formed into organic 'sectors'. Joining-up between sector groups was driven horizontally as overlapping interests arose and joint strategies and arrangements were entered into to achieve process and outcome success (Scott & Boyd 2017).

In 2005, central direction was strengthened when the State Services Commissioner's powers were expanded and that role was given broader responsibilities to provide leadership and develop capabilities. The State Service Commission subsequently introduced 'Development Goals' that formed the basis of aspirations for how state services in NZ would be configured and performed (State Services Commission 2005). The State Services Commission (2005) identified six goals to guide practice, summarised here as: (1) the state becomes an employer of choice; (2) the development of a strong commitment to constant learning; (3) the adaptive use of information technology to support planning and coordination; (4) increased coordination between agencies; (5) increased quality of service; and (6) strengthened trust and reinforcement of the spirit of service. A subsequent inquiry undertaken and focused on the core central agencies (Department of the Prime Minister and Cabinet; State Services Commission; Treasury) found that while these core agencies had a role in aligning agencies and providing goals, this role was insufficiently developed to support the joining-up of a whole-of-government integrated approach (Treasury New Zealand 2006; see also Halligan, Buick & O'Flynn 2011, pp. 87–88).

There were, however, successful initiatives designed to coordinate policy and delivery launched in this period. These included the creation of the Government Economic and Urban Development Office and Urban Design Panels that fostered an emerging third-party institutional infrastructure (Wetzstein 2007). In 2005, the Family Violence Funding Circuit Breaker process was created (Ministry of Social Development 2005). This was a collaborative funding initiative that aimed to reduce transaction and compliance costs for community services providers who were funded across multiple agencies. Mechanisms of accountability were put in place to encourage funding providers to work collaboratively to meet joint outcomes, which was seen as the reduction of compliance costs to improve 'providers' capacity to achieve good outcomes for families experiencing violence' (Ministry of Social Development 2005, n.p.).

Governance issues in NZ after the global financial crisis in 2008 were framed by the need to find ways to provide effective service delivery given tight budget constraints. The NZ government formed the Better Public Services Advisory Group (BPSAG) in 2011 which was notable for the inclusion of leaders from the public, private and non-profit sectors. The BPSAG report (2011) had significant implications for the way agencies were organised, governed and held accountable. In response to that report, the NZ government developed a new programme that made groups of agencies collectively responsible for achieving results. This programme was built around the 'Better Public Services Results Programme' and listed ten issues, many centred on wicked problems, for which groups would be accountable. By 2017, the programme had proved highly successful as a collaborative exercise and many lessons had been learned in JUG related to effective coordination and accountability design (Scott & Boyd 2017).

Conclusion

The Australian and NZ governments' experiences of JUG are separated by different political and financial contexts. NZ, as a unitary state, may be assumed to represent a simpler challenge in relation to the achievement of the utopia of JUG as it does not have to contend with a combination of sovereign states and multiple interests within a federal constitutional settlement. Australia, with its three levels of government and multiple arrangements within those levels in relation to the constitutional settlement, might be assumed to represent a much more complex challenge in this regard.

However, both have a shared history of the Westminster system of government, bureaucracy and siloed departmental formation (refer to Chapter 5 for a more detailed look at the Westminster system of government). Both countries experienced levels of fragmentation during the NPM reforms of the late 1980s and early 1990s that witnessed a trend driving the devolution of responsibilities to government agencies. This was more marked in the case of the NZ experience. JUG has evolved in different ways in each country, but modifications to horizontal management and a stronger JUG narrative and role for central agencies that have included providing principles, guidance frameworks and accountability practices, has been a shared experience.

The overall impact of the work of successive governments and public sectors in both countries over four decades has been to establish both the aspiration and practice of JUG at the centre of the national discourse relating to public sector effectiveness, financial efficiency in the context of the expenditure of public money, and the delivery of services that meet both policy requirements and the needs of service users. The framework for these aims has also changed over time, with quasi-market funding arrangements being used to ration financial resources to those non-government agencies that are increasingly used to deliver government policy and services on the basis of efficiency and effectiveness. Overall, the need for further exploration of government experiences in this area, and the identification and exemplification of instances of success, are critical to widening the opportunity for achieving the utopia of JUG.

Notes

1 University of Western Australia, Perth WA, Australia (David.gilchrist@uwa.edu.au)
2 In 1983 David Ashworth changed his name to Perri 6. For this book we are using the word Six as the surname rather than the number 6 to avoid any confusion.

References

Better Public Services Advisory Group (BPSAG) 2011, 'Better public services advisory group report', viewed 16 January 2018, www.ssc.govt.nz/sites/all/files/bps-report-nov2011_0.pdf

Bogdanor, V (ed) 2005, *Joined-up government*, Oxford University Press for the British Academy, Oxford.

Boston, J, Martin, J, Pallot, J & Walsh, P 1996, *Public management: the New Zealand model*, Oxford University Press, Auckland.

Briggs, L 2012, 'Commissioner's foreword', *Tackling wicked problems: a public policy perspective*, viewed 16 January 2018, www.apsc.gov.au/publications-and-media/archive/publications-archive/tackling-wicked-problems

Carey, G, Crammond, B & Riley, T 2014, 'Top-down approaches to joined-up government: examining the unintended consequences of weak implementation', *International Journal of Public Administration*, vol. 38, no. 3, pp. 167–168.

Carey, G & Dickinson, H 2017, 'A longitudinal study of the implementation experiences of the Australian National Disability Insurance Scheme: investigating transformative policy change', *BMC Health Services Research*, vol. 17, no. 1, p. 570.

Carey, G, McLoughlin, P & Crammond, B 2015, 'Implementing joined-up government: lessons from the Australian social inclusion agenda', *Australian Journal of Public Administration*, vol. 74, no. 2, pp. 176–186.

Christensen, T & Laegreid, P 2007, 'The whole-of-government approach to public sector reform', *Public Administration Review*, vol. 67, no. 6, pp. 1059–1066.

Commonwealth Department of Family and Community Services 2005, *Joining up services for homeless jobseekers. Final report for the national homelessness strategy*, Australian Commonwealth Government, Canberra.

Data Linkage Western Australia 2018, 'Developmental pathways project', viewed 16 January 2018, www.datalinkage-wa.org.au/projects/developmental-pathways-project

Davies, JS 2009, 'The limits of joined-up government: towards a political analysis', *Public Administration*, vol. 87, no. 1, pp. 80–96.

Department of Infrastructure Regional Development and Cities 2003, '2002–2003 report on the operation of the Local Government, (Financial Assistance) Act 1995', viewed 16 January 2018, http://regional.gov.au/local/publications/reports/2002_2003/index.aspx

Eppel, EA, Gill, D, Lips, AMB & Ryan, B 2008, *Better connected services for Kiwis: a discussion document for managers and front-line staff on joining up the horizontal and the vertical*, Institute of Policy Studies, Victoria University of Wellington, Wellington.

Gregory, R 2003, 'All the king's horses and all the king's men: putting New Zealand's public sector back together again', *International Public Management Review*, vol. 4, no. 2, pp. 41–58.

Halligan, J, Buick, F & O'Flynn, J 2011, 'Experiments with joined-up, horizontal and whole-of-government in Anglophone countries', in A Massey (ed), *International handbook on civil service systems*, Edward Elgar, Cheltenham, pp. 74–102.

Hill, M & Hupe, P 2009, *Implementing public policy*, 2nd edn, Sage, London.

Hood, C 2005, 'The idea of joined-up government: a historical perspective', in V Bogdanor (ed), *Joined-up government*, The British Academy, Oxford, pp. 19–42.

Hunt, S 2005, 'Whole-of-government: does working together work?' *Policy and Governance Discussion Paper 05–01*, Asia Pacific School of Economics and Government, Australian National University, Canberra, viewed 16 January 2018, https://openresearch-repository.anu.edu.au/bitstream/1885/43012/2/PDP05-1.pdf

Keast, R 2011, 'Joined-up governance in Australia: how the past can inform the future', *International Journal of Public Administration*, vol. 34, no. 4, pp. 221–231.

Ling, T 2002, 'Delivering joined-up government in the UK: dimensions, issues and problems', *Public Administration*, vol. 80, no. 4, pp. 615–642.

Management Advisory Committee (MAC) 2004, 'Connecting government: whole of government responses to Australia's priority challenges', viewed 16 January 2018, www.apsc.gov.au/__data/assets/pdf_file/0006/7575/connectinggovernment.pdf

Matheson, C 2000, 'Policy formulation in Australian government: vertical and horizontal axes', *Australian Journal of Public Administration*, vol. 59, no. 2, pp. 44–55.

McDermott, S, Bruce, J, Fisher, KR & Gleeson, R 2010, 'Evaluation of the integrated services project for clients with challenging behaviour: final report', viewed 16 January 2018, www.adhc.nsw.gov.au/__data/assets/file/0006/236499/43_ISP_Evaluation_Final_Report-JUNE_2010.pdf

Meyrer, MK & Dillon, N 1999, 'Institutional paradoxes: why welfare workers can't reform welfare', in G Frederickson & J Johnston (eds), *Public administration as reform and innovation*, University of Alabama Press, Tuscaloosa.

Ministerial Advisory Group 2001, 'Report of the Advisory Group on the review of the centre', viewed 16 January 2018, www.ssc.govt.nz/upload/downloadable_files/review_of_centre.pdf

Ministry of Social Development 2005, 'Statement of intent 2005 – families and whanau', viewed 16 January 2018, www.msd.govt.nz/about-msd-and-our-work/publications-resources/corporate/statement-of-intent/2005/families-and-whanau.html

New South Wales Government 2011, 'Whole of government ageing strategy ideas pack', viewed 13 March 2018, www.adhc.nsw.gov.au/__data/assets/file/0012/241122/Ageing_strategy_ideas_pack.pdf

Office of the Government Chief Information Officer 2017a, 'The Western Australian whole of government interoperability policy', viewed 16 January 2018, http://gcio.wa.gov.au/wp-content/uploads/2016/06/Interoperability-Policy.pdf

Office of the Government Chief Information Officer 2017b, 'Western Australian enterprise architecture framework (WEAF) 1.0', viewed 16 January 2018, http://gcio.wa.gov.au/wp-content/uploads/2017/12/WA-Enterprise-Architecture-Framework-WEAF-1.0.pdf

O'Flynn, J, Buick, F, Blackman, D & Halligan, J 2011, 'You win some, you lose some: experiments with joined-up government', *International Journal of Public Administration*, vol. 34, no. 4, pp. 244–254.

Peters, BG 1996, 'Managing horizontal government: the politics of coordination', *Public Administration*, vol. 76, no. 2, pp. 298–311.

Pollitt, C 2003, 'Joined-up government: a survey', *Political Studies Review*, vol. 1, no. 1, pp. 34–49.

Pollitt, C & Bouckaert, G 2004, *Public management reform: a comparative analysis*, 2nd edn, Oxford University Press, Oxford.

Queensland Government 2001, *Smart state – investing in people and communities*, Goprint, Brisbane.

Richards, S 2001, 'Four types of joined up government and the problem of accountability', in National Audit Office, *Joining up to improve public services*, HC 383 Session 2001–2002, House of Commons, London.

Ross, S, Frere, M, Healy, L & Humphreys, C 2011, 'A whole of government strategy for family violence reform', *The Australian Journal of Public Administration*, vol. 70, no. 2, pp. 131–142.

Royal Commission on Australian Government Administration (RCAGA) 1976, *Report of the Royal Commission on Australian government administration*, Government of Australia, Canberra.

Sandfort, J 1999, 'The structural impediments to human service collaborations: examining welfare reform at the front lines', *Social Service Review*, vol. 73, no. 3, pp. 314–339.

Scott, R & Boyd, R 2017, 'Interagency performance targets: a case study of New Zealand's results programme', viewed 16 January 2018, www.ssc.govt.nz/sites/all/files/Case-Study-Interagency-Performance-Targets-IBMCCAG-2017.pdf

Senior Management Council 2016, *Working together: a joined-up policy guide*, Government of South Australia, Adelaide.

Six, P 2004, 'Joined-up government in the western world in comparative perspective: a preliminary literature review and exploration', *Journal of Public Administration Research and Theory*, vol. 14, no. 1, pp. 103–138.

Smyth, P, Reddel, T, & Jones, A 2004. 'Social inclusion, new regionalism and associational governance: the Queensland experience', *International Journal of Urban and Regional Research*, vol. 28, no. 3, pp. 601–615.

Stanley, F, Glauert, R, McKenzie, A & O'Donnell, M 2011, 'Can joined-up data lead to joined-up thinking? The Western Australian developmental pathways project', *Healthcare Policy | Politiques de Santé*, vol. 6, special issue, pp. 63–73.

State Services Authority 2007, 'Victorian approaches to joined up government: an overview', viewed 16 January 2018, http://apo.org.au/system/files/1465/apo-nid1465-99716.pdf

State Services Commission 2005, 'State services development goals', viewed 16 January 2018, www.ssc.govt.nz/node/4180

Stewart, J 2002, 'Horizontal coordination – how far have we gone and how far can we go? The Australian view', *The Public Interest*, pp. 21–26.

Tasmania Together Progress Board 2006, 'Tasmania together 2020', viewed 16 January 2018, www.tasmaniatogether.tas.gov.au

Treasury New Zealand 2006, 'Treasury report: review of central agencies' role in promoting and assuring state sector performance', viewed 16 January 2018, www.treasury.govt.nz/publications/informationreleases/exgreviews/ca

Vincent, I 1999, 'Collaboration and integrated services in the NSW public sector', *Australian Journal of Public Administration*, vol. 58, no. 3, pp. 3–12.

Wetzstein, S 2007, 'Networked governance for global economic participation: the case of New Zealand's largest service city', in PW Daniels & JW Harrington (eds), *Services and economic development in the Asia-Pacific*, Routledge, London and New York, pp. 199–220.

Wilkins, P 2002, 'Accountability and joined-up government: abstract', *Australian Journal of Public Administration*, vol. 61, no. 1, pp. 114.

Wintringham, M 2002, 'State Services Commissioner's annual report on the state services', viewed 16 January 2018, www.ssc.govt.nz/sscer-report-state-services-2002

12 Conclusion and globalising accounting, accountability and governance

Robyn Pilcher[1]

In Chapter 1, we introduced the three main themes of the book—accounting, accountability and governance—themes which are relevant to the public sector in all countries. Accounting can be traced as far back as Pacioli and Cotrugli (Yamey 1994) and today continues to develop as new standards, policies, procedures and legislation are introduced into both the private and public sectors. Under New Public Management (NPM), the distinction between these two sectors became blurred as private sector performance criteria and ideas were transferred to the public sector. This blurring was very evident with the worldwide shift in the last 40 years or so from cash accounting to the accrual basis of accounting in much of the public sector—in particular, governments (Carlin 2005; Tickell 2010).

The alleged reason for the introduction of accrual accounting was to improve the efficiency and effectiveness of management practices and reporting in the public sector. The development of NPM was seen as a means by which to enhance accountability and transparency of governments and this, in turn, required financial information that was more comparable, relevant and useful for decision-making within the public sector. Following on from this, according to Bolivar and Galera (2007), the International Financial Reporting Standards (IFRS) could provide the benchmark for improving the quality of financial reporting.

Hence, we have (allegedly) improved financial reporting and generated more transparent and accountable organisations, all under the umbrella of improved governance. In the private sector there was an attempt to define corporate governance and establish guidelines with the release of several reports, including Cadbury (1992); Greenbury (1995), Hampel (1998) and OECD (1999). According to Goddard (2005), the principles contained in these reports and underlying the private sector guidelines were extended to the public sector by Nolan (1995), Sharman (2001) and Langlands (2005), to name a few.

Traditionally, governments have used cash-based accounting systems and input-based budgeting systems. New Zealand (NZ), Australia, Canada and the United States (US) were the first to transition to accrual accounting. They were closely followed by the United Kingdom (UK), Europe and Sweden (van der Hoek 2005). So, in the western world at least, accrual accounting in some form has been adopted by governments. These countries did so in order to improve the efficiency and effectiveness of the public sector—and hence its accountability and transparency. Many other countries have also adopted a form of accrual accounting, but here we are concentrating on developed countries.

Accounting, accountability and governance in the global world

Since the introduction of accrual accounting (in its many forms) in the public sector, we have seen the development of IFRS and another push for change. This has proven to again be controversial and Chapter 2 examines a potential way to deal with the complexities of IFRS by analysing a modified form considered in Australia. This form comes under the concept of differential reporting – a topic that became more prominent with the introduction of the International Accounting Standards Board's (IASB's) *IFRS for Small and Medium-sized Entities (SMEs)* in July 2009 (IASB 2009). For countries like Australia and NZ that had been pioneers in adopting IFRS for the public sector, it provided an avenue to reduce the complexity of IFRS for organisations struggling with fulfilling all the standards' requirements.

Differential reporting began to be debated in countries such as the UK, the US and Australia back in the 1980s. According to Ceustermans, Branson and Breesch (2012), differential reporting is simply the idea that there are different reporting requirements for different types of entities. What is different in the financial reporting chain needs to be decided, as does how the 'new' reporting requirements should be derived. Whether different measurement and recognition principles should also be considered is a controversial opinion debated by those such as Eierle 2005; Knutson and Wichmann 1985; Marriott, Collis and Marriott 2006.

Apart from Australia and NZ, Europe, the UK, Ireland, the US and Africa are amongst those countries and continents considering differential reporting. As explored in Chapter 2, financial reporting requirements become an issue when costs of compliance and implementation exceed benefits for particular entities. Given IFRS was originally produced with the private sector in mind, smaller businesses and the public sector often struggle with its complexity. The IASB (2014) argued that the simplicity of IFRS for SMEs came about by excluding standards such as those associated with earnings per share and segment reporting. Policies were also simplified, as was the measurement of assets with the option to revalue no longer required (IASB 2014).

Unfortunately, it was immediately obvious that there would be issues with adoption of IFRS for SMEs as one of the original aims of IFRS was harmonisation. As soon as the IASB (n.d., in Bouvier 2013) indicated that selection of entities allowed to use the standard would be jurisdictional, then any hope of comparability between countries was lost. The IASB also claimed that publicly accountable organisations (such as many public sector entities) would not be able to adopt IFRS for SMEs (confirmed in a meeting by the IFRS Advisory Council 10 June 2013 (IASB 2013)).

In 2011, the UK government released policies claiming that the UK would become one of the premier places in Europe for small businesses to develop and grow (HM Treasury 2011). One way of doing this was to reduce complexity of financial reporting. Hence, in both the UK and Ireland differential reporting was adopted by way of IFRS for SMEs with the IASB's 2009 standard revised and released in 2015 as *FRS 102 The Financial Reporting Standard Applicable in the UK and Republic of Ireland* (UK Financial Reporting Council 2015a) and *FRS 105 The Financial Reporting Standard applicable to the Micro-entities Regime* (UK Financial Reporting Council 2015b).

Prior to the release of these two standards, an interesting article was published in *Accounting and Business Research* providing early evidence of the due process associated with adoption of IFRS for SMEs in various countries. Kaya and Koch (2015) found that in Europe the implementation decision had been a controversial one with the European Commission (EC) releasing an Accounting Directive stating 'IFRS for SMEs would not appropriately serve the objectives of simplification and reduction of administrative burden' (EC 2013, para. 12). Kaya and Koch (2015) forecasted, based on their findings, that the UK and Ireland would not adopt the IASB's version of IFRS for SMEs but would first modify it to suit their economic and political needs (Ball 2006). This forecast proved to be accurate, as witnessed above.

On the other side of the world, the US has not implemented differential reporting as it is yet to adopt IFRS (Negash, Holt & Hathorn 2017).

From considering overall accounting standards, we move on to deliberate international treatment of just one standard—that of depreciation. There has been considerable research on asset management and depreciation of infrastructure in Australia and NZ as detailed in Chapter 3. Depreciation is a topic that has been debated for many centuries with possibly one of the earliest theories, that of falling price, being expressed by the Roman Vitruvius who described annual depreciation as 'the price of passing of each year' (Chatfield 1977, p. 96). Depreciation is a topic that every few years raises its head and becomes an issue for debate, goes quiet for a while, then comes to the fore once again. The inability to obtain overall agreement on depreciation was succinctly summarised by Sterling (1975, p. 28) who claimed the topic and its related problems have been debated, pushed aside and debated again and would continue to be so in the future—'recycled ideas without resolving issues'.

Concentrating on depreciation of infrastructure in a global environment, in the US there was very little mention of depreciation prior to 1830 and the invention of the steam engine (Woodward 1956). In September of 1835, the Baltimore and Ohio Railroad annual report (as cited in Woodward 1956, p. 71) mentioned the concept 'after carrying $75,000 to the debit of profit and loss to make good deterioration of the railway and machinery'. Unfortunately, there was never any consistency to the way depreciation was accounted for by the railways. For example, while Baltimore and Ohio accounted for depreciation as a separate provision, others charged the replacement cost as an expense (Woodward 1956).

Then, in 1878, the US Supreme Court criticised the practice of reducing operating expenses by depreciation and would only allow expenditure actually incurred to be deducted from overall gross earnings (*US v Kansas Pacific Railway*

Company, [1878] 99 US 455). Turning to current issues in the 21st century, from a practical perspective it has been indicated in the US that by not putting money aside to cover depreciation, infrastructure replacement cost could be in the trillions of dollars (see as follows). Surowiecki (2016,p. n.p.) encapsulated it as follows:

> From the crumbling bridges of California to the overflowing sewage drains of Houston and the rusting railroad tracks in the Northeast Corridor, decaying infrastructure is all around us.

In 2017, the American Society of Civil Engineers (ASCE) gave America's overall infrastructure a D+ rating, claiming US$3.6 trillion needed to be spent by 2025 to bring it to an acceptable standard (in other words a B rating) (ASCE 2017) If American politicians do not follow this advice, then the ASCE (2017, p. 7) forecast:

- US$3.9 trillion in losses to the US GDP by 2025;
- US$7 trillion in lost business sales by 2025;
- 2.5 million lost American jobs in 2025.

Here is a very real consequence of years of mis-management for political and other reasons as examined in Chapter 3. Another potential area ripe for more research.

Moving briefly onto the UK and Europe, Pitts's (1998) study of British coal companies 1864–1914 found that a large variety of depreciation policy and disclosure policy existed and that the practice for depreciation varied from company to company and within a company over time. Sound familiar? Healy and Wahlen (1999, p. 368) suggested that earnings management:

> occurs when managers use judgment in financial reporting and in structuring transactions to alter financial reports to either mislead some stakeholders about the underlying economic performance of the company or to influence contractual outcomes that depend on reported accounting numbers.

It appears that infrastructure management figures are known by some in the UK to be manipulated for reasons, such as political (Giles 2005). Given the lack of resources in most countries, infrastructure deterioration is expected. However, ideas raised in Chapter 3 combined with information such as that provided in the UK news media (Lancefield 2017, p. 1)—'thousands of UK bridges at risk of collapse, warns RAC'—means there is still a lot of work to do in this area of research.

As would have become obvious in Chapter 3's discourse on depreciation (and in many of the other chapters as well as from the multitude of references provided), accountability and transparency are essential qualities for both the private and public sectors. We have seen in the US the corporate catastrophes of Enron, WorldCom and Tyco; in the UK, examples include the Bank of Credit and Commerce International and Barings Bank; in Italy there was the collapse of Parmalat;

whilst in Australia HIH and One.Tel were also disasters. Investigations into the collapses uncovered evidence of fraud, malpractice by senior officials, irresponsible business practices and, more often than not, indications of creative accounting, manipulation and miscommunication (Porter 2009). From this we saw an outcry from the public for better accountability and transparency and auditors put under pressure to perform to a much higher standard.

For the public sector, accountability is just as important, if not more so—after all, it is the taxpayers' funds that are at stake. As well, in the public sector, accountability from parliament to its multiple stakeholders is complex. It is 'not a simple one-to-one relationship between a principal and agent' (Mayston 1993, p. 77) but a relationship between a number of different groups with overlapping economic and political interests (Pilcher et al. 2013). As Dobel (2015, p. 304) claimed, to ensure transparency and integrity 'public institutions should be enmeshed in a web of accountability'.

Chapter 4 examines a framework of accountability, designed to ensure financial accountability does not preclude public accountability. The Australian political system is based on the Westminster doctrine of responsible government. This doctrine holds a key assumption that parliament is the dominant body in a chain of accountability allowing the electorate to hold those who govern accountable for their actions. Thus, as the central player in the chain of accountability, parliament is accountable to the public (Davis et al. 1993).

To capture the changes in government reporting over a period of 30 years, thus encapsulating the move from cash accounting to accrual accounting and NPM, Chapter 4 uses a case study approach. What is apparent from the case study is that accounting reforms have introduced uncertainty and, more particularly, confusion in government reporting both in terms of what is reported and where it is reported. There is now detailed information presented in a variety of formats and reports, ironically resulting in a lack of clarity. This clearly affects the use of the various reporting processes as accountability mechanisms. The portfolio budget statements are diminished in their capacity to perform an accountability function since they no longer include the capacity to compare budget to actual figures—something essential to compare future performance.

Mack (in Chapter 4) refers to research in the UK on the introduction of accrual accounting (badged as resource accounting). When referring to the multiple corporate collapses above, the fraudulent behaviour and publicised scandals in the not-for-profit (NFP) sector (for example, in charities) were not mentioned. Connolly and Hyndman (2013) provided a case study approach to their exploration of the need to increase accountability and transparency in this sector in the UK. They (2013, p. 259) explained that under the *Charities Act 2006* (UK), the Charity Commission in England and Wales had been 'charged with responsibility for: enhancing charitable accountability; increasing public trust and confidence; and promoting the effective use of charitable funds'. Comparable legislation exists in both Scotland and Northern Ireland. Similar to the findings in Chapter 4, it was determined that not only financial accountability needs to be discharged, but there is also a requirement for more emphasis on non-financial indicators and performance.

With countries like the Netherlands, Iran and China also beginning to question public sector accountability and the place of accrual accounting and budgeting, this area still provides an abundance of research opportunities to be explored (Abolhallaje 2014; Ma & Hou 2009; van der Hoek 2005).

Chapter 4's reference to the Westminster system and responsible government provides readers with a smooth transition into Chapter 5. That chapter considers this system in far more depth. It details the original development of British colonies in Australia, NZ, Canada and South Africa and with this the transference of English culture, education, economic thinking, political thought, religion and literature. Great Britain, being the Imperial centre, also influenced the type of government and how resources were used and accounted for. As the years went by, this influence faded somewhat as the colonies became more independent and developed their own political power and subsequent accounting systems.

Although Chapter 5 is based on the Westminster system and hence constrained in its applicability to some countries, the findings themselves are not limited. Gilchrist (Chapter 5) determines that where politicians could exploit the weaknesses inherent in the Westminster system in order to win over their electorate, they would and will continue to do so. One interesting idea speculated was that accountability mechanisms may not be linked as closely to historical roots as originally thought—bringing into question many perceptions about the influence of history. Greenaway (1995) also questioned these perceptions as he dissected the Thatcher government in the UK and the changing face of parliament.

Chapter 5 considers practical problems associated with sovereignty and this raises an interesting point when it comes to dual sovereignties. Thompson (2004), in his article on the takeover of Hong Kong and the move from English sovereignty to Chinese sovereignty, raised multiple issues. Unlike in Chapter 5, it did not just have internal political and local electorates to contend with, but such a change in sovereignty impacted on many other jurisdictions as well. I would also suggest that governments were less interested in responsible government and the well-being of citizens and more interested in political advantages to be gained elsewhere. Canada, as a former UK colony, is another country ripe for research on the basis of some of the findings in Chapter 5.

Still on politics, we move onto Chapter 6 and voter turnout which *is* an area applicable to any democratically governed country. Finding an association with something such as pre-election reporting is just one method of trying to increase voter turnout, especially in countries where voting is not compulsory. The idea that governments are appearing more transparent by releasing these reports should be seen as a positive attempt at an accountability mechanism. This is not always the case.

There are many other reasons for people deciding whether to vote or not in political elections. These reasons can include age, education, residential mobility, region, media exposure, mobilisation (partisan and non-partisan), voting in a previous election, party identification, political interest and political knowledge (Smets & van Ham 2013). In the political science arena there has been a lot of research on voter turnout in the UK, US and Europe. However, in the economic and business area, there is far less research and, in the specific area examined in

Chapter 6, there is very little, if anything. This not only makes this chapter unique but provides the catalyst for multiple areas of future research to occur in all countries worldwide.

If we consider what has been researched in the accounting arena, Ingram and Copeland (1981) examined the usefulness of current municipal financial reports when it came to voters making a decision about whom to elect as mayor. Their research was not trying to find a direct link between accounting numbers and election decisions, but Ingram and Copeland (1981) were more interested in whether financial reports had any impact on decisions made by users. Given 'financial reporting objectives should consider the needs of users and the decisions they make' (GASB 1987, p. 1), it makes sense for this topic to be considered by global researchers now. As explained in Chapter 6, the findings will contribute to practice by way of additional mechanisms for government accountability.

Parliamentary accountability via transparent reporting is considered in Chapter 6 in regards to voter turnout. However, the financial reporting is only reliable if the audit process is above reproach. To ensure this, it is important that the audit offices (those doing the checking) are also accountable and that there is oversight of their performance. Chapter 7 provides us with insight into audit offices in Australia and the statutory review process.

Throughout the world, public sector oversight bodies—supreme audit institutions (SAIs), parliamentary ombudspersons, auditors-general, anti-corruption commissions, public service commissions and so on—are responsible for improving public sector performance (Kells & Hodge 2009). They are also responsible for ensuring the integrity of all processes, financial and non-financial. Researchers have begun to show a keen interest in monitoring information from these oversight bodies and analysing the impact on public sector organisational performance (Kells & Hodge 2009). However, more analysis needs to be done in order to determine exactly what is being achieved with these performance audits.

In Canada, Ferguson and Rafuse (2004) provided an insight into the integrity of an SAI with the aim of their research being to assess and review the performance audit practice of the Office of the Auditor-General. An external review was conducted with representatives of SAIs from the UK, Norway, the Netherlands and France. Obviously this type of review is expensive and time consuming, so the process in Australia of statutory reviews may be a more achievable way of 'watching the watchdog'.

Chapter 7 demonstrates just how much accounting, accountability and governance are linked—in particular the last two. Chapter 8 also considers performance audit but this time from a governance perspective. It compares performance audits with operational audits and links both to governance within an NPM framework. Globally, both performance audits and operational audits have a long history in the public and private sectors. However, these terms have been applied interchangeably both in theory and practice. Ambiguities are claimed, in Chapter 8, to exist around their similarities and differences which, in turn, potentially impact the quality of their performance and, therefore, of the outcomes associated with these important assurance activities (Vafaei 2016).

It is this ambiguity as well as lack of a clear definition that Chapter 8 raises as an important area for future research. This assertion supports previous research internationally. For example, Kells and Hodge (2009, p. 34) claimed a lack of clarity about the nature and definition of performance audit is a barrier to progress in this field of research. Performance audits (often referred to as value-for-money audits) became popular after the Second World War, particularly in the UK and Sweden. Unfortunately, if we consider operational audits, more of the confusion contended in Chapter 8 is, once again, prominent. However, adding to the confusion is how the term 'operational audit' is used. Flesher and Zarzeski (2002) treated the two terms—performance and operational audit—interchangeably, dependent on the country. So, we can see, research opportunities still abound in this area.

Performance audits can provide both an external and internal accountability mechanism, thus improving the overall governance of the organisation. Performance indicators can provide the data by which to judge the organisation's overall performance as well as enhance the accountability and transparency of that specific sector. At least, that is the theory behind performance indicators. Performance management links into this discussion as well as NPM and the public sector reforms of the 1980s and 1990s. The move for the public sector to borrow many of the management strategies from the private sector was a worldwide trend that resulted in the transformation of the public sector (Akbar, Pilcher & Perrin 2012). Accountability is linked very closely to governance in much of the NPM literature interlinked with performance (Akbar, Pilcher & Perrin 2012; Keasey & Wright 1993). As detailed in Chapter 9, much of the prior literature on public sector performance management is pessimistic. For example, Lee and Fisher (2007) found that perceived usefulness of performance information in the Australian public sector was higher than actual usefulness. This claim was supported by de Bruijn (2007) and, earlier, Berman (2002).

Performance management and the use of performance indicators has been a source of much research globally over the years. Unfortunately, it is too easy, still, to manipulate figures to fit the ratio required, including in governments. If an organisation is being judged based on their performance indicators, then the temptation is always there to enhance those results. As Kravchuk and Schack (1996, p. 349) claimed:

> Ultimately, a system of performance measures does no good if it does not inform decision makers. Worse, it can do great harm if it misrepresents, misleads, or introduces perverse behavioural incentives.

Pilcher (2009) found depreciation was being manipulated in local governments in Australia to produce several of their key performance indicators. This was supported by Pilcher and Van der Zahn (2010). Although we are concentrating on developed countries, it is interesting to note that developing countries, such as Indonesia, have also been at the forefront of much of the research around performance indicators. For example, Mimba, van Helden and Tillema (2007) found that many government agencies focused on the compliance of formal requirements rather than the functional use of the performance information. Back to developed countries, there has been a lot of work in looking into why public sector organisations respond to the pressure of performance indicators as they do. Oliver (1991) found that manipulation was one such response as the organisations tried to cope with multiple constituent demands and expectations. In the public sector, political influence is usually lurking in the background (Johnsen 1999).

The previous two chapters considered performance audits and Chapter 9 also suggests this method as one which may be able to assist with the problem of, for example, gaming (defined by Bevan and Hood (2006) as the exploiting of grey areas to present a more favourable impression of performance than might otherwise be warranted). When billions of dollars are at stake (as in the case study in Chapter 9), then more research in this area is required.

Another area where manipulation and fraud have often been in the media is the use of resources, and accounting for such resources, in charities and other not-for-profit (NFP) organisations (Dhanani & Connolly 2012). Like the public sector, the NFP sector has also gone through a reform period, with accountability, transparency and governance a major component of the change. In fact, the purpose, mission and/or objects of an association (the area of NFP organisations that is the focus for Chapter 10) have become central to debates regarding governance, sustainability, efficiency and arrangements associated with government procurement from NFP organisations (Frumkin 2005; Wilkins & Gilchrist 2016). From a definitional perspective, there is a lot of debate surrounding the NFP sector, but Chapter 10 concentrates on the omission, in many definitions, of the sector's mission.

Like the public sector, the NFP sector is now subject to accounting standards and regulations. In the US, the Financial Accounting Standards Board (FASB 2006) released *FASB Statement No. 157 Fair Value Measurements*, adapted for the NFP sector under FASB (2010) ASC Topic 820 *Fair Value Measurements*. This standard is, as would be expected, causing much angst for NFP organisations as it expects items such as gifts-in-kind to be given a value (Brenner 2013). The adoption of a standard far more suited to the private sector is in conflict with the mission of many charities. This is another example of where taking on commercial foci (or private sector concepts) is over-riding the basic mission of NFP organisations.

Another example of NFP organisations managing their numbers can be found in the work of Connolly, Hyndman and McConville (2013). Again, with the introduction of accrual accounting, the call by stakeholders for more accountability and transparency, and hence the need for greater governance, saw the introduction of efficiency ratios into the sector. Unfortunately, the results reported in Connolly, Hyndman and McConville (2013) indicated non-compliance with the latest standards and legislation; questionable quality in regards to what disclosures were provided; and limited visibility of ratios (and, therefore, less chance of outside scrutiny). Adding to these disturbing findings was the fact that auditors often failed to report non-compliance (Connolly, Hyndman & McConville 2013). One suggestion provided by the authors was that performance of managers be judged against the NFP's mission, not financial ratios. Therefore, this need to recognise and reward the achievement of a NFP organisation's mission is one that needs more research globally.

We finish the book with one final chapter—Chapter 11—that provides, like the other chapters, experiences in Australia and NZ which can form the basis for more global research. In fact, the topic—joined-up government (JUG)—is one that actually began in the UK. As we saw in previous chapters, NPM became popular in the UK with the Thatcher government in the 1980s. At that time government was seen to be becoming 'increasingly defined not as the solution to societal problems, but instead the very root and cause of these problems' (Peters & Pierre 2000, p. 62). Hence, solutions for a better type of service delivery were sought. JUG was used as a label for service reform under the Blair government and entailed the combining of public, private and voluntary sector bodies to achieve a common goal. In the Blair government's second term, there was a change of focus for JUG from agency creation to good governance (Matthews 2008).

With good governance came the need for improved accountability (which, under JUG, was proving to be a nightmare) and so there arose a distinction between vertical and horizontal accountability (Hodges 2012). This issue with accountability was highlighted in Christensen, Fimreite and Laegreid (2014) where ambiguity in accountability relations was still apparent. Christensen, Fimreite and Laegreid (2014) also found problems with political control and, thus, overall governance of the operation. Unfortunately, there were very few positive outcomes experienced in Norway in regards to welfare administrative reform. Christensen, Fimreite and Laegreid (2014, p. 452) claimed:

> The idea behind the reform – to increase the capacity of government to cut across existing policy fields and in that way handle 'wicked issues' in the various welfare fields – is still struggling to be implemented.

Conclusion

One can see there are still multiple areas of research to be conducted and brought to the attention of the world. Our book has formed the basis for future research with experiences in Australia and NZ laying the foundation for research in years to come. Look to history and it will inform the present and the future. Accounting, accountability and governance are all linked and, as Uhr (2015) claimed, we can take a lesson from Shakespeare's *Macbeth*. By 'aligning the challenges of personal and public integrity', accountability and governance in the public sector can only improve (Uhr 2015, p. 280). I'll leave you with this thought from Dobel (2015, p. 305):

> Shakespeare reminds us that . . . a realistic public service needs transparency, multiple accountability mechanisms, and active reassertion of the importance of public service as a calling to counteract the limits of the public service and human nature.

Note

1 Curtin University, Perth WA, Australia (r.pilcher@curtin.edu.au).

References

Abolhallaje, M 2014, 'Financial management reforms in the health sector: a comparative study between cash-based and accrual-based accounting systems', *Medical Journal of the Iranian Red Crescent*, vol. 16, no. 10, pp. 1–5.

Akbar, R, Pilcher, R & Perrin, B 2012, 'Performance measurement in Indonesia: the case of local government', *Pacific Accounting Review*, vol. 24, no. 3, pp. 262–291.

American Society of Civil Engineers (ASCE) 2017, 'Infrastructure report card: a comprehensive assessment of America's infrastructure', viewed 20 February 2018, www.infrastructurereportcard.org/

Ball, R 2006, 'International financial reporting standards (IFRS): pros and cons for investors', *Accounting & Business Research*, vol. 36, supp. 1, pp. 5–27.

Berman, E 2002, 'How useful is performance measurement', *Public Performance & Management Review*, vol. 25, no. 4, pp. 348–351.

Bevan, G & Hood, C 2006, 'What's measured is what matters: targets and gaming in the English public health care system', *Public Administration*, vol. 84, no. 3, pp. 517–538.

Bolivar, M & Galera, A 2007, 'Could fair value accounting be useful, under NPM models, for users of financial information?', *International Review of Administrative Sciences*, vol. 73, no. 3, pp. 473–502.

Bouvier, S 2013, 'IASB ends review of IFRS for SMEs, maintains stance to prevent wider use', *Accounting, Policy & Practice Report*, vol. 9, no. 14, pp. 572–573.

Brenner, J 2013, 'Gifts-in-kind: what are they worth?' *Journal of Accountancy*, vol. 216, no. 2, pp. 44–48.

Cadbury, A 1992, *Report of the committee on the financial aspects of corporate governance*, Gee Publishing, London.

Carlin, T 2005, 'Debating the impact of accrual accounting and reporting in the public sector', *Financial Accountability & Management*, vol. 21, no. 3, pp. 309–336.

Ceustermans, S, Branson, J & Breesch, D 2012, 'Differential financial reporting requirements: developing a framework using a multi-actor multi-criteria analysis', *SSRN Electronic Journal*, https://ssrn.com/abstract=2005053

Chatfield, M 1977, *A history of accounting thought*, Robert E Krieger Publishing Company, New York.

Christensen, T, Fimreite, A & Laegreid, P 2014, 'Joined-up government for welfare administration reform in Norway', *Public Organization Review*, vol. 14, no. 4, pp. 439–456.

Connolly, C & Hyndman, N 2013, 'Charity accountability in the UK: through the eyes of the donor', *Qualitative Research in Accounting & Management*, vol. 10, no. 3/4, pp. 259–278.

Connolly, C, Hyndman, N & McConville, D 2013, 'Conversion ratios, efficiency and obfuscation: a study of the impact of changed UK charity accounting requirements on external stakeholders', *Voluntas*, vol. 24, no. 3, pp. 785–804.

Davis, G, Wanna, J, Warhurst, J & Weller, P 1993, *Public policy in Australia*, 2nd edn, Allen & Unwin, St Leonards, NSW.

de Bruijn, H 2007, *Managing performance in the public sector*, Routledge, Taylor and Francis Group, London.

Dhanani, A & Connolly, C 2012, 'Discharging not-for-profit accountability: UK charities and public discourse', *Accounting, Auditing & Accountability Journal*, vol. 25, no. 7, pp. 1140–1169.

Dobel, JP 2015, 'The fragility of public service: a study of *Richard II* and *Measure for Measure*', *Public Integrity*, vol. 17, no. 3, pp. 291–307.

Eierle, B 2005, 'Differential reporting in Germany: a historical analysis', *Accounting, Business & Financial History*, vol. 15, no. 3, pp. 279–315.

European Commission (EC) 2013, 'Financial reporting obligations for limited liability companies', *Accounting Directive*, viewed 20 February 2018, http://europa.eu/rapid/press-release_MEMO-13-540_de.htm

Ferguson, A & Rafuse, B 2004, 'Who audits the auditor? the international peer review of the Office of the Auditor General of Canada', *International Journal of Government Auditing*, vol. 31, no. 4, pp. 10–15.

Financial Accounting Standards Board (FASB) 2006, 'Statement of financial accounting standards No. 157, fair value measurements', September, Financial Accounting Foundation, Norwalk, Connecticut.

Financial Accounting Standards Board (FASB) 2010, 'Fair value measurements topic 820, An amendment of the Accounting Standards Codification (ASC)', January, Financial Accounting Foundation, Norwalk, Connecticut.

Financial Reporting Council (UK) 2015a, 'FRS 102 the financial reporting standard applicable in the UK and Republic of Ireland', July, Financial Reporting Council, London.

Financial Reporting Council (UK) 2015b, 'FRS 105 the financial reporting standard applicable to the micro-entities regime', July, Financial Reporting Council, London.

Flesher, DL & Zarzeski, MT 2002, 'The roots of operational (value for money) auditing in English speaking nations', *Accounting & Business Research*, vol. 32, no. 2, pp. 93–104.

Frumkin, P 2005, *On being nonprofit: a conceptual and policy primer*, Harvard University Press, Cambridge.

Giles, C 2005, 'Statistics revision "difficult" ahead of election', *Financial Times*, 23 February, Financial Times Limited, London.

Goddard, A 2005, 'Accounting and NPM in UK local government – contributions towards governance and accountability', *Financial Accountability & Management*, vol. 21, no. 2, pp. 191–218.

Governmental Accounting Standards Board (GASB) 1987, *Concepts statement no. 1 of the Governmental Accounting Standards Board – Objectives of Financial Reporting*, GASB, Stamford, CT.

Greenaway, J 1995, 'Having the bun and the halfpenny: can old public service ethics survive in the new Whitehall?' *Public Administration*, vol. 73, no. 3, pp. 357–374.

Greenbury, R 1995, *Directors' remuneration: report of a study group chaired by Sir Richard Greenbury*, Gee Publishing, London.

Hampel, R 1998, *Committee on corporate governance: final report*, Gee Publishing, London.

Healy, P &Wahlen, J 1999, 'A review of the earnings management literature and its implications for standard setting', *Accounting Horizons*, vol. 13 no. 4, pp. 365–383.

HM Treasury 2011, 'The plan for growth', viewed 20 February 2018, www.gov.uk/government/uploads/system/uploads/attachment_data/file/31584/2011budget_growth.pdf

Hodges, R 2012, 'Joined-up government and the challenges to accounting and accountability researchers', *Financial Accountability & Management*, vol. 28, no. 1, pp. 26–51.

Ingram, RW & Copeland, RM 1981, 'Municipal accounting information and voting behavior', *The Accounting Review*, vol. 56, no. 4, pp. 830–843.

International Accounting Standards Board (IASB) 2009, 'International financial reporting standard for small and medium-sized entities (IFRS for SMEs)', viewed 30 August 2015, http://ifrs.org

International Accounting Standards Board (IASB) 2013, 'IASB update', June 2013, viewed 20 February 2018, www.ifrs.org/-/media/feature/news/updates/iasb/2013/iasb-update-june-2013.pdf

International Accounting Standards Board (IASB) 2014, 'About the IFRS for SMEs', viewed 30 August 2015, www.ifrs.org/IFRS-for-SMEs/Pages/IFRS-for-SMEs.aspx#

Johnsen, Å 1999, 'Implementation mode and local government performance measurement: a Norwegian experience', *Financial Accountability & Management*, vol. 15, no. 1, pp. 41–66.

Kaya, D & Koch, M 2015, 'Countries' adoption of the International Financial Reporting Standard for small and medium-sized entities (IFRS for SMEs) – early empirical evidence', *Accounting & Business Research*, vol. 45, no. 1, pp. 93–120.

Keasey, K & Wright, M 1993, 'Corporate governance: issues and concerns', *Accounting & Business Research*, vol. 23, no. 91A, pp. 301–313.

Kells, S & Hodge, G 2009, 'Performance auditing in the public sector: reconceptualising the task', *The Journal of Contemporary Issues in Business & Government*, vol. 15, no. 2, pp. 36–60.

Knutson, DL & Wichmann, H 1985, 'The accounting standards overload problem for American small businesses', *Journal of Business Finance & Accounting*, vol. 12, no. 3, pp. 387–397.

Kravchuk, RS & Schack, RW 1996, 'Designing effective performance-measurement systems under the *Government Performance and Results Act* of 1993', *Public Administration Review*, vol. 56, no. 4, pp. 348–358.

Lancefield, N 2017, 'Thousands of UK bridges at risk of collapse, warns RAC', *Independent*, 10 March, viewed 23 May 2017, www.independent.co.uk/news/uk/home-news/thousands-uk-bridges-substandard-at-risk-of-collapse-not-fit-to-take-weight-lorries-hgvs-a7621661.html

Langlands, A 2005, *Good governance standard for public services: the independent commission on good governance in public services*, OPM (Office for Public Management) and CIPFA (Chartered Institute of Public Finance and Accountancy), London.

Lee, J & Fisher, G 2007, 'The perceived usefulness and use of performance information in the Australian public sector', *Accounting, Accountability & Performance*, vol. 13, no. 1, pp. 42–73.

Ma, J & Hou, Y 2009, 'Budgeting for accountability: a comparative study of budget reforms in the United States during the progressive era and in contemporary China', *Public Administration Review*, vol. 69, no. 1, pp. 553–559.

Marriott, N, Collis, J & Marriott, P 2006, *Qualitative review of the accounting and auditing needs of small and medium-sized companies and their stakeholders*, Professional Oversight Board for Accountancy, London.

Matthews, F 2008, 'Ensuring the capacity to deliver – new Labour and the public service agreement framework, 1997–2007', *The International Journal of Leadership in Public Services*, vol. 4, no. 3, pp. 37–52.

Mayston, D 1993, 'Principals, agents and the economics of accountability in the new public sector', *Accounting Auditing & Accountability Journal*, vol. 6, no. 3, pp. 68–96.

Mimba, NPSH, van Helden, G & Tillema, S 2007, 'Public sector performance measurement in developing countries', *Journal of Accounting & Organisational Change*, vol. 3, no. 3, pp. 192–208.

Negash, M, Holt, A & Hathorn, J 2017, 'The changing IFRS debate in the USA: a rejoinder', *Journal of Accounting & Organizational Change*, vol. 13, no. 1, pp. 65–84.

Nolan, M 1995, *First report of the committee on standards in public life*, CMND 2850(1), HMSO, London.

OECD 1999, *OECD principles of corporate governance*, Organisation for Economic Co-operation and Development, Paris.

Oliver, C 1991, 'Strategic responses to institutional processes', *Academy of Management Review*, vol. 16, no. 1, pp. 145–179.

Peters, BG & Pierre, J 2000, *Governance, politics and the state*, Palgrave Macmillan, Basingstoke.

Pilcher, R 2009, 'Deconstructing local government performance and infrastructure measurement', *Asian Review of Accounting*, vol. 17, no. 2, pp. 163–176.

Pilcher, R, Gilchrist, D, Singh, H & Singh, I 2013, 'The interface between internal and external audit in the Australian public sector', *Australian Accounting Review*, vol. 23, no. 4, pp. 330–340.

Pilcher, R & Van der Zahn, M 2010, 'Local governments, unexpected depreciation and financial performance adjustment', *Financial Accountability & Management Journal*, vol. 26, no. 3, pp. 299–324.

Pitts, MV 1998, 'Did dividends dictate depreciation in British coal companies 1864–1914?' *Accounting History*, vol. 3, no. 2, pp. 37–67.

Porter, B 2009, 'The audit trinity: the key to securing corporate accountability', *Managerial Auditing Journal*, vol. 24, no. 2, pp. 156–182.

Sharman Lord 2001, *Holding to account: the review of audit and accountability for central government*, HM Treasury, London.

Smets, K & van Ham, C 2013, 'The embarrassment of riches? A meta-analysis of individual-level research on voter turnout', *Electoral Studies*, vol. 32, no. 2, pp. 344–359.

Sterling, RR 1975, 'Toward a science of accounting', *Financial Analysts Journal*, vol. 31, no. 5, pp. 28–36.

Surowiecki, J 2016, 'System overload', *The New Yorker Financial Page*, 18 April, viewed 1 February 2018, www.newyorker.com/magazine/2016/04/18/inside-americas-infrastructure-problem

Thompson, E 2004, 'The political economy of national competitiveness: "One country, two systems" and Hong Kong's diminished international business reputation', *Review of International Political Economy*, vol. 11, no. 1, pp. 62–97.

Tickell, G 2010, 'Cash to accrual accounting: one nation's dilemma', *International Business & Economics Research Journal*, vol. 9, no. 11, pp. 71–78.

Uhr, J 2015, 'Investigating public integrity in *Macbeth*', *Public Integrity*, vol. 17, no. 3, pp. 279–290.

Vafaei, E 2016, 'Operational auditing within Australian internal audit departments: developing a framework', doctoral thesis, Curtin University, Perth, Australia.

van der Hoek, MP 2005, 'From cash to accrual budgeting and accounting in the public sector: the Dutch experience', *Public Budgeting & Finance*, vol. 25, no. 1, pp. 32–45.

Wilkins, P & Gilchrist, D 2016, 'Accountability for the public policy contribution of not-for-profit organisations: who is accountable to whom and for what?' in R Pablo Guerrero & P Wilkins (eds), *Doing public good? Private actors, evaluation and public value*, vol. 23, Comparative Policy Evaluation, Routledge, New York, pp. 49–66.

Woodward, PD 1956, 'Depreciation – the development of an accounting concept', *The Accounting Review*, vol. 31, no. 1, pp. 71–76.

Yamey, B 1994, 'Benedetto Cotrugli on bookkeeping (1458)', *Accounting, Business & Financial History*, vol. 4, no. 1, pp. 43–50.

Legislation

Charities Act 2006 (UK)

Cases

US v Kansas Pacific Railway Company, US Supreme Court [1878] 99 US 455.

Index

Note: Page numbers in *italics* indicate figures and in **bold** indicate tables on the corresponding pages.

Printed and bound by CPI Group (UK) Ltd, Croydon, CR0 4YY

18/10/2024

01776022-0015